HARVARD UNIVERSITY
STUDIES AND NOTES IN
PHILOLOGY AND LITERATURE
VOLUME VI

THE ORIGINS
AND SOURCES OF THE
COURT OF LOVE

THE ORIGINS
AND SOURCES OF THE
COURT OF LOVE

BY

WILLIAM ALLAN NEILSON, 1869-1946

NEW YORK / RUSSELL & RUSSELL

FIRST PUBLISHED IN 1899
REISSUED, 1967, BY RUSSELL & RUSSELL
A DIVISION OF ATHENEUM HOUSE, INC.
L. C. CATALOG CARD NO: 66–24738

PRINTED IN THE UNITED STATES OF AMERICA

PREFACE.

THIS volume is substantially a dissertation presented to the Faculty of Arts and Sciences of Harvard University in May, 1898, to fulfil a requirement made of candidates for the degree of Doctor of Philosophy.

The investigation was begun as an inquiry into the pseudo-Chaucerian *Court of Love;* and in the first chapter a rearrangement of the text of that poem, and in the seventh certain conclusions as to its sources, represent the main results of this inquiry. But the search for sources led naturally to a wider and wider extension of the field, until the dissertation finally included a general account of the rise and development of some of the leading features of mediæval love-allegory.

The number of instances I have found of the central conception of a court held by the God or Goddess of Love and attended by personifications of abstract qualities is so large as almost to justify the treatment of this class of allegory as a separate literary *genre.* The chapter on the Statutes of Love attempts to trace the origin and indicate the extent of one of the most interesting features of this *genre*, and at the same time presents a body of material for the study of mediæval social ideals. The chapter on Philobone is devoted to a short analysis of a familiar type in the literature of the Middle Ages ; and that on the Birds' Matins contains a collection of evidence possessing interest other than literary in its bearing on the mediæval attitude towards religion.

The section which most nearly approaches the controversial, and which is put forth with the greatest diffidence, is that in which I have ventured to deal with the vexed question of the existence of the institution known as a Court of Love. The view which is here advocated occurred to me as the result of a study of the prevailing literary and social occupations of the earlier Middle Ages, and I have endeavored to present it in the light of those considerations which first suggested it. What I attempt to do is not to make any fresh attack upon either of the parties already in the field, but to propose a change of issue. The question, that is, as it appears to me, is not whether or not Courts of Love ever existed, but whether the practices on which some have based the belief in the existence of such an institution were serious or playful. That they were playful, but yet socially important and influential, is the conclusion to which the evidence here collected seems to point.

I owe acknowledgment to the work of scholars who have preceded me in parts of the same field, and of whose results I have freely availed myself. Such are the contributions of Gaston Paris to mediæval studies generally, and, with Trojel and Rajna, to the controversy on the institution of the Court of Love ; of Raab to the history of patristic allegory ; of Dammann to that of Provençal allegory ; of E. Langlois to the study of the *Roman de la Rose;* of A. Piaget to the history of French literature in the fifteenth century ; of L. F. Mott to the study of Courtly Love ; and of many others. Such obligations I have tried to make explicit as they occur, but I cannot expect to have avoided omissions. For these and for the other errors which are sure to have escaped me I can only plead inadvertence.

The subject of the investigation was suggested to me by Professor George Lyman Kittredge of Harvard University. To him I am indebted, not only for his kindness in reading the whole work in proof and for constant help and suggestion, but also for the greater part of

the training which enabled me to undertake the task at all.   To him
and to Professors E. S. Sheldon and A. R. Marsh of Harvard, who
also have read the book in proof and given much valuable aid, I owe
more than I can adequately express for the generosity with which
they have permitted me to draw on their time and their scholarship.
To Professors Charles Eliot Norton and Josiah Royce, and to
Mr. J. B. Fletcher, all of Harvard, to Professor C. M. Bakewell
of Bryn Mawr College, to Dr. N. C. Brooks of the University of
Illinois, to Dr. W. D. Howe of the University of Indianapolis, and
to the late Dr. R. A. Small of Brown University, I am grateful for
various services which are recorded in their appropriate places.

WILLIAM ALLAN NEILSON.

BRYN MAWR COLLEGE, PENNSYLVANIA,
     June 30, 1899.

CONTENTS.

—◦—

		PAGE
PREFACE		iii
I.	THE MIDDLE ENGLISH *COURT OF LOVE*	1
II.	THE BEGINNINGS OF MODERN ALLEGORY	8
	A. Pagan	8
	B. Christian	17
III.	THE CENTRAL CONCEPTION OF THE COURT OF LOVE	23
	A. Provençal	24
	B. Latin and Old French	31
	C. Italian	109
	D. German	120
	E. English	135
IV.	THE STATUTES OF LOVE	168
	4. The Ovidian Tradition	170
	B. Provençal	181
	C. French	184
	D. Italian	202
	E. German	204
	F. English	205
V.	THE CHARACTER OF PHILOBONE	213
VI.	THE BIRDS' MATINS	216
	A. Birds and the Love-Divinities	217
	B. Parodies of Religious Services	220
	C. Parodies Sung by Birds	225
VII.	THE IMMEDIATE SOURCES OF THE *COURT OF LOVE*	228
VIII.	THE RELATION OF THE ALLEGORY TO THE INSTITUTION AND THE PAGEANT OF THE COURT OF LOVE	240
IX.	THE COURT OF LOVE AFTER 1520	256
	INDEX	271

THE ORIGINS AND SOURCES OF THE
COURT OF LOVE.

———◦◦———

CHAPTER I.

THE MIDDLE ENGLISH *COURT OF LOVE.*

THE only extant MS. of the *Court of Love* is now in the Library of Trinity College, Cambridge, and is marked R. 3. 19. This MS. is a "miscellaneous collection of Middle English pieces of various dates," and of these our poem is No. 59.[1] From this source it was printed in 1562, by Stow, in his *Woorkes of Geffrey Chaucer, newly printed with diuers Addicions which were neuer in printe before.* From the fact that this volume included poems ascribed by Stow himself to Lydgate, it is clear that the editor did not intend to imply that the "diuers Addicions" were necessarily Chaucer's ; but the title proved misleading, and, as a result, the *Court of Love* has been included in the complete editions of Chaucer down to our own time. The baselessness of the ascription has been completely demonstrated by Professor Skeat,[2] and need not be discussed here.

The part of the MS. containing the *Court of Love* is in a hand of the sixteenth century, and Skeat is now inclined to place the composition of the poem after 1532, the date of Thynne's edition of Chaucer, which he thinks the author probably used. This he supports by an

---

[1] For an account of the age and contents of this MS., see Skeat, *Chaucerian and Other Pieces*, Oxford, 1897, pp. lxxii ff.

[2] See *Athenæum*, Nov. 4, 1876 ; *Academy*, June 3, 1878 ; Aug. 3, 1878 ; July 18, 1891 ; *Chaucerian Pieces*, loc. cit.

instance of parallelism between the translation of the *Roman de la Rose*, printed by Thynne, and the *Court of Love.* The passages are these :

> *R. R.*, 2819–20 . . . or of hir chere
> That to thee made thy lady dere,
> *C. of L.*, 496–7 . . . and all the chere
> That thee hath mad thy lyves lady dere.

He mentions also the five or six poems by Chaucer which, as will be shown later, influenced the *Court of Love*, and suggests that he may have learned his metre from Scottish authors such as Henryson and Dunbar. On these grounds, and from the general impression produced on him by the poem, he inclines to place the author with Sackville, Surrey, Grimoald, and other forerunners of the Elizabethans.

These arguments do not seem to me very cogent. The parallel with the *Roman de la Rose* passage has no force. The author of the *Court of Love* could have known the Chaucer poems before the publication of Thynne's edition ; Henryson was dead before 1500, and Dunbar had written all his most important work before 1510. Again, if a passage of the *Court of Love* be read with one from Surrey or Sackville, the earlier date of the former becomes immediately evident. Not only is the language manifestly older, but the literary attitude of the author is so distinctly mediæval that one feels at once that his place is rather with Hawes than with Surrey. Allowing an interval to account for the loss of some of Hawes's inflections, we shall probably be not far astray in fixing the date about the end of the first quarter of the sixteenth century.

The *Court of Love* in its present state consists of 1442 verses in rhyme royal.[1] The plot of the poem is in outline as follows :

After a prologue containing a dedication to his lady, for whose pleasure he has written the poem, an invocation of the Muses, and an apology to "metriciens" for his "lak of science," the poet tells how, when he was eighteen, he was summoned by Mercury to the Court of Love. Setting out on his journey, he overtook people swarming like bees in the same direction ; and, following them, he

---

[1] All quotations and references in the following pages will be according to the text in Skeat's *Chaucerian Pieces*, pp. 409–47.

came to a gorgeous castle glittering with gold and precious stones, and painted outside and in with daisies to signify that Alcestis dwelt there, who, with Admetus, acted as vicegerent for Venus. He entered a hall hung with arras and cloth of gold, and found the King and Queen sitting in state, wearing their crowns, and surrounded by many courtiers, including Danger and Disdain and "the ladies gode ninetene." He was particularly struck with admiration for the Queen's beauty, and for her eyes, the beams of which "were shapen lich a dart." "In mewet" he uttered a stanza expressing his wonder. As he looked round, he saw Philobone, the Queen's "chamberer" and a friend of his, who came and asked his errand. She particularly wanted to know whether he came of his own accord ; and when he confessed that Mercury had been sent for him, she warned him that the anger of the King would be sure to fall on him for his long delay in coming to Court. He ought to have come as soon as he was wise enough to tell a woman from a swan.

Trembling and repentant, the poet was led by Philobone into a temple where, in a raised tabernacle, sat Venus and Cupid [apparently in effigy, v. 223]. The windows and walls of the temple were painted with the stories of Dido and Æneas, of Anelida and Arcite, and many other princely lovers ; and the building itself was thronged with people. There were true lovers in blue, unfortunate ones in black, priests, nuns, and hermits in white, russet, and green, all bewailing their woful condition (v. 266).

But now a messenger summoned all new-comers before the King. When the poet, trembling and pale, presented himself, the King beheld him with stern visage and asked :

> What doth this old,
> Thus fer y-stope in yeres, come so late
> Unto the court?

On the plea of bashfulness, and on condition of future fidelity, he was pardoned, and handed over to an officer called Rigor, that he might take the oath to the Statutes of the Court of Love. After reading the twenty Statutes for men [which will be discussed later in detail], he turned over to the Statutes for women ; but just then Rigor noticed him and sharply stopped him.

The oath having been taken, Rigor sent him back to the temple with his fellow-neophytes, instructing them to pray, — those who had met their fate, for wisdom to guide them in service, those who were yet "unpurveyed," for grace that their destiny might be honorable and happy. Round the shrine they found thousands on their knees : unfortunate lovers offering prayers for pity and vengeance, and fortunate ones singing praises, extolling the omnipotence of love and its power as "exyler ay of vice and sin." The poet himself made confession and prayer, and told how one night in a vision he had seen a beautiful lady who made his heart dance a little. Who she was he did not know, but her he should like to serve and win.

Close by he noticed a jewelled shrine which Philobone told him was the sepulchre of Pity, who died from "tender herte" because she saw an eagle tear a fly to pieces. Formerly, his guide informed him in closest confidence, Pity was more serviceable to lovers than any one in Court, but now nothing availed but "hot corage."

Now he is to meet the fairest lady under the sun, and Philobone instructs him in modest behavior, warning him against forwardness, and making rather obscure allusions to some previous little affairs of his. They enter a chamber and behold Rosial, who is described after the traditional fashion, with straight nose, lily brow, full red lips, even teeth, golden hair, sweet breath, slender figure, and so on. He is deeply wounded by Love's dart, and retires to write a "bill" in seven stanzas. He returns and presents this, but the lady says she does not know anything about him. He describes himself as Philogenet, clerk of Cambridge, maker of love songs, and writer "in art of love." She tells him he expects success far too soon, and her coldness causes him to faint. This moves her to relent somewhat, and she promises to set his heart at ease ; but she charges him to keep the Statutes, granting, at his request, with a blush that makes her name appropriate, a modification of the objectionable sixteenth.

The lines (vv. 1020-2) which follow here sound like the end of the tale:

> Thus have I won, with wordes grete and small,
> Some goodly word of hir that I love best,
> And trust she shall yit set myne harte in rest.

But instead of closing, the narrative begins again thus :

> ' Goth on,' she said to Philobone, ' and take
> This man with you, and lede him all about.'

So the poet sets out on another round of sight-seeing, and Philo-
bone shows him Attendaunce, Diligence, Esperaunce, Dred-to-offend,
Despair, Hope (the last two of whom offer advice to him), Lust and
Delyt engaged in debate, Liar and Flattery.

In the midst of a speech made by Flattery, probably with reference
to Philogenet, the next stanza (v. 1093) begins with a question as to
why some people dressed in black and white and gray are so sad.
This introduces the description of a series of groups of complainants
— friars, nuns, poverty-stricken and deformed lovers, and, lastly, a
company who are " waried and misseid " by the Fates, and who
curse Nature for giving them life.

At this point we suddenly find Philogenet back among the allegorical personages (v. 1177)— Contrite, Dissemble, Shamefastness,
Avaunter, Envy, Privy-thought, and Golden Love and Leaden Love.

Just as these last two enter (v. 1316), another break occurs, and
we find Rosial explaining how Pity had come to life again and
induced her to take mercy on Philogenet. The lover bursts out
into thanks to Pity and Rosial, and Rosial tells him to dwell with
her till the feast held in May by the King of Love.

The remainder of the poem (vv. 1352– end) consists of a parody of
the Matins and Lauds of the Hours of the Blessed Virgin, sung by
the birds in honor of the God of Love. After the service all the
court go forth to gather hawthorn, and pelt one another with flowers,
and the poet is smitten through the heart with a " trew-love, plited
many-fold," thrown by his lady.

In this outline it will be observed that several breaks are noted in
the continuity of the poem. Two of these are remarked by Professor Skeat : that at v. 1022, where Rosial first relents, and where
I have quoted three lines which might conceivably end the poem;
and that at v. 1316, where, after the entrance of Leaden Love and
Golden Love, Rosial abruptly begins her full confession of love.
To account for these, Professor Skeat suggests that " probably six

stanzas are lost in each case, owing to the loss of the two corresponding leaves in the original from which the existing copy was made." [1] But I am by no means convinced that at v. 1022 anything has dropped out at all. The appearance of a conclusion in the use of a perfect tense in v. 1020 is indubitable; but it seems to me much more probable that at one time the poem did actually end here, and that, when the author decided to continue the allegory, he neglected to remove the trace of his earlier close.

As for the gap at v. 1316, it does not seem possible to avoid the inference that some stanzas are lost, in which the second round of the Court was completed, and Philogenet brought again into the presence of Rosial.

But this by no means exhausts the evidence of mutilation of the text. In the second round of the Court, which occupies exactly those stanzas between vv. 1022 and 1317, *i.e.* between the gaps recognized by the editor, we have (1) a group of allegorical figures described; (2) a group of typical figures — complainants; (3) another group of allegorical figures; and at v. 1092, where (2) begins, and at v. 1177, where (3) begins, the transition is so abrupt that we are led to suspect some confusion. As the poem at present stands, the second round seems a somewhat meaningless and confused repetition of features occurring in the earlier part. If, however, we remove the twelve stanzas dealing with the complainants (vv. 1093–1176), and spell Contrite with a capital, making it the name of one of the allegorical figures, parallel with Dissemble who immediately follows, we find that this part of the poem runs on without interruption.[2] The second round of the court is now seen to have the definite object of introducing a new kind of allegory, that dealing with abstractions,

---

[1] *Chaucerian Pieces*, p. lxxiv, note 2. This explanation is hardly satisfactory, for, allowing, as Professor Skeat does, six stanzas to each leaf, we find that the forty-two stanzas of which the passage between the two *lacunae* consists would occupy seven leaves, which, since seven is an odd number, is clearly not possible. No number which exactly divides forty-two works any more satisfactorily.

[2] Bell, in his edition of Chaucer (Lond., n. d., IV, 173), saw the appropriateness of making Contrite another of the allegorical courtiers, but thought it necessary to alter the line to " And there eek was Contrite, and gan repent," but this change does not seem to be required.

there being none of these in what I take to have been the earlier form of the poem except the two or three conventional figures grouped round the King and Queen — Danger, Disdain, and Rigor.

The twelve stanzas thus excised find a natural place after v. 266. There they would follow and complete a passage of a very similar character in the account of Philogenet's first visit to the temple, and would immediately precede the summons to the King's presence. No changes are necessary to make them fit here except a few in punctuation, which are required to make sense in any case. Professor Skeat prints vv. 1093–1103 without any quotation marks whatever ; but if we read them punctuated as follows, supposing that Philogenet asks the first question and Philobone answers him, the whole passage becomes intelligible, and the poem, except for the hopeless lacuna at v. 1316, is now continuous.

> " This is the court of lusty folk and glad,
>   And wel becometh their habit and array :
>   O why be som so sorry and so sad,
>   Complaining thus in blak and whyte and gray ? "
> " Freres they ben, and monkes, in good fay :
>   Alas, for rewth ! great dole it is to seen,
>   To see thaim thus bewaile and sory been.
>
> See how they cry and wring their handes whyte,
>   For they so sone went to religion !
>   And eke the nonnes, with vaile and wimple plight,
>   There thought that they ben in confusion. . . ."

It will be observed that the only accident to the MS. which we have to assume to account for the misplacement of these twelve stanzas (vv. 1093–1176) is the detachment of, say, two leaves and the copying in of these at the wrong place by a later scribe.

Such are the main facts about the contents and text of the poem into whose origins and sources we are to inquire. The characteristic features which will form the main lines of the investigation are these : *first*, the general idea of a Court like that of a feudal lord — sometimes in its social, sometimes in its legal aspect — held by Cupid or Venus, or by representatives of these divinities, and attended by a throng of personified abstractions acting as courtiers; *second*, the Statutes of Love — a series of commandments to be observed by those who owe allegiance to the Lord of Love; *third*, the figure of Philobone — the person who acts as guide and adviser to the hero of the allegory; *fourth*, the association of birds with Venus; *fifth*, the parody of Church services as exemplified in the Birds' Litany which closes the *Court of Love*. After an attempt to indicate the beginnings of this kind of allegory in general before the mediæval period, each of these features will be followed through the chief mediæval European literatures that dealt with such forms; next, a chapter will be devoted to a consideration of the immediate sources used by the author of the *Court of Love;* another to the relation of the allegory to the institutions and pageants known by similar names; and finally, some account will be given of the development of certain of these ideas after the date of our poem.

CHAPTER II.

THE BEGINNINGS OF MODERN ALLEGORY.

A. PAGAN.

ALTHOUGH the term *allegory* is commonly used to cover a considerable number of literary types — types differing as much from one another as, e.g., the Beast-fable, *The Pilgrim's Progress*, and the parable of the Prodigal Son — it will be convenient to limit it for the present purpose to that kind of symbolical narrative or description in which the main characters are personifications of abstract ideas and qualities.

The study of the instances of this kind of allegory in the classical literatures is beset with peculiar difficulties, chiefly on account of its relation to mythology. Beginning as symbols of natural phenomena,

the Greek gods gradually gathered to themselves more and more definite personalities, until they reached a pitch of anthropomorphism.
But along with this growth in individuality there was an extension
of their sovereignty into the domain of moral and intellectual qualities ; so that when in. the later, more sceptical times there came a
decay of the belief in their separate, concrete, personal existence,
their numbers continued to receive additions from a great variety of
sources, additions made by men who found the old forms of language
and even of worship convenient means of expression long after they
had ceased to be bound by the implications of these forms. | The
Neo-Platonists, for example, found room in their system for an
indefinite number of minor divinities, embodiments of various moral
and spiritual ideas, which they regarded as subordinate to the Supreme
Being, and which *in name* they identified with the ancestral deities of
the Greeks and Romans.[1] The generous hospitality offered by the
Roman Pantheon to the gods of alien nations, and the deification of
the Emperors, are other instances ; and perhaps more striking from
the present point of view is the practice of raising statues to the
separate qualities of individual heroes, as to the Valor of Cæsar or
the Clemency of Augustus.

It is clear that in this last class of cases we have something very
far from the conception of the gods in Homer, and within measurable
distance of the ideas of Beauty and Pity as courtiers of Love ; yet
nothing is harder than to say where mythology ends and allegory
begins. Even if we go back to Homer we find the difficulty ; for he
places abstractions like Fear, Rumor, and Strife side by side with the
great gods, though the former have no regular place in the theogony,

---

[1] Cf. Arthur Richter, *Neu-Platonische Studien*, Heft III, *Die Theologie und
Physik des Plotin*, Halle, 1867, p. 18: " Im Allgemeinen lässt sich darüber sagen :
Mythen bewegen sich in der Sphäre der Vorstellung, Plotins Standpunkt ist der der
Idee. Er schreibt den Mythen daher nicht als solchen Wahrheit zu, sondern sucht
die in ihnen ausgesprochenen Vorstellungen auf einen Ideengehalt zurückzuführen.
Dies geschieht: 1) dadurch, dass er sich der mythischen Namen der Götter ziemlich
willkührlich zur Bezeichnung seiner fundamentalen Begriffe bedient. . . ." Richter
goes on to give instances of the use of the names of Aphrodite, Apollo, Eros,
Nemesis, etc., in the manner described.

and it is hard to think that any one ever believed in them as actual persons. Thus in the *Iliad*, iv, 439–44, we have:

ὦρσε δὲ τοὺς μὲν Ἄρης, τοὺς δὲ γλαυκῶπις Ἀθήνη
Δεῖμός τ᾽ ἠδὲ Φόβος καὶ Ἔρις ἄμοτον μεμαυῖα,
Ἄρεος ἀνδροφόνοιο κασιγνήτη ἑτάρη τε,
ἥ τ᾽ ὀλίγη μὲν πρῶτα κορύσσεται, αὐτὰρ ἔπειτα
οὐρανῷ ἐστήριξε κάρη καὶ ἐπὶ χθονὶ βαίνει.

While in one line Ἔρις is called the sister and companion of Ἄρης, in the next she is described in such terms as seem quite in keeping with their context when we find them two thousand years later in the fantastic allegory of Chaucer's *Hous of Fame:*

> For altherfirst, soth for to seye,
> Me thoughte that she was so lyte,
> That the lengthe of a cubyte
> Was lenger than she semed be ;
> But thus sone, in a whyle, she
> Hir tho so wonderliche streighte,
> That with hir feet she th' erthe reighte,
> And with her heed she touched hevene.[1]

These personifications in the passage from Homer are further differentiated from the established divinities if we note, as Mr. Leaf does in his commentary on the passage, that "the three half-personified spirits of battle must not be regarded as siding with either party, but as arousing alike τοὺς μέν and τοὺς δέ."[2]

Examples of such figures from the classics could be multiplied indefinitely ;[3] but instances pointing more directly to the mediæval development are found in such passages as the description of the

---

[1] Chaucer, *Hous of Fame*, vv. 1368–75. See below, p. 13.

[2] *The Iliad*, ed. by W. Leaf, London, 1886, vol. I, p. 140, note on iv, 440.

[3] Such are the personifications of Fear in *Iliad*, xv, 119 ; of Strife in *Iliad*, xviii, 535 ; of Fame in *Iliad*, ii, 93; *Odyssey*, xxiv, 412 ; Hesiod, *Works and Days*, vv. 761–4 ; Virgil, *Aeneid*, iv, 173–188 ; Ovid, *Met.*, ix, 137 ff.; of Envy in Callimachus, *Hymn to Apollo*, v. 105 ; Ovid, *Met.*, ii, 768 ff.; of Faith in Virgil, *Aen.*, i, 292 ; Horace, *Carm.* I, xxxv, 21–24 ; of Rage in Virgil, *Aen.*, i, 294.

Triumph of Love in the second elegy in Book I of Ovid's *Amores*, where, after confessing himself the new-made prey of Cupid, the poet addresses the god thus :

> Necte comam myrto, maternas iunge columbas :
> Qui deceat, currum uitricus ipse dabit ;
> Inque dato curru, populo clamante triumphum,
> Stabis et adiunctas arte mouebis aues.
> Ducentur capti iuuenes captaeque puellae :
> Haec tibi magnificus pompa triumphus erit.
> Ipse ego, praeda recens, factum modo uulnus habebo
> Et noua captiua uincula mente feram.
> *Mens Bona* ducetur manibus post terga retortis
> Et *Pudor* et castris quidquid Amoris obest.
> Omnia te metuent : ad te sua bracchia tendens
> Vulgus ' io ' magna uoce ' triumphe ' canet.
> *Blanditiae* comites tibi erunt *Error*que *Furor*que
> Adsidue partes turba secuta tuas.
> His tu militibus superas hominesque deosque.
> Haec tibi si demas commoda, nudus eris.
> Laeta triumphanti de summo mater Olympo
> Plaudet et adpositas sparget in ora rosas.
> Tu pinnas gemma, gemma uariante capillos
> Ibis in auratis aureus ipse rotis.

Here the personifications are actually in the train of Love, and the god himself in these lines and the rest of the elegy is represented with all the accompaniments of wings, quiver, torch, bow and arrows, which we shall constantly find in the mediæval allegories, and which are too common in classical art to need special illustration. Note, too, the association with birds and roses.

This Triumph of Cupid leads us to another feature of mediæval treatment of the love divinity which finds its beginnings in the classics — the Palace of Love.

It will be noticed that in the *Court of Love* the temple and the palace of Venus are both introduced — the temple being a kind of appendage to the palace. When we come to the mediæval period further instances of this will be produced, and the connection of the two — even amounting to a confusion — goes very far back. In the

Homeric *Hymn to Venus*, vv. 58–63, the goddess is described as going to her *shrine* in Cyprus and there being bathed, anointed, and adorned by the Graces, in preparation for her wooing of Anchises. Similarly in *Aeneid*, i, 415, Venus leaves Æneas for Paphos, where she has "sedes" as well as a temple :

> Ipsa Paphum sublimis abit, sedesque reuisit
> Laeta suas, ubi templum illi, centumque Sabaeo
> Ture calent arae sertisque recentibus halant.

Tibullus (i, 3, 57–64) has a passage which has very plausibly been considered[1] as the direct source of the scene with which the *Roman de la Rose* opens, and which was so widely imitated :

> Sed me, quod facilis tenero sum semper Amori,
> Ipsa Venus campos ducet in Elysios.
> Hic choreae cantusque uigent, passimque uagantes
> Dulce sonant tenui gutture carmen aues :
> Fert casiam non culta seges, totosque per agros
> Floret odoratis terra benigna rosis :
> Ac iuuenum series teneris inmixta puellis
> Ludit, et adsidue proelia miscet Amor.

In Homer all the gods have houses, and from these doubtless the later descriptions are elaborated. The palace of Apollo in the beginning of Book ii of Ovid's *Metamorphoses* is an example, and may also be a source, of the gorgeous descriptions of castles such as we have in the *Court of Love :*

> Regia Solis erat sublimibus alta columnis,
> Clara micante auro flammasque imitante pyropo,
> Cuius ebur nitidum fastigia summa tegebat ;
> Argenti bifores radiabant lumine ualuae.
> Materiam superabat opus ; nam Mulciber illic
> Aequora caelarat medias cingentia terras
> Terrarumque orbem caelumque, quod inminet orbi —

and so on, describing in detail the decorations. A further parallel with the *Court of Love* occurs in vv. 23 ff. :

---

[1] E. Langlois, *Origines et Sources du Roman de la Rose*, Paris, 1891, p. 10, note.

> . . . Purpurea uelatus ueste sedebat
> In solio *Phoebus* claris lucente smaragdis.
> A dextra laevaque *Dies* et *Mensis* et *Annus*
> *Saecula*que et positae spatiis aequalibus *Horae*
> *Ver*que novum stabat cinctum florente corona ;
> Stabat nuda *Aestas* et spicea serta gerebat ;
> Stabat et *Autumnus* calcatis sordidus uuis,
> Et glacialis *Hiems* canos hirsuta capillos.

Alongside of this " Court of Apollo," as it may be called, may be placed the House of Fame in *Met.*, xii, 39–63, which, through the imitation in Chaucer's *Hous of Fame*, is a source with which our *Court of Love* author had a double chance of being familiar :

> Orbe locus medio est inter terrasque fretumque
> Caelestesque plagas, triplicis confinia mundi,
> Unde quod est usquam, quamuis regionibus absit,
> Inspicitur, penetratque cauas uox omnis ad aures.
> *Fama* tenet, summaque domum sibi legit in arce
> Innumerosque aditus ac mille foramina tectis
> Addidit et nullis inclusit limina portis.
> Nocte dieque patet.   Tota est ex aere sonanti ;
> Tota fremit uocesque refert iteratque quod audit :
> Nulla quies intus nullaque silentia parte.
> Nec tamen est clamor, sed paruae murmura uocis,
> Qualia de pelagi, siquis procul audiat, undis
> Esse solent, qualemne sonum, cum Iuppiter atras
> Increpuit nubes, extrema tonitrua reddunt.
> Atria turba tenet : ueniunt, leue uulgus, euntque
> Mixtaque cum ueris passim conmenta uagantur
> Milia rumorum confusaque uerba uolutant.
> E quibus hi uacuas implent sermonibus aures,
> Hi narrata ferunt alio, mensuraque ficti
> Crescit, et auditis aliquid nouus adicit auctor.
> Illic *Credulitas*, illic temerarius *Error*
> Vanaque *Laetitia* est consternatique *Timores*
> *Seditio*que repens dubioque auctore *Susurri*.

After the beginning of the Christian era these traditions continued in the pagan poets.   Exactly the same kind of personifications are found in Statius, e.g., *Theb.*, iii, 426, and *Silvae*, iii, 3, 1–7. In Apuleius we have them not infrequently. In the story of Cupid and Psyche in Book vi of his *Metamorphoses* we have several instances. Thus Venus threatens Cupid that she will call to her aid his enemy Sobrietas, and where Venus is persecuting Psyche these passages occur : "Jamque fores ei dominae proximanti occurrit una de famulitio Veneris nomine *Consuetudo* statimque quantum maxime potuit exclamat, 'Tandem, ancilla nequissima, dominam habere te scire coepisti'"[1]; and "'Ubi sunt,' inquit [Venus], '*Sollicitudo* atque *Tristities*, ancillae meae?'"[2] — and forthwith these servants come forth and proceed to torture Psyche.

In Apuleius, too, we have a suggestion of the Palace of Love. Psyche, immediately after her mysterious marriage, falls into a sleep, and awaking finds herself in a grove in the midst of which is a fountain with crystal waters. "Prope fontis adlapsum domus regia est, aedificata non humanis manibus sed divinis artibus. . . . Summa laquearia citro et ebore curiose cauata subeunt aureae columnae, parietes omnes argenteo caelamine conteguntur. . . . Enim uero pauimenta ipsa lapide pretioso caesim deminuto in uaria picturae genera discriminantur."[3] The grove, the fountains, the precious building materials, and the picture decorations all become regular features of the mediæval House of Venus.

But as early as Apuleius there is a change in the mental attitude of authors towards even the most august divinities, and what Puech says of Claudian begins to be true long before : "Whatever care Claudian took to conserve the traditions of the past, he yielded in spite of himself to the influence of his age, — an age in which mythology had ceased to be more than a poetic convention, when theology, striving after a vague deism or pantheism of the Stoic kind and re-establishing the fabulous divinities only as attributes, as hypostases, deprived them of their life and their humanity. At times, also, he seems to have planned to substitute for these ancient gods so mocked by the Christians, less compromising abstractions."[4]

This treatment of mythology as a poetic convention is indeed

---

[1] Apuleius, *Met.*, vi, 8.   [2] *Ibid.*, vi, 9.   [3] *Ibid.*, v, 1.
[4] Puech, *Prudence*, Paris, 1888, pp. 241–2.

more and more evident in the later pagan literature. Personifications occur with greater frequency. In one passage[1] in Claudian (flor. A.D. 400) Alecto appears surrounded by Discord, the nurse of war; imperious Hunger; Old Age, neighbor of Death; Disease; Jealousy; Grief, mourning in a ragged veil; Fear; blind Audacity; Luxury, and Poverty, her inseparable companion; Avarice, and the Curae. Later in the same poem :

> *Concordia, Virtus,*
> Cumque *Fide Pietas* alta ceruice uagantur,
> Insignemque canunt nostra de plebe triumphum (i, 52–4).

In another poem[2] are Patience, Temperance, Prudence, Constancy, Avarice, and Ambition, and after an interval[3]:

> Lictorque Metus cum fratre Pauore
> Barbara ferratis innectunt colla catenis.

With a still bolder symbolism he pictures the cave of Eternity, where

> Vestibuli custos, uultu longaeua decoro,
> Ante fores *Natura* sedet, cunctisque uolantes
> Dependent membris animae.[4]

Most interesting of all to us at present is the account of the dwelling of Venus to which Cupid goes in the poem *De Nuptiis Honorii et Mariae* to announce to his mother his conquest of the heart of Honorius. The abode of the goddess is in Cyprus, in a flat plain on the top of a mountain inaccessible to the foot of man, and surrounded by a golden wall built by Vulcan as the price of his wife's kisses. Here there blows no wind nor does winter bring snow, but in perpetual spring the flowers bloom, and among the trees sing only those birds whose song has been approved by Venus. The very leaves love, *omnisque vicissim Felix arbor amat.* There are two fountains, one sweet and one bitter, in which the arrows of Cupid receive their temper :

> Mille pharetrati ludunt in margine fratres,
> Ore pares, habitu similes, gens mollis Amorum.
> Hos Nymphae pariunt, illum Venus aurea solum
> Edidit (vv. 72–5).

---

[1] Claudian, *In Rufinum,* i, 25 ff.
[2] Claud., *De Laudibus Stilichonis,* ii, 100 ff.
[3] *Ibid.,* ii, 373 ff.   [4] *Ibid.,* ii, 431–3.

To gods and kings the Venus-born Cupid confines his attention, while the amours of the crowd of common men are the charge of the lesser Loves. Other divinities dwell there — Licentia, Irae, Excubiae, Lacrymae, Pallor, Audacia, Metus, Voluptas, Perjuria, Juventus. The description of the Palace itself may be compared with the Ovidian Palace of Apollo [1]:

> . . . . Procul atria diuae
> Permutant radios, siluaque obstante uirescunt.
> Lemnius haec etiam gemmis exstruxit et auro,
> Admiscens artem pretio, trabibus smaragdis
> Supposuit caesas hyacinthi rupe columnas.
> Beryllo paries, et iaspide lubrica surgunt
> Limina, despectusque solo calcatur achates.[2]

In this gorgeous place Amor finds Venus seated " corusco solio," engaged in making her toilet with the assistance of the Graces.[3] She needs no mirror, for the admiration of all around sufficiently reflects her beauty. She receives her son warmly, and at his request sends for Triton and, seated on a couch of roses on his back, and attended by a train of Loves, she crosses the waves to bless the marriage of Honorius and Maria.

To some extent parallel to this marriage poem by Claudian is the *De Nuptiis Philologiae et Mercurii* of Martianus Capella (flor. A.D. 425). Here the aim is didactic instead of panegyric, and the attendant figures are Virtus, Phronesis, and the like.[4]

Much closer, and very evidently an imitation, is the *Epithalamium dictum Ruricio et Hiberiae* of Apollinaris Sidonius (A.D. 430–483). Here again the dwelling is the work of Vulcan, and the precious stones are even more elaborately described [5]:

> Profecit studio spatium ; nam Lemnius illic
> Ceu templum lusit Veneri fulmenque relinquens

---

[1] See p. 12, above.

[2] Claud., *De Nuptiis Honorii et Mariae*, 85 ff.

[3] Cf. the Homeric *Hymn to Venus*, 58–63, and p. 12, above.

[4] See especially bks. i, ii, and ix.

[5] C. Sollius Apollinaris Sidonius, *Carm.*, xi, 14 ff., ed. by P. Mohr, Leipzig, 1895, p. 307.

Hic ferrugineus fumauit saepe Pyragmon.
Hic lapis est, de quinque locis dans quinque colores,
Aethiops, Frygius, Parius, Poenus, Lacedaemon,
Purpureus, uiridis, maculosus, eburnus et albus.
Postes chrysolithi fuluus diffulgurat ardor ;
Myrrhina, sardonyches, amethystus, Hiberus, iaspis
Indus, Chalcidicus, Scythicus, beryllus, achates
Attollunt duplices argenti cardine ualuas,
Per quas inclusi lucem uomit umbra smaragdi ;
Limina crassus onyx crustat propterque hyacinthi
Caerula concordem faciunt in stagna colorem.

B. CHRISTIAN.

When we begin to deal with the Christian writers of allegory, it becomes necessary to take account of another stream of influence than the classical, to which hitherto we have devoted exclusive attention, *viz.*, that from the Scriptures.

Of allegory in the limited sense in which we have defined it there is not a great variety in the Bible. By far the most frequent personification in the Old Testament is that of Wisdom. In the *Proverbs* we have her crying aloud in the streets,[1] holding length of days in her right hand and riches and honor in her left,[2] making subtilty her dwelling,[3] building her house and sending forth her maidens.[4] In the Apocryphal *Wisdom of Solomon* she is radiant and fadeth not away,[5] is easily beheld of them that desire to know her,[6] goeth about herself seeking them that are worthy of her,[7] is the artificer of all things,[8] and is sought by the speaker as a bride.[9] In *Ecclesiasticus* she exalteth her sons, and taketh hold of them that seek her.[10]

We have no other figure of this kind nearly so elaborately pictured. The people of Israel, and more particularly the city of Jerusalem, are not infrequently represented as female figures : e.g., " Shake thyself

---

[1] *Proverbs*, i, 20.   [4] *Proverbs*, ix, 1.   [7] *Wisdom*, vi, 16.
[2] iii, 16.   [5] *Wisdom*, vi, 12.   [8] vii, 22.
[3] viii, 12.   [6] *Ibid.*   [9] viii, 2.
[10] *Ecclesiasticus*, iv, 11, and *passim.*

from the dust; arise, sit thee down, O Jerusalem; loose thyself from the bands of thy neck, O captive daughter of Zion." [1]   Again, in *Psalm* lxxxv, 10–11, occur some instances that were worked very hard by the Fathers :

> Mercy and Truth are met together;
> Righteousness and Peace have kissed each other.
> Truth springeth out of the earth,
> And Righteousness hath looked down from heaven.

From the mass of symbolism in the *Apocalypse* a few instances can be selected : the figure on the pale horse representing Death,[2] another on the red horse apparently representing War,[3] the scarlet woman who personifies Babylon,[4] and most important, the figuring of the Church as the Bride of Christ.[5]   The allegorical significance of these was increased, and many passages not originally figurative were made so, by the well-known allegorizing tendency of the Church in the Early and Middle Ages.[6]   One instance of the kind of allegorical story which the early Fathers sometimes founded upon the merest hints will be given later [7] from a parable ascribed to Bernard of Clairvaux. Meantime we have to consider instances in which the Fathers turned to Christian uses the kind of personifications the tradition of which had come down from classical sources.

Tertullian in his book *De Patientia*, cap. 15,[8] describes Patience as a woman of calm and tranquil countenance, with forehead free from wrinkles of sadness or anger, eyes cast down in humility, not in unhappiness, a silent mouth, and an expression of peaceful and innocent joy.   She is clad in a close-fitting snow-white garment, and is seated on the throne of the calmest and sweetest spirit, "for where God is, there is his foster-daughter, Patience."   Of a similar

---

[1] *Isaiah*, lii, 2.   [2] *Revelation*, vi, 8.   [3] *Ibid.*, vi, 4.   [4] xvii, 3.   [5] xix, 7.

[6] For instances of the elaboration of the passage from Psalm lxxxv, and of the personification of Faith, Hope, and Charity from *I Cor.*, xiii, see Raab, *Ueber vier allegorische Motive in der lateinischen und deutschen Literatur des Mittelalters*, chap. iii.   He cites Heinzel, *Zt. f. deutsches Alt.*, XVII, 43–51.

[7] See p. 21, below.

[8] Quoted by Ebert, *Allgemeine Geschichte der Literatur des Mittelalters im Abendlande*, Leipzig, 1874–87, I, 49–50.

nature are the figures of Irene and Agape in Cyprian, and of Avarice and Luxury in Augustine.   Soon, however, one literary type begins to predominate in the Christian allegorical literature, — that which later becomes familiar as the Battle of the Vices and the Virtues, which found its first extended treatment at the hands of the Spaniard Prudentius about A.D. 400, and its last and greatest, after an almost continuous tradition of twelve hundred years, in the works of Bunyan.

According to Puech,[2] Prudentius probably received the suggestion for his *Psychomachia* from a passage in the *De Spectaculis* of Tertullian (c. 29).   The passage runs thus :

> Si scenicae doctrinae delectant, satis nobis litterarum est, satis uersuum, satis sententiarum, satis etiam canticorum, satis uocum ; nec fabulae, sed ueritates ; nec strophae, sed simplicitates. Vis et pugillatus et luctatus? praesto sunt, non parua, sed multa. Adspice impudicitiam deiectam a castitate, perfidiam caesam a fide, saeuitiam a misericordia contusam, petulantiam a modestia obumbratam, et tales sunt apud nos agones, in quibus ipsi coronamur.

This last sentence does indeed contain, as Puech says, "le programme même de la *Psychomachia*." The same idea is found in Cyprian also, in a passage not noted by Puech. "Obsessa mens hominis et undique diaboli infestatione uallata uix occurrit singulis [uitiis], uix resistit : si auaritia prostrata est exsurgit libido," etc.[3]

The subject was first treated by Prudentius in his *Hamartigenia* (vv. 394 ff.) in which the human soul is described as besieged by Satan, under whom fight a crowd of vices — Anger, Superstition, Melancholy (Maeror), Discord, Luxury, Thirst of Blood, Envy, Adultery, Cheating, Violence, etc. In the *Psychomachia*[4] the soul is a battle-field where a series of duels is being fought ; as, e.g., that between the Christian Faith and Paganism, "the worship of the old gods."

---

[1] Augustine, *Sermon 86*, chap. vi, cited by Ebert, I, 237, n. 2.

[2] A. Puech, *Prudence*, Paris, 1888, pp. 245 ff. — an admirable account of the works and influence of Prudentius, from which I have received help.

[3] Cyprian, *De Mortalitate*, 4 ; Ebert, I, 59, n. 1.

[4] *Psychomachia*, 21 ff.

> Prima petit campum dubia sub sorte duelli
> Pugnatura *Fides*, agresti tuɪbida cultu,
> Nuda humeros, intonsa comas, exerta lacertos ;
> Namque repentinus laudis calor ad noua feruens
> Proelia, nec telis meminit, nec tegmine cingi :
> Pectore sed fidens ualido, membrisque retectis,
> Prouocat insani frangenda pericula belli.
> Ecce lacessentem collatis uiribus audet
> Prima ferire *Fidem, ueterum cultura Deorum*, etc.

Similarly Pudicitia fights with Libido, Patientia with Ira, Superbia with Humilitas, Luxuria with Sobrietas, Avaritia with Largitas, Concordia with Discordia. One group has some Court of Love figures. After the death of Luxuria at the hands of Sobrietas :

> Caede ducis dispersa fugit trepidante pauore
> Nugatrix acies. *Jocus* et *Petulantia* primi
> Cymbala proiiciunt: bellum nam talibus armis
> Ludebant, resono meditantes uulnera sistro.
> Dat tergum fugitiuus *Amor :* lita tela ueneno,
> Et lapsum ex humeris arcum, pharetramque cadentem
> Pallidus ipse metu sua post uestigia linquit.[1]

Justitia, Honestas, Jejunia, Pudor, Spes, Pompa, Vetustas, Voluptas, and others also occur.

The influence of this work was very great not only in Spain, where, according to Puech, it inspired the *autos sacramentales* (which are often only " Psychomachies dramatiques "[2]) and other works, but in many foreign countries as well. Features which may plausibly be derived from it are to be seen in the sermons of the later Fathers, and one cannot fail to notice how strongly it suggests the Morality Play. It would take us too far afield to follow the descendants of the *Psychomachia* down through the theological and didactic literature of the following centuries, but one instance may be quoted to show the persistence of that kind of allegory which Prudentius indeed did not invent, but of which he was the first great exponent.

---

[1] *Psychomachia*, 432 ff.

[2] See Puech, *Prudence*, p. 255. For the *autos sacramentales*, see *Biblioteca de Autores Españoles*, LVIII, Madrid, 1865.

In connection with the allegorizing of passages of Scripture originally free from any intentional parabolic signification, a sermon by Bernard of Clairvaux (d. 1153), the preacher of the Second Crusade, was mentioned.   We have five *Parables*[1] ascribed to St. Bernard, and all of them, though founded upon different passages of Scripture, approach the type of the Battle of the Vices and the Virtues.   In one of these, starting from St. Paul's chapter on Charity, he tells of a King who had three daughters, Fides, Spes, and Caritas, whom he puts in charge of the town of Mansoul, in which are three castles, Rationabilitas, Concupiscibilitas, and Irascibilitas.   To each daughter is assigned a castle, and each sets a guardian with attendants to watch over it.   Fides appoints Prudentia and gives her as associates Obedientia, Patientia, Dispensatio, Ordo, and Disciplina ; Spes appoints Sobrietas and gives her Discretio, Continentia, Constantia, and Humilitas, with Silentium as doorkeeper; Caritas appoints Pietas (who is accompanied by Munditia Corporis and " congruas exercitationes, videlicet lectiones, meditationes, orationes, et spirituales affectiones") and Beatitudo, with Peace as doorkeeper.   The whole town is governed by Liberum Arbitrium.   These arrangements having been made, the daughters retire, and the town is attacked by the Adversary at the head of an army of wickedness.   They gain entrance by the doors of Rationabilitas and Concupiscibilitas, Liberum Arbitrium is bound, and Blasphemia, Luxuria, and Superbia hold sway.   The three daughters seek help from their father, who sends Timor and Gratia with an army of Virtues.   Liberum Arbitrium is liberated, and, it is hoped, will remain under the dominion of Gratia forever.

But the Christian writers of Allegory were not exclusively occupied with biblical subjects, and their knowledge of pagan literature is shown in other ways than the *Psychomachia* might indicate.   Thus we find them turning their ingenuity in interpretation to the symbolism of the God of Love himself, though in no very friendly spirit. The features dwelt on are the usual conventions of classical art, but they are so constantly used in that class of mediæval poems that

---

[1] See Raab, *Ueber vier allegorische Motive*, pp. 10, 13, 29, etc., for other Church writings of the same kind.   The present summary is based on Raab, p. 10.

we are to study that it is worth while to note one or two instances of their treatment.

Fulgentius[1] (A.D. 540) thus interprets the stock attributes of Venus :

Hanc etiam nudam pingunt, siue quod nudos sibi affectatores dimittat, siue quod libidinis crimen nunquam celatum sit, siue quod nunquam nisi nudis conueniat.   Huic etiam rosas[2] in tutelam adiiciunt.   Rosae enim et rubent et pungunt, ut etiam libido.   Rubet uerecundiae opprobrio, pungit etiam peccati aculeo.   Et sicut rosa delectat quidem, sed celeri motu temporis tollitur : ita et libido libet momentaliter, et fugit perenniter.   In huius etiam tutelam columbas ponunt, illa uidelicet causa, quod huius generis aues sint in coitu feruidae.

In a similar strain is a passage by Theodulfus, Bishop of Orléans about A.D. 800 :

> Fingitur alatus, nudus, puer esse Cupido,
>   Ferre arcum et pharetram, toxica, tela, facem.
> Quod leuis, alatus, quod aperto est crimine, nudus,
>   Sollertique caret quod ratione puer.
> Mens praua in pharetra, insidiae signantur in arcu,
>   Tela, puer, uirus, fax tuus ardor, Amor. . . .[3]

Other passages of this sort could be quoted, but these are sufficient to show the attitude of the early Churchmen towards even the least serious of the old divinities.| It was about a thousand years before it was easy for a Christian clerk to regard the winged god without a frown ; and when we again come upon poets describing the House of Venus without deprecating gestures, we realize that we are in a new world, that of the love-allegories of the Middle Ages.

---

[1] *Mythologicum,* ii, 4 (on Venus).

[2] Muncker in a note to this passage quotes Jerome : " Flos Veneris rosa est ; quia sub eius purpura multi latent aculei." *Mythographi Latini,* ed. by A. van Staveren, Amsterdam, 1742, p. 670, n. 4.   Cf. also in same vol., pp. 903-4, Albricus Philosophus, *De deorum imaginibus Libellus,* v.

[3] Theodulfus, *De libris quos legere solebam et qualiter fabulae poetarum a philosophis mystice pertractantur,* 33 ff.   See edition in *Monumenta Germaniae Historica, Poet. Lat.,* I, 543, and cf. parallel from Isidore quoted in note 8.

In the present chapter we have attempted to discover how much of the common material of the Court of Love allegory was a legacy from preceding literatures. The investigation has dealt mainly with two points — the source of those allegorical figures that form the courtiers of Venus, and the beginnings of the descriptions of the Palace of Venus. Of both of these we have found evidence of much more than a trace. The Palace seems to be derived almost entirely from the classics, unless we suppose that the account of the New Jerusalem in the *Revelation* may also have given suggestions. The personifications, as was perhaps to have been expected, are found both in the classics and in Hebrew literature. The Christian contribution is increased by the patristic tendency to force an even fourfold meaning out of all Scripture, so that the clerical mind had its familiarity with personification increased by many instances which would never have been recognized as such by their authors.

This matter of personification[1] has been dealt with much more fully than will be possible or desirable in the succeeding chapters. We have, as it were, been collecting material to show from what soil the allegory of the Court of Love sprang ; having realized that, we can now confine our attention more exclusively to the growth of the plant itself.

CHAPTER III.

THE CENTRAL CONCEPTION OF THE COURT OF LOVE.

THE general principle of arrangement in this and the following chapter will be according to language : Provençal, Old French, Italian, Middle-High German, and English. Latin documents, belonging as they do to various, and often to uncertain, nationalities, will be discussed at points where their relation to vernacular pieces makes it most convenient.

---

[1] For further instances of personification after Prudentius, see E. Langlois, *Origines et Sources du Roman de la Rose*, Paris, 1891, pp. 63 ff.

A. PROVENÇAL.

GUIRAUT DE CALANSO.

We begin with the work of a troubadour of the end of the twelfth century, Guiraut de Calanso, who wrote his *A leis cui am de cor e de saber* [1] to pay homage to a lady. It deals with three kinds of love, to be understood as carnal, natural (*i.e.* that of relatives), and celestial, but the second and third together get only three lines. The first kind is personified as a very powerful being, conquering nobles, princes, and kings. Not Reason but Impulse rules her court, and never will justice be done there. So subtle is she that no man can see her; so swiftly she runs that none can escape; so straight she strikes that none can guard by hauberk however stout against the dart of steel with which she gives the "colp de plazer," against the golden arrows which she shoots from her bow, or against her finely sharpened dart of lead. She wears a crown of gold. Though she sees nothing, yet where she wishes to strike she never misses. She flies lightly and is much feared. When she does evil it seems as if it were good. Descent or wealth she does not regard.

She dwells in a palace with five portals, two of which having been passed, the other three are easy of entrance; but the exit is hard. Whoever can remain there lives in joy. The entrance is at the top of four very smooth steps, which no villain can climb. Those who fail to ascend are lodged without in the "barri," which holds more than half the world. Outside there is a stone seat where one may sit and play on a board any game one pleases; but the play is not without risks.

Love makes the whole universe serve her. One she makes rich, another to languish; one she holds down, another she makes suc-

---

[1] Edited, with discussions, by O. Dammann, Breslau, 1891. Guiraut Riquier wrote a commentary on this poem which Dammann thinks is the only thing of its kind preserved. Dammann's book contains a collection of valuable material to which I owe some suggestions.

The text may also be found in Bartsch's *Chrest. Prov.*, 4th ed., Elberfeld, 1880, col. 163, and in Appel's *Prov. Chrest.*, Leipzig, 1895, p. 75. For translation see Diez, *Leben u. Werke der Troubadours*, 2d ed., p. 428.

cessful. She is unstable, proving faithless to her fair promises. Naked she goes, girt with a little gold embroidery, and all her race spring from a fire, of which they are formed [the last word is doubtful].

Several of the features in this wonderfully condensed little poem are repeated in another by the same author[1]:

> Sapchas d'Amor
> Com vol' e cor
> E com jai nuda ses vestir
> E non ve ren,
> Mas fer trop ben
> Ab sos dartz c'a fatz gen forbir;
> Dels dos cairels
> L'us es tan bels
> De fin aur c'om ve resplandir;
> L' autr'es d'acier,
> Mas tan mal fier
> C'om nos pot del sieu colp guerir;
> Comandamens
> Nous, si l' aprens,
> I trobares, senes mentir, etc.

The all-powerful character of the divinity here goes back to the Homeric *Hymn to Venus*, which attributes to her power over even the gods, except Diana, Minerva, and Vesta. At the other extreme of our period, this omnipotence forms the chief theme of the happy lovers' praise of Venus in the English *Court of Love*. The arrows are, of course, also a classical tradition; but the division of them and of the darts according to material, — steel, gold, and lead, — is peculiar. Two classes we shall find frequently in Old French; and the "Golden Love" and "Leaden Love" that enter the Court just where one of the breaks in the *Court of Love* occurs are doubtless of a similar signification. What that signification is we shall find explained in later poems. Of the Palace[2] we have already had

---

[1] K. Bartsch, *Denkmäler der Provenzalischen Litteratur*, Stuttgart, 1856, p. 100.

[2] Additional classical parallels to the Palace are quoted by Dammann : House of the Winds, *Aen.*, i, 50–63 ; of Vulcan, *Aen.*, viii, 416; of Envy, Ovid, *Met.*, ii, 760 ; of Cold, etc., *ibid.*, viii, 788 ; of Sleep, *ibid.*, xi. 592 ; Statius, *Theb.*, x, 84 ; of Mars, Statius, *Theb.*, vii, 40.

instances, and for the doors a parallel will be found in Andreas Capellanus.

The most important characteristic in these poems by Guiraut de Calanso is his attributing to the goddess the conventional features of Cupid, — wings, nakedness, blindness, and the bow and arrows. The explanation doubtless lies in the fact that *amor* is feminine in Provençal.

JAUFRE RUDEL.

The conventional features of the landscape in which the God of Love usually has his court occur frequently in Provençal poems that are not allegorical. Such a passage as the following from the troubadour Jaufre Rudel is typical:[1]

> Quan lo rius de la fontana
> S' esclarzis, si cum far sol,
> E par la flors aiglentina,
> El rossignolitz el ram
> Volf e refraing et aplana
> Son dous chantar et afina,
> Dreitz es qu'eu lo meu refraigna.

PEIRE GUILHEM (?).

A similar setting of flowers and streams and nightingales occurs, in a more elaborate form, in a fragmentary poem by a certain Peire, whose surname is uncertain (the MS. evidence being indecisive). The poet, who speaks in the first person throughout,[2] was out riding one day, accompanied by his knights and squires, when he met a very handsome and magnificently equipped cavalier conducting a beautiful lady. Both of them rode strangely-colored horses whose

---

[1] Bartsch, *Chrest. Prov.*, 4th ed., col. 55.

[2] For text see Raynouard, *Lexique Roman*, Paris, 1838, I, 405–17, and Mahn, *Werke*, I, 241 ff. For translation (imperfect) into modern French see *Hist. litt. des Troubadours* [Sainte-Palaye], Paris, 1774, II, 297 ff. These editors call the author "Pierre Vidal," but Bartsch (*Chrest. Prov.*, 4th ed., col. 265) and Stimming (*Gröber's Grundriss*, Band II, Abt. 2, art. *Provençal Litt.*, p. 46) call him "Peire Guillem" or "Peire Guilhem"; see also Bartsch, *Peire Vidal*, p. xciv.

trappings were rich with jewels. They were attended by a squire and a damsel whose long hair almost hid her from view. The poet offered them hospitality, and, as they seemed to prefer the open air, he led them to a sequestered garden enclosed by a hedge of reeds, shaded by laurels, and watered by a clear fountain. The lawn was enamelled with fresh flowers, and the trees were full of birds singing. The damsel spread a pavilion richly worked with gold, on which were represented all sorts of animals and flowers. A thousand knights could stand in it without touching each other, and yet the damsel carried it folded up in her purse.[1] After some conversation the poet was informed that the knight is the God of Love, the lady Mercy, and the squire and damsel Loyalty and Modesty. The squire carried a bow of *alborn* with three arrows in his girdle, one of gold, one of Poitou steel, one of lead. The last part of the poem is occupied with discussions of the origin and nature of love ; of the grounds which justify a man in putting away his wife, as the King of Navarre had just done, and of the reason why the God of Love was leading Mercy and her attendants away from the court of Alphonso of Castile; but as the MS. is not complete, not all the answers to Peire's questions have come down to us.

The squire, and not the god, it should be noted, has the bow and arrows. This was doubtless suggested by the custom of the squire's carrying the knight's spear when no fighting was to be done ; but in the poem the squire not only carries the bow but does the shooting. The arrows, we are told, enter by the eyes and by the ears, and serve to unite, not to separate, hearts. Observe also the different kinds of arrows — gold, steel, and lead, like the darts and arrows in Guiraut de Calanso.

ROMAN DE FLAMENCA.

In the romance of *Flamenca*,[2] though as a whole it is a quite realistic picture of fashionable life about 1200, several allegorical personages occur. In one passage we have Jovens, Avolesa, Proesa, and

---

[1] Van Bemmel, *De la langue et de la poésie prov.*, Brussels, 1846, p. 186, thinks this a proof of Arabic influence.

[2] *Roman de Flamenca*, ed. by Paul Meyer, Paris, 1865.

Cobezesal,[1] in another Malvestatz, Valor, Jois, Vergona, and Conois-sensa,[2] all these qualities being distinctly personified ; and the hero soliloquises at length on the power of Love.[3]

CHASTEL D'AMORS.

The troubadours of the north of Italy who imitated Provençal models and used the Provençal language, have also contributed to the growth of the Court of Love tradition. One of these, whose name is unknown, but whose nationality is betrayed by Italianisms in his style,[4] has left, in a unique and imperfect MS., an extreme example of the metaphorical type of the House of Love. In the beginning of this *Chastel d'Amors* the speaker announces his intention of building a noble castle. The high towers are to be hard-hearted ladies, and no lady is to be admitted who loves unworthily, or who is not or does not intend to be engaged in love. The gates of speech are the entrances, and the courteous open the doors with the keys of prayer. Immediately inside are the houses where rings and other love-tokens are sold. The next door is fastened by sweet private love-kisses, and this is the point where a stand must be made if the fortress is not to be yielded. Inside all is sweetness and youth and welcome, and up in the tower are secluded chambers for the secret joys of love. The butlers and the cooks "son tuit de ris e de joec et de parlar ses ennuec," and no fire is required but love, which makes perpetual summer. No bargaining is permitted ; and mortal war is waged against husbands and jealous persons. Slanderers are constantly attacking the ladies, who defend themselves by shooting proverbs at them. Evasions are their bucklers, oaths their lances, and they are able to lie with an air of truth. He who can get a dwelling place in this castle can go there and live in safety, and need never fear to lose what he has gained.

The particular kind of metaphor which is used in this poem is

---

[1] vv. 740 ff.   [2] vv. 231 ff.   [3] vv. 3326 ff.

[4] So A. Thomas in his edition of the text in *Annales du Midi*, 1889, pp. 183-96. See also Bartsch, *Chrest. Prov.*, 4th ed., col. 273 ff ; *Jahrbuch f. rom. und engl. Lit.*, XI, 23. On the MS. see *Archiv f. d. Stud. d. neueren Spr. u. Lit.*, XXXIV, 418 ff., and Gröber, *Romanische Studien*, II, 433–42.

found not infrequently in Old French poems, where palaces are described as founded upon sighs and surrounded with moats filled with tears; but I have found no example where this method is carried so far as here. It is a specially pernicious kind of allegory, for it is so impossible to visualize the things described that the concrete side of the parable goes to confusion, and the poem is inconsistent and incoherent throughout.

BERTOLOME ZORZI.

Very different is the romance of another Italian troubadour, Bertolome Zorzi.[1] This poem connects itself with the Court of Love conception on the other side altogether — through the idea of the God of Love as judge in lovers' quarrels.

The poet, wandering in search of a flower to cure him of his amorous pains, came upon a pair of lovers under the shade of an abbey. The man was appealing to the God of Love against being condemned unheard, when the voice of the God was heard saying that he had already passed judgment on the case, but would recall his sentence till he had listened to both sides.

The lady complained that the lover had brought shame on her by babbling of the favors she had granted him. This the man denied, accusing her of having listened too readily to slanderers. She next charged him with having attempted her honor, and he protested that, though he had been carried away by her beauty, he had never thought of dishonoring her, but that she, by obeying Love's command, could, without shame, have saved him from his suffering.

When the pleading was finished, the voice of Love was heard again saying that the lover was guiltless of babbling, but that he had been wrong in being so immoderate in his striving, yet that he deserved pardon on account of his sufferings while waiting for reconciliation, and that he should continue in the lady's service and she should reward his faithfulness. The sentence was executed.

The chief importance of this romance lies in its forming a link

---

[1] *Der Troubadour Bertolome Zorzi*, ed. by Emil Levy, Halle, 1883, p. 63. See also Diez, *Ueber die Minnehöfe*, pp. 23 ff.

between the pure allegory and the much disputed institution of the Court of Love.[1]

The most extended instance of a Court of Love allegory in Provençal is a poem contained in a MS. of the first half of the thirteenth century, formerly in the library of Sir Thomas Phillipps. This time Love is a regular feudal over-lord, who one fine day in spring calls together his barons at his dwelling on the top of Parnassus. The barons are ten in number: Joi, Solatz, Ardiment, Cortesia, Bon' Esperanza, Paor, Largueza, Domnei, Celament, and Dolsa Companhia. To each of them in turn Love makes a speech, thanking him for his services in the past and allotting new tasks for the furtherance of the lordship of Love. The background is the familiar one, with violets and other flowers, a pleasance hedged in with laurels and pines, fountains playing into golden basins, and a hundred fair damsels being kissed and embraced by their lovers. The door-keepers are Pretz and Drudaria.[2]

Most of the other Provençal material which has a connection with the Court of Love will come under the chapter on *Statutes.* References to the "cort del ver dieu d'amor"[3] or the "cortz de lejals amadors"[4] occur not infrequently in the lyrics of the troubadours, but there is no elaboration of the idea, and the meaning is little more than merely "the sphere of courtly love."

---

[1] See chap. viii, below.

[2] For the text see L. Constans, *Les Manuscrits provençaux de Cheltenham,* Paris, 1882, pp. 66-115; or *Revue des Langues Romanes,* 1881, Series 3, VI, 157 ff., 209 ff., 261 ff. Cf. also A. Thomas, *Franc. da Barberino,* in *Bibl. des Écoles franç. d'Athènes et de Rome,* fasc. 35, p. 65.

[3] Rich. de Tarascon, cited by Diez, *Ueber die Minnehöfe,* p. 21. Cf. *Parnasse occitanien,* p. 385.

[4] Gaucelm Faidit, cited by Trojel, *Middelalderens Elskovshoffer,* Copenhagen, 1888, pp. 199-200.

B. LATIN AND OLD FRENCH.

The most considerable group of Court of Love poems in the early period of Old French literature is bound together by an important identity of subject-matter : *viz.,* the discussion of the comparative merits of clerks and knights as lovers. The existence and wide prevalence of this discussion throw a significant light upon the social situation, in reading which it must be remembered that all the Latin and most of the vernacular poems were written by clerks, who, of course, gave the victory to their own side.

ROMARICIMONTIS CONCILIUM.

The *Romaricimontis Concilium,* or *Concile de Remiremont*[1] is a Latin poem by an unknown clerk. It is preserved in a MS. dated by Waitz, its editor, as "soweit ich mich jetzt erinnere, von einer hand des 11n oder spätestens 12n jh. geschrieben," though it is probably later. The place "Remiremont" and the names "de Granges" and "de Falcon" occurring in the poem, the same authority thinks point to the southern part of the diocese of Toul, in Lorraine. The poem is one of remarkable interest in itself; and is so important to us as containing the earliest instances of certain features of the Court of Love *genre* which were soon to become traditional, that a full account of its contents is justifiable.

On the Ides of April, an assembly of ladies [of religion] was held at Remiremont, where nothing but Love was discussed. For "puellae amantes" it was held, and no men except a few honest clerks were admitted. The doorkeeper was that Sibilia who had been a soldier of Venus from her tender years, and had without reluctance done whatever Love commanded.

Old ladies past the age of joy having been shut out, and all the bands of virgins admitted, Eva de Danubrio, universally affirmed to be "potens in officio artis amatoriae," read for gospel the precepts of the famous doctor Ovid, and two others sang songs of love.

---

[1] Printed by G. Waitz in *Zt. f. deutsches Alt.,* VII, 160–7 (cf. also XXI, 65 ff.), from Trèves MS., 1081 (LXXI). Cf. Pertz, *Archiv,* VII, 598, cited by Waitz.

After this the " cardinalis domina " stood up in the midst and called for silence. She was becomingly dressed in a many-colored gown, brighter than gems, more precious than gold, and hung with a thousand flowers of May. This royal maid, the flower and glory of the world, eloquent and learned, announced that she had been sent by the God of Love, at the suggestion of April and May, to inquire into the lives of those who were present. Elisabet de Granges rose and stated that they served Love as well as they could. " Nothing that he wishes displeases us, and if we neglect anything, it is unwittingly. Thus we choose to keep no regular bond with any man, nor do we know any unless he be of our order." Elisabet de Falcon followed and more distinctly declared that they loved the favor, praise, and memory of clerks, whose "rule" alone held them, and whom they knew to be "affabiles, gratos et amabiles." Clerks were courteous and honorable, and knew not deceit or slander ; they had experience and diligence in loving. They gave beautiful gifts and kept agreements well; if they loved anything sweetly, they did not relinquish it lightly. The breaking of foolish vows was not mortal sin. The love of knights she declared detestable and unstable ; and, though confessing that once she and her sisters sought their notice, she asserted that they soon discovered their guile and transferred themselves to the jolly clerks whose love was without vice, strong, firm, and stable.

This view was approved by the lady cardinal; but a new speaker, Elisabet Pompona, came forward on behalf of the knights "who go boldly to battle for our sakes, and to please us fear neither hardships, wounds nor death. Such we choose, such we make ours; their prosperity is our happiness, their sadness disturbs our joy." " Such an occupation," continues one Adeleyt, "pleases me more than the psalter. . . . Compared with this tie, I hold our rule light."

But the weight of opinion was on the other side. "We have given ourselves to the clerks and we will not change. . . . The whole country smiles with their mirth : they praise us in all kinds of verses. Such men do I love above all others, by the command of Venus." Knights are blamed for levity and foolish talkativeness; they like to slander and reveal secrets. " I have known the life and manners of all lovers. . . .

There is no happiness, no faithfulness in the love of knights. It is good and wise to choose clerks; their love is a great delight."

Then the chief lady summed up, and decreed the expulsion of all who did not disown the love of knights. Faithfulness to one lover, under pain of heavy penance, was enjoined. Never must they give to vile knights "tactum vestri corporis, vel colli, vel femoris." Pleasure taken with knights gave rise to scandal: clerks knew how to arrange things and could keep secrets.

All responded in support of this decision and declared that the decrees should be announced through all the churches to the convent girls. An " Excommunicatio Rebellarum " was drawn up : " By the command of Venus, to you and others everywhere who yield to the love of knights let there remain confusion, terror, contrition, and many other curses, unless you repent and are forgiven." " Ad confirmacionem omnes dicimus Amen. . . . Militibus victis, cessit victoria clero."

The following features of this poem are specially to be noted :

(1) The time of meeting, — the Ides of April. Note also that it ﹖ is April and May who suggest to the God of Love the sending of the *cardinalis domina.*

(2) The parody of the church service, — reading Ovid for the gospel and singing love songs for hymns, and the Excommunication.

(3) The association of Sibilia, as a single person, with Venus.

(4) The function and dress of the *cardinalis domina.*

(5) The qualities for which Elizabeth of Falcon praises the clerks and those for which she blames the knights.

(6) The unmistakably sensual nature of the love discussed.

(7) The " clerk *v.* knight " debate.

The second, third, fifth, and seventh points will be treated in subsequent sections. The first, the placing of a Court of Love in the spring, hardly needs explanation. Finding its root in a natural phenomenon, the association of love with the springtime is probably as old as love poetry, and is constantly appearing, — in the *Pervigilium Veneris*, in practically all mediæval love allegories, down to the robin and the lapwing, the dove and the young man of the " Locksley Halls " of our own time. The association of May 1st with Venus, which finds its finest expression in the Latin poem just mentioned, and the May-day festivities which have not yet quite died out, are the outcome of the same natural causes.[1]

In the case of the fourth point, we may remark that though this poem is not in a strict sense a Court of Venus or Cupid, yet the God of Love is represented by the Lady Cardinal in a fashion slightly analogous to that of Alcestis in the *Court of Love;* and that her dress, though not elaborately described, is of the same kind as is to be found in the usual descriptions of the occupant of the throne of Love. The figure throughout, however, is clearly taken rather from the ecclesiastical than the feudal side of mediæval life ; and this ecclesiastical element continues to appear, alone or mixed with the feudal, down to the sixteenth century.

THE *DE PHYLLIDE ET FLORA* GROUP.

The *Altercatio*, as it is sometimes called, *De Phyllide et Flora*[2] is the next poem on the "clerk *v.* knight" theme, and it also is in Latin. The exact date of the poem, the name and even the nationality of the writer, are unknown, though M. Gédéon Huet[3] has attempted to prove by parallelisms from the *chansons de geste* that the author was a Frenchman. Its influence upon French poetry is, however, sufficient justification for introducing it at this point.

One fine morning in spring Phyllis and Flora walk out into the meadows.

> Erant ambae uirgines et ambae reginae
> Phyllis coma libera Flora compto crine.

---

[1] See Lucretius, i, 1–40, and cf. H. A. J. Munro's ed. of Lucretius, Cambridge, 1886, II, 23, n. on ll. 10, 12 ; and G. Paris, *Les Origines de la poésie lyrique en France*, in *Journal des Savants*, 1891, p. 686 ; 1892, pp. 156–8. This last reference I owe to Professor Marsh.

[2] *Carmina Burana*, Stuttgart, 1847, pp. 155 ff., or in *Latin Poems commonly att. to W. Mapes*, ed. by T. Wright, for Camden Soc., Lond., 1841, p. 258. It has been printed also by J. Grimm, *Gedichte des Mittelalters*, etc., in *Abhand.* of Berlin Acad., 1843, p. 218; by Von Aretin, *Beyträge zur Gesch. u. Lit.*, Munich, 1806, VII, 301. Cf. Hauréau, *Notices et Extraits des MSS.*, Paris, 1880, XXIX, pt. 2, 305–9.

[3] *Romania*, XXII, 536 ff.

They are alike in all respects save one — Phyllis loves a knight, Flora a clerk. Coming to a brook, they sit down in the shade of a great pine on the bank. Sighs betray them to each other, and they exchange love-confidences. Phyllis apostrophizes Paris, and magnifies the soldier's life, while Flora longs for Alcibiades, and praises "sola felicia clericorum jura." Phyllis says that clerks are epicures who care only to sleep, eat, and drink, while love and youth are the soldier's food and drink. Flora ascribes such charges to envy, and contrasts the clerk's ease and affluence with the knight's poverty and hardship.

> Sentit tela Veneris et amoris ictus,
> Non tamen est clericus macer et afflictus.

Phyllis thinks she must be blind who does not see the superior glory of the knight riding armor-clad to battle as contrasted with the lazy clerk rising reluctantly at dawn ; but Flora insists that the knight is merely driven to his strenuousness by poverty. Finally she appeals to Cupid, and Phyllis acquiesces.

So to Cupid they go, and many stanzas are filled with a description of the mule and the horse they ride. Soon they reach the Paradise of Love, at the entrance of which murmurs a river, and the air is laden with sweet odors and the sounds of music.

> Sonant omnes uolucrum lingua uoce plena :
> Vox auditur merulae dulcis et amena,
> Corydalus garrulus, turtur, philomena,
> Quae non cessat conqueri de transacta poena.

They enter and approach the god.

> Circa siluae medium locus est occultus,
> Ubi uiget maxime suus deo cultus ;
> Fauni, Nymphae, Satyri, comitatus multus
> Tympanizant, concinunt ante dei uultus.

> *   *   *   *   *

> Inter haec aspicitur Cythereae natus,
> Vultus est sidereus, uertex est pennatus,
> Arcum laeua possidet et sagittas latus :
> Satis potest coniici potens et elatus.

The god holds a flower-wreathed sceptre, and three Graces, on bended knee, offer him a cup. (Cf. the Graces attending on Venus in the Homeric Hymn and in Claudian. See pp. 12 and 16 above.) The maidens approach and state their case.

> Amor habet iudīces, Amor habet iura;
> Sunt Amoris iudices Usus et Natura.
> Istis tota data est curiae censura,
> Quoniam praeterita sciunt et futura.

Judgment is in favor of the clerk.

This poem had a wide popularity. Two English translations of the time of Elizabeth still exist, one by "R. S.,"[1] and one by Chapman.[2] Four Old French poems on the same model survive, and of these, two seem to have been written in England.

Florance et Blancheflor, or *Le Jugement d'Amour*[3] is exactly the same in plot as *De Phyllide et Flora* up to the point where the ladies arrive at the palace of the God of Love. The description of the dwelling is here much more elaborate, and we have the beginnings of a new type of palace, even more fantastic than the bejewelled mansion of the type of Ovid's palace of Apollo. The walls are not of stone, but of roses and other flowers, and the grounds are fenced in with Cupid's bows. No "vilain" can pass the gates : all must bear the seal of love. On arriving, the damsels dismount under a pine, and two birds come down from the tree and lead them to the palace. When the God of Love sees them he leaps from his bed, salutes them courteously, and, taking them by the hand, seats them beside himself and asks their needs. Blancheflor states the case, and the king [he was a god a moment before] assembles his barons to decide the question. When the court, which consists of birds, has assembled, the king lays the question before them. The side of the knight is taken by Sire Esperviers, Sire Faucons, and the Gais ; that of the clerk by Dame Kalandre, Dame Aloë, and the Rossignox. The jay

---

[1] See Wright's *Lat. Poems att. to W. Mapes*, Lond., 1841, p. 363.

[2] *Works of Chapman*, Lond., 1875, II, 43–9, *The Amorous Contention of Phillis and Flora*, "trans. out of a Latin copy written by a Friar, anno 1400." The Latin text is also given.

[3] Barbazan et Méon, *Fabliaux et Contes*, Paris, 1808, IV, 354–65.

thinks the clerk's business is to pray for souls, and the knight's to love ladies. The nightingale offers to fight in support of the clerk's claim, and the parrot accepts the challenge. After a fight in which the armor consists of rose-petal helmets and the like, the nightingale wins, and the parrot yields up his sword, confessing that the clerk is valiant, and more courteous than any other.

At this decision Florance weeps and tears her hair. Three times she faints and recovers : the fourth time she dies. The birds assemble for the funeral, and make her a rich grave scattered with flowers, and write as epitaph :

> Ici est Florance enfoïe,
> Qui au Chevalier fu amie.

The second Old French poem of this group is fragmentary, but so far as it is preserved it is very close to the foregoing. It is called *Hueline et Aiglantine*,[1] from the names of the heroines. The particular quality that each insists that her lover has most of is courtesy, and the discussion almost takes the form of a *tenson*. They set off to seek an umpire and meet two bachelors, who direct them to the God of Love. Shortly after they come within a wall which no snow or rain or fire can pass,[2] and they see a palace built of flowers and spices. They dismount by a tree in whose branches singing birds "d'amors movent lo cenbel." Here the MS. breaks off.

The following extract from *Hueline et Aiglantine* will serve as an example of the fantastic palace introduced in this group of poems :

> Et après voient lo palais,
> Ainz tel ne fu, ne n'ert jamais.
> La closture est de flor de lis,
> Soef en flaire li païs ;
> Et tuit li tré sont de cristal,
> Li paleron de garingal ;
> Di ginbregien sont li chevron,
> Et de ciprès lo freste en son.
> De canele est l'antravéure,
> Et de basme la coverture ;
> Moult par est biax sanz nul redout.

---

[1] Méon, *Nouveau Recueil de Fabliaux et Contes*, Paris, 1823, I, 353–63.
[2] Cf. passage from Claudian on p. 15, above.

Li conpas est de requelice,
Qui aportez fu d'outre Grice :
Li pavement sont tuit de flors,
Mil libres valent li péors ;
Et moult est granz la doçors, etc. (vv. 293-308).

The two Old French poems of this group that were written in England are the *Geste de Blancheflour et Florence,*[1] in which a king again presides and birds form the court, deciding the question by combat in favor of the knight ; and *Melior et Idoine,*[2] in which the scene is laid near Lincoln. Here there is no god of Love, and the author himself overhears the damsels dispute as he is riding to Lincoln. The appeal is simply to the birds and the verdict is in favor of the clerk.

The Debate which forms the central motive of this group of poems is a literary form that we shall find frequently associated with the machinery of the Court of Venus. The more remote results of this association will be discussed in the chapter on the Relation of the Allegory to the Institution of the Court of Love (chap. viii, below). For the origin of the Debate itself see A. Jeanroy, *Les Origines de la Poésie Lyrique en France au Moyen Age.*[3]

The wide circulation of the Latin form of *De Phyllide et Flora* has already been noted. Besides the late English translations, there is a dramatized French version whose date is probably between 1490 and 1550.[4]

The inconsistency in the use of "king" or "god" for the central personage in *Florance et Blancheflor,* which has been noted above, is suggestive of the process by which the classical divine court took on a feudal character. The birds are just about to be brought in, not merely as attendants on the God of Love, but as barons with delib-

---

[1] In a unique MS. at Cheltenham. See P. Meyer, *Rom.,* XV, 332 ff., and Langlois, *Origines et Sources du Roman de la Rose,* Paris, 1891, p. 15. The last stanza states it was written in English by Wanastre and translated into French by Brykholle.

[2] P. Meyer, *Rom.,* XV, 333; and Langlois, *Origines et Sources,* etc., p. 14.

[3] Paris, 1889. See especially pp. 45 ff.

[4] See p. 108.

erating power, and almost unconsciously, it might seem, the poet begins to speak of a king instead of a god.

Before going on to our next Old French author, we may notice one or two other passages from the same collection as *De Phyllide et Flora* — the *Carmina Burana.* References to Cupid's arrows and other paraphernalia are frequent in the love songs of the collection, as

> Venus me telo uulnerauit
> Aureo, quod cor penetrauit (p. 145),

or in more detail,

> Est Amor alatus puer et leuis, est pharetratus.
> Ala recessurum demonstrat, tela cruentum,
> Aetas amentem probat et ratione carentem.
> Vulnificus pharetra signatur, mobilis ala.
> Nudus formatur, quia nil est quo teneatur.
> Mittit pentagonas neruo stridente sagittas,
> Quod sunt quinque modi quibus associamur amori,
> Visus, colloquium, tactus, compar labiorum.[1]

The resemblance of this interpretation to those quoted from Fulgentius, Jerome, and Theodulfus on p. 22, above, is clear, though there is here an appropriate absence of the grave severity of the churchmen.

Of more significance than these is a poem [2] which is interesting because it seems to indicate that the allegorical machinery with which we have become familiar in the poems lately described was already so well known as to allow of its becoming a medium for burlesque. The poet, speaking in the first person, tells how he was a guest, "vino debachatus," at an inn beside the temple of Venus. From out of the doors of the "almum templum" came a sound of sweet singing, — from sirens, many thought, — and going up to the porter, "virgo nobilis, pulchra, statu brevi," he asked for admission. In answer to her questions he told her he was wounded with the arrow of Venus and sought a speedy cure. Venus summoned him to her

---

[1] *Carmina Burana*, Stuttgart, 1847, no. 116 b.   [2] *Ibid.*, no. 49.

presence, and trembling with fear he approached and knelt before her. She asked him questions, and when he sought a cure she promised him

> Si tu das denarios monetae electae,
> Dabitur consilium salutis perfectae.

The money was forthcoming, and hand in hand they went to where they found many beautiful creatures, all alike in nature and dress, who rose in welcome and offered seats. But Venus said, "aliud volumus explere."

> Innuens his omnibus ipsa abire cito
> Pariter remansimus in loco munito.
> Solis quiescentibus strato redimito
> Plura pertractavimus sermone polito.

After further details of his entertainment which leave no doubt as to the nature of the "templum," the author says that he and his companion went to bathe in a garden bath consecrated to Jove, and thence he emerged refreshed and hungry. A feast, chiefly of fowls, was served, and he stayed till "a Venere sum nunc allevatus nummis." The poem ends with an admonition to young men to heed his experience.

The phrase "templum Veneris," the sound of singing, the porter, the arrow, the way in which the hero is led to the goddess, the throng of beautiful maidens — all these point to a familiarity with exactly that kind of allegory which we are studying. The cloak of the double meaning falls off when the poem is about half finished, and the second part is realistic rather than allegorical.

If the date of the poem were to be neglected, one might suggest that the author had in mind rather the obscene rites that were in some cases observed in the worship of the earthly Aphrodite, and the practice of prostitution in connection with the temples of that goddess in several cities, notably in Corinth; but the knowledge of antiquity current in the middle ages was not of such a nature as to make this at all probable. If any general inference is to be drawn from this poem at all, it is more likely that, as has been said, the Court of Venus allegory was already familiar enough to give point to a parody.

LI FABLEL DOU DIEU D'AMOURS.

There is less uncertainty as to the relations of our next example. *Li Fablel dou Dieu d'Amours*[1] is, as Langlois makes out with considerable certainty, a somewhat clumsy imitation of some form of the story of which *De Phyllide et Flora* is our earliest surviving example. It gains a separate importance, however, from the greater elaboration of some features, and from the fact that it is probably the medium through which the preceding group influenced the *Roman de la Rose.* It is the first poem of its class, too, which is in the dream-setting that afterwards becomes almost the rule.

The author, who writes in the first person, had a vision that he was walking one bright May morning in a fair garden watered by a clear brook and surrounded by a ditch and a marvellous wall within which no " vilain " was admitted. He seated himself under a tree with healing powers, and listened to the songs of the birds until he almost thought himself in paradise. The nightingale called the other birds round him, and complained of the degeneration of love. The hawk laid the blame on the "villaine gent," but the thrush objected to the hawk's confining love to clerks and knights. The jay, too, was democratic, and thought that to love and be well loved was to be as worthy and wise as a clerk. The nightingale agreed and dismissed the assembly, leaving the lover lying delightless under the tree.

From this dream the lover fell into another. He saw approaching a maiden, whom he recognized as his lady. They met with affectionate embraces; but in the midst of their talk a dragon descended and carried her off, leaving him lamenting and declaring the folly of serving the God of Love. Just then the god himself came riding up, and, after some conversation, promised succor. He carried off the lover to his palace, Champ Fleuri, leaving him here while he went to hunt the dragon. In the description of the palace the metaphorical element is carried one step farther than in *Florance et Blancheflor.* The ditches were of sighs, the water was lovers' tears

---

[1] Ed. by A. Jubinal, Paris, 1834. For its derivation from the *Florance et Blancheflor* debate, see Langlois, *Origines*, pp. 17 ff.

and so on. The gate was guarded by the Phœnix. The hero entered and found the palace supported by pillars representing the Months. The hall was filled with youths and maidens playing chess and tables for kisses, but they all stopped to give him welcome, which he acknowledged by singing a love-song. Then a girl took him by the hand to show him the glories of the mansion, and they visited the chamber of the god, where hung two quivers, one with arrows tipped with lead, the other with arrows having points of gold.

> Li diex d'amors qant se va deporter,
> De ces saietes cui il en velt navrer,
> Contre ses dars ne se puet nus tenser :
> L'un fait haïr et l'autre fait amer (p. 31).

Out in a meadow under a tree his guide showed him the grave of a king's son, over whom the birds sang of true love. This had been her own lover who had died for her.

On returning to the house, they found the god just arrived with the hero's lady. The hero thanked him with great joy, but immediately awoke and found it but a dream.

DE VENUS LA DEESSE D'AMOR.

A great part of the *Fablel dou Dieu d'Amours* is reproduced in another poem, which, though changing many details and modifying the plot, is yet manifestly founded on it. *De Venus la Deesse d'Amor*[1] is written in the third person, but otherwise follows the model closely till we come to the dispute among the birds. When the nightingale is describing the symptoms of lovers,[2] the hero exclaims that he is such a man, and frightens the bird away. Here a gap in the text occurs, and this is followed by a long lament on the miseries of the lover, whose lady is absent. After this appears the Goddess of Love attended by three damsels, all riding on mules. The birds, who have returned, now proclaim the lover's distress and get the goddess to promise her assistance. After inquiries concerning his loyalty, Venus leads him to the Court of the God of Love,

---

[1] *De Venus la Deesse d'Amor*, ed. by W. Foerster, Bonn, 1880.
[2] See p. 185, below.

where they are admitted on showing the seal of love. Venus is warmly welcomed; and, going to the god's chamber, they find him on a bed of flowers. He rises, and embraces and makes much of the goddess. The hall is described: roses and other flowers are everywhere; the door is of coral, the building itself of crystal, the water "qui enclot le palais sont lerme: de pities." Then a girl acts as guide, as in the model, and the lover sees the chamber, the arrows, and the tomb. When they return to the palace, ten maidens bring in a bier with the body of a true lover, which is given a rich funeral.

Now the goddess leads the hero before the God of Love, who embraces her and seats her beside him, while the true languishing lover kneels before them. A prince sounds a golden "sifflet" and calls for silence. The goddess rises and makes a plea for the lover, and the god grants her what she seeks, and his seal. The nightingale offers to devise the charter, and gets the commission. This charter orders the lady to return the passion of the loyal lover on pain of fearful vengeance. But when the lover, having taken leave of the Court, and having come to his lady, presents it, she yields at once, and the poem ends.

Several of the features of these two poems will be spoken of in special chapters; but at present we may note the extending use of birds and flowers, the persistence of the two kinds of arrows and of the guide, and the growing distinctness of the picture of a feudal court in its double aspect of a social and a legal institution. The courts of the feudal lords were, of course, not only the social centres of their territories, but were also the places where justice was administered, and even in *De Phyllide et Flora* this double function is indicated. On the arrival of the hero or heroine, the lord and his retinue are usually found enjoying themselves; but they are always ready for business when a case turns up, the decision sometimes lying with the lord himself, as in *De Venus la Deesse*, sometimes being handed over to his barons, as in the *Altercatio*. In the poem just outlined it is to be remarked that the god is not called Cupid, and that he seems to be the husband or lover of Venus rather than her son.

CHRESTIEN DE TROYES.

In the extant works of Chrestien de Troyes we have no extended
allegory, but there occur throughout his romances allusions to the
God of Love which point to a familiarity with the conception of him
as a feudal lord.   Thus in *Yvain*,[1] vv. 5375 ff. we read : —

> Et s'estoit si tres bele et jante
> Qu'an li servir meist s' antante
> Li Deus d'Amors s' il la veïst
> Ne ja amer ne la feïst
> Autrui se lui meïsmes non.
> Por li servir devenist hon,
> S' eissist de sa deïté fors
> Et ferist lui meïsme el cors
> Del dart don la plaie ne sainne
> Se desleaus mires n' i painne.

Again in *Cligès*,[2] vv. 3865 ff. : —

> Vos qui d'Amor vos feites sage,
> Qui les costumes et l'usage
> *De sa cort* maintenez a foi . . .

and a little later, vv. 3886 ff.,

> De peor doit serjanz tranbler,
> Quant ses sire l'apele ou mande.
> Et qui a Amor se comande,
> Son mestre et son seignor an fet,
> S'est droiz qu'an reverance l'et
> Et mout le crieme et mout l'enort,
> S'il viaut bien estre *de sa cort*.

A number of such passages could be gathered from Chrestien ; others
will be found in the chapter on the Statutes.

JEAN DE HAUTEVILLE.

Contemporary with the great romance writer was a Latin poet
whose affiliations are with the allegorists of the fourth and fifth

---

[1] Ed. by W. Foerster, Halle, 1891, p. 142.
[2] Ed. by W. Foerster, Halle, 1888, p. 102.

centuries, and who has a place as one of the links between these early writers and the *Roman de la Rose.* The *Architrenius*[1] of Jean de Hauteville contains numerous figures belonging to the same class of personifications which Claudian delighted in. Thus his House of Venus (bk. i, p. 252) has quite clear evidence of his acquaintance with that poet's works:

> Jamque fatigato Veneris domus aurea, rerum
> Flosculus, occurrit, monte superedita, qualem
> Cantat odorifero Philomena poetica uersu.
> Quae quibus intorsit odii certamina liuor
> Ruffinum uitiis, Stiliconem moribus, armat,
> Alternansque stylos, istum premit, erigit illum ;
> Neutrum describit, tacet ambos, fingit utrumque.
> Hic dea uirginibus roseum cingentibus orbem
> Praesidet, et rudibus legit incentiua puellis ;
> Inque uiros faculas accendit, et implicat hamos.

His description of Cupid[2] and of Dame Nature[3] are also in the direct line of tradition.

ANDREAS CAPELLANUS.

The *De Arte Honeste Amandi*[4] of Andreas Capellanus is so largely devoted to the jurisprudence of love that its detailed treatment falls under the head of Statutes of Love. Yet there occur in it certain allegorical passages treating especially of the Palace of Love, so that some account of it comes in at this point.

The book as we have it was probably compiled about 1200, though there remain several difficult problems about its date, original form, and the identity of its author.[5] The evidence for an earlier form lies

---

[1] For this reference I am indebted to Professor Kittredge. For edition see T. Wright's *Anglo-Latin Satirical Poets of the 12th Century,* Lond., 1872, I, 240 ff.

[2] Wright's ed., bk. ii, pp. 260 ff.   [3] *Ibid.,* bk. viii, p. 369.

[4] *Andreae Capellani Regii Francorum De Amore,* ed. by E. Trojel, Copenhagen, 1892.

[5] On the question of date, etc., see G. Paris, *Romania,* XII, 526 ff., XIII, 403 ; P. Meyer, *Les derniers Troubadours,* Paris, 1871, p. 68 ; Brakelmann, *Jahrbuch f. rom. u. engl. Lit.,* IX, 429 ; P. Rajna, *Tre Studj per la Storia del Libro di Andrea Capellano* in *Studj di filol. rom.,* 1891, V, 193-272 ; Trojel, Introduction to his edition.

in such facts as that in one of the decisions which it gives regarding a question of love, the Countess of Flanders quotes the " Capellani doctrinam." [1]

On pp. 89 ff. of Trojel's edition there is a description of the palace of Love differing in many interesting details from those already quoted. This building stands in the centre of the world, and has four fronts, each front having a beautiful portal. Here dwell the God of Love himself and "dominarum collegia." The eastern doorway is kept for the god; the other three are used by three classes of ladies respectively. The ladies of the south door are always dallying about the threshold, the door being kept open. Those of the west perpetually wander beyond the entrance. Those of the north stay within closed doors and never look beyond the limits of the palace.

Meridianae sunt illae, igitur, quae amare uolunt et dignos non repellunt amantes, et merito, quia, quum sint in meridie cunctae dispositae, ab ipsius in oriente habitantis amoris meruerunt radio coruscari. Occidentales uero sunt meretrices, quae uix aliquem amant nec ab aliquo probo inueniuntur amari, et merito, quia quum in occidente ipsarum reperiatur habitatio sita, igneus amoris radius ab oriente ad illas usque peruenire non potest. Septentrionales uero sunt illae mulieres, quae amare recusant, quamuis illae amentur a multis, et merito, quia in sinistra positas deus non respicit ipsas, quia sunt maledictae. Ex his uero uerbis amoris patet palatii dispositio manifesta.

This description is given by a knight to a lady whom he wishes to frighten out of her coldness, and it is reinforced by the account which follows of a procession of the inmates of this palace. In his vision, the speaker says, he saw a procession led by a man crowned with a golden diadem and riding a beautiful horse. He was followed, first, by a great troop of women gorgeously arrayed and each seated " in equo pinguissimo et formoso." A knight was in attendance on each side, and a third led the horse by the bridle. The second troop of women were also attended, but were in great discomfort through the noise and confusion of the many who wished to wait on them. The third rode in miserable garments on wretched limping horses, and

---

[1] P. 283 of Trojel's ed. For other instances of the book's quoting itself, see pp. 106 and 148.

were without attendants. One of this last class acted as guide and interpreted thus :

Miles quem uides cuncto populo aureo diademate coronatum praecedere, deus est amoris, qui singulis septimanis una die praesenti cernitur adiunctis militiae et cuique, prout bene uel male gessit in uita, mirabiliter pro cuiusque retribuit meritis.

But this is not all. Led by his unfortunate interlocutor, the knight follows the procession to a beautiful meadow surrounded by " pomiferous and odoriferous " trees, and divided by concentric circles into three parts. In the centre of the innermost circle stood a wonderful tree bearing all kinds of fruits, and having at its root a fountain of nectar in which all kinds of fishes swam. Beside the tree,

in throno quodam ex auro et omni lapidum ornatu constructo regina sedebat amoris splendidissimam suo capite gerens coronam, et ipsa pretiosissimis sedebat vestimentis ornata auream manu virgam retinens.

At her right hand stood another gorgeous seat, empty. The streams from the central fountain pleasantly watered the first part, but flooded the second, which was called " humiditas," and the water there became very cold, though overhead the sun blazed and there was no tree to shelter. The third zone was called " siccitas " : there everything was arid, and the air was full of fiery vapors as from a red-hot furnace. All about lay bundles of thorns with a log through the midst of each, and a strong man stood at each end of the log. But through the third and second regions a pleasant road led to the centre, encumbered with none of these things.

Now the King of Love entered and, after embracing the Queen, took his seat on the vacant throne. The three bands followed and took possession of their respective regions, the members of the third being forced to sit on the bundles of thorns while the men in attendance kept the axles in motion. The knight now asked leave to go ; but his guide sent him before the God of Love, and instructed him to pay great attention and not to forget to pray for her. So to the god he went and sought mercy and advice, and favor for his guide. The deity instructed him to use this vision for the salvation of all such women as he should find resisting love ; enumerated the twelve chief precepts of love, and made some concessions to the guide. Then the knight returned to the world.

Some of the features of this story are merely conventional, — the dream form, the meadow with its trees and fountain, the gorgeous costumes, and the guide. Since in date Andreas probably comes between *Li Fablel dou Dieu d'Amours* and *De Venus la Deesse d'Amor*, it is worth noting that the relation of the God and the Goddess is the same in Andreas as in the second of the two poems, neither of the names Cupid or Venus being used in the prose work. Again, though in the scene in the meadow of the Paradise of Love the God and the Goddess are called King and Queen, the whole conception here is borrowed from the religious rather than the feudal world ; the rewards and punishments are not such as a sovereign might inflict, but are an adaptation of the theological conceptions of paradise, purgatory, and hell. It is important also to remember that all this was written a century before the *Divine Comedy*. Observe, too, that the palace and the meadow scene are quite separate.

HUON DE MERY.

In *Le Tornoiement d'Antéchrist*[1] by Huon de Mery (ca. 1235) we have a poem which as a whole belongs to the Prudentius-Bunyan line of allegorical tradition, but which has one passage containing a good deal of the Court of Love machinery.

In the army of Christ, made up of Virtues and their followers, comes Love, riding with Prowess, Courtesy, and Largess. They are arming Love with a shield painted with flowers and adorned with other emblems.

> L'escu, qui est sanz vilenie,
> A .iiii. roussignous d'argent,
> A l'esprevier courtois et gent,
> Qui de voler ne se repose (vv. 172–225).

Love bears also "l'arc turcois encordé d'argent," and a quiver full of amorous darts, furnished with feathers which Love had bound to the wood with a "blanc chevol d'Aliance." Every one would wish

---

[1] *Le Tornoiement de l'Antechrist*, par Huon de Mery, ed. by P. Tarbé, Reims, 1851, especially pp. 51 ff. I follow the ed. of Wimmer, Marburg, 1888 (*Ausg. u. Abh.*, no. 76).

to be wounded with such an arrow, so that the point should remain in his heart, for it is called "douz anemis," and no heart is proud enough to resist its force and refrain from becoming "douz et atempréz et courtois."

> Car Amours a si courtois non,
> Que se vileins de li s'acointe,
> Amours le fet courtois et cointe,
> Et le felon fet franc et douz,
> Et l'orgeillous met a genouz,
> Et [donte] les outredoutez (vv. 1768-73).

When the battle is joined, Virginity and Chastity are found making successful war against Fornication and Adultery, but Cupid and Venus come to the aid of the latter. Cupid draws his bow and Chastity turns in flight. Venus holds the bow of Temptation which Love has strung with the tresses of damsels, and shoots with a barbed arrow at Virginity. The poet himself is struck to the heart with this arrow, and he stretches himself on the grass while Bras-de-Fer comforts him. Esperance holds his head, and they begin to work necromancy on him without avail. So much is he grieved with Desperance that he swoons and sees a vision of Venus and a great procession of goddesses coming to help him in his pain, — a pain in the heart worse than toothache, he says. Venus, Temptation, and Amor administer a potion in a silver phial which he drains at one draught, with such effect that if Esperance had not put a plaster of good hope on his left side his soul would have been drawn out of his body. But now his spirit returns and he calls for justice. The judge acquits Venus and puts the blame on his eyes, the porters of the castle, who left the gate open. The eyes protest, Reason replies, and all approve. Virginity, Chastity, and their followers are put to flight. In the long run, the Vices are overthrown.

In this passage Love, of course, instead of being the supreme power, is only one of the abstractions taking part in the tournament, so that it is not so absurd to find Venus herself complained of before a judge. But the whole matter is very much confused. Love is introduced on the side of Christ, and in excellent company, — his attendants Prowess, Courtesy, and Largess being the regular knightly virtues which are so constantly insisted on in the Statutes. The moral influence of love is also dwelt on here as in the later poems : yet when the fighting once begins Love is on the side of the Vices. This confusion is really the result of the influence of the two classes of models which Huon de Mery had before him. On the one hand was the growing mass of literature in praise of Love which we are particularly studying ; on the other was the didactic allegory with a purely moral and religious aim, and a tendency to treat love from the ascetic point of view. When Love comes riding in, Huon is thinking of the favorable representations ; but when the fight begins he falls into the clerical attitude and naturally enough ranges him against Virginity and Chastity. The confusion is interesting as being another instance of the two tendencies in this allegorizing of love, — the feudal and the religious.

The metaphor of the eyes as the porters at the gate of the castle of the soul, which adds to the confusion of the figures at the close, is one which occurs later. The bird and arrow motives reappear.

ALANUS DE INSULIS.

Another Latin poem which contributes to the collection of allegorical houses and persons from which the authors of the *Roman de la Rose* had to draw is the *Anticlaudianus*[1] of Alanus de Insulis (Alanus Anglicus).[2] The type is easily recognizable in the following description of the House of Nature :

> In medio nemoris euadit in aera montis
> Ardua planities, et nubibus oscula donat.
> Hic domus erigitur Naturae. . . .
> Nec sibi dignetur conferre palatia regum,
> A nostris laribus excepta beatior aula.
> Aera metitur, altis suspensa columnis ;
> Sidere gemmarum prefulgurat, ardet in auro.
> Nec minus argenti proprio donatur honore (i. 4).

It is adorned with paintings too, and portraits of Aristotle, Plato, and others. In lib. i, cap. 3, also occurs a somewhat similar descrip-

---

[1] T. Wright, *Anglo-Latin Satirical Poems*, etc., II, 268 ff.

[2] For influences other than those taken up here, see E. Langlois, *Origines*, etc., pp. 148–50.

tion of the palace where Nature deliberates with the Virtues; in i, 7, a portrait of Prudentia, "lilia nupta rosis"; in i, 10, of Ratio, and in viii, 1, the House of Fortune, half on a hill and half in a valley, at once ruinous and gorgeous, stormed against by Boreas and breathed on by Zephyrus.

> Hic est Fortunae sua mansio, si tamen usquam
> Res manet instabilis, residet uaga, mobilis haeret.

ROMAN DE LA ROSE.

We now arrive at the consideration of a poem of vastly greater importance than any mediæval document that we have yet discussed. The *Roman de la Rose* is so compendious that there are few motives of any importance in the class of poems we are here concerned with, which are not found represented in it; and its influence was so extensive and so profound that there are few of these poems in the two or three centuries following which do not give evidence of their authors' acquaintance with it. Yet M. Langlois is undoubtedly right when he points out [1] the error of supposing that the authors of the *Roman* are responsible for the prodigious predominance of allegory in the imaginative work of the succeeding centuries. The appearance of a masterpiece in any literary *genre* does undoubtedly lead to a more extensive cultivation of that *genre* by the great crowd of minor authors; and in this way Guillaume de Lorris and Jean de Meun must bear their share of the blame, if blame it must be called, of making allegory so universal in France and the countries under her literary influence from 1250 to 1550. But we have already produced sufficient instances of exactly the kind of thing of which the *Roman de la Rose* is the supreme example to show that allegory was an increasingly favorite form before Guillaume began his poem, and to justify the assumption that it would have been more and more extensively employed though he had never lived. It does not require a very profound knowledge of the working of the mediæval mind to feel that in this elaborating of double meanings and this classifying

---

[1] *Histoire de la Langue et de la Littérature française*, ed. by Petit de Julleville, Paris, 1896–7, II, 154.

and labelling of emotional states, that mind found a naturally con-
genial field for those subtle exercises in which it took delight.

It will not be necessary for our present purpose to give a complete
analysis of the 22,000 lines of the *Roman de la Rose*, since the poem
itself is much better known than most of those with which we have
to deal, and since such an analysis is easily accessible.[1] Our ends
will be sufficiently served if we select those features which find a
parallel in the English *Court of Love* or to any large extent in the
other poems of its class.

I. The dream setting is used. We have already found this in
Li Fablel dou Dieu d'Amours, and the author himself declares his
knowledge of Macrobius's commentary on the *Somnium Scipionis* of
Cicero. But after this poem the framework of a vision is much
more a matter of course, and the use of it by Chaucer, and through
Chaucer, by many other poets in Britain is the direct result of the
Roman de la Rose. The Middle English *Court of Love*, curiously
enough, is not a vision.

II. The description of a May morning at the opening of the poem
is already a tradition of long descent, and has been commented on
above (pp. 33–4). The *Roman*, however, has much more detail here,
and the detail becomes henceforth part of the tradition. This
feature also is lacking in the English *Court of Love*.

III. The placing of the Court in a meadow surrounded by fine
trees, with streams and fountains, with abundance of all kinds of
flowers, and with birds singing — all this had already become familiar,
though here, too, the generous scale of the poem allowed a great
deal of detail. The *Court of Love* uses the flowers in describing the
decoration of the palace, and the birds in the litany at the end, but,
except in the reference to the gathering of hawthorn by the court in
the last few stanzas, the action is all in-doors.

IV. The painting on the walls is suggested probably by the
mediæval fashion of decorating with some kind of fresco instead of
tapestry. The house of Nature in the *Anticlaudianus* has portraits
of famous men on the walls, and a lay by Marie de France (to be

---

[1] See Langlois in Petit de Julleville's *Hist.*, etc., II, 111–6, and 130–44.

cited in the chapter on Statutes) has further evidence of the practice. This appears frequently in later poems, including the *Court of Love*.

V.   The porter Idleness is another point probably suggested by common usage.   In ballads and romances the porter is a frequent and often an important figure, and the least original poet describing an allegorical castle might be expected to furnish a representative. Thus little stress need be laid on the presence of a porter in the predecessors of the *Roman*, and just as little upon Idleness here as suggesting later instances.   Yet it may be worth noting in passing that Chaucer has what seems like a direct allusion to this particular porter :

> The ministre and the norice unto vyces,
> Which that men clepe in English Ydelnesse,
> That porter of the gate is of delyces.[1]

VI.   The origin of the personifications of abstract ideas acting as courtiers has already been discussed in some detail, and further instances have appeared in nearly all the poems analyzed.   But here again this device receives a great expansion, and several new creations, henceforth to be indispensable, appear for the first time.   The figures appearing both in the *Roman de la Rose* and in the *Court of Love* are these : Daunger (probably original with Guillaume de Lorris), Shame, Pity, Delight, Hope, Envy, Despair, Lust, and the goddesses Venus and Fortune.   Some qualities that appear in the *Roman* as persons (e.g., Bien-Celer, Hardement, and Seürté, the Warriors of Love) become Statutes in the *Court of Love*.   Other characters (not occurring in the English poem) which were probably first put into circulation by the *Roman* are Bel Acueil, Male Bouche, Deduit, Dous Regart, Dous Penser,[2] and Dous Parler.   In all, the French poem has about fifty of these personifications.

VII.   The Fountain of Love, into which no one can look without falling in love, and which is here specially associated with the Narcissus myth, is in this special form probably original with Guillaume de Lorris.   We have found a fairly constant tradition of a clear

---

[1] Prologue to the *Seconde Nonnes Tale*, vv. 1–3.

[2] Yet Privy Thought in the *Court of Love* may be regarded as an equivalent of Dous Penser.

river or crystal fountain as one of the regular features of the flowery meadow in which the courtiers of Love disport themselves ; and the Narcissus story would suggest the fatal quality which is here made of general application. The magic fountain of the romances and fairy stories may also have contributed. The motive is frequent in the later poets, and in one or two cases becomes central. It does not occur in the *Court of Love.*[1]

VIII. The arrows of Cupid are more elaborately treated than hitherto. The idea of two kinds of arrows Langlois traces to the quivers in the god's chamber in *Li Fablel dou Dieu d'Amours.* But an indication of some similar idea we have seen in the passage in the *De Nuptiis Honorii et Mariae* of Claudian, where in the abode of Venus in Cyprus are two fountains, one sweet and one bitter, in which Cupid's arrows are dipped. In Guiraut de Calanso we had the same idea : in his *A leis cui am de cor* there were three metals, steel, gold, and lead, and in his *Sapchas d'Amor* two, gold and steel. But the earliest instance is probably that noted by Professor Skeat[2] from Ovid, *Met.*, i, 468 ff. :

> Prompsit duo tela pharetra
> Diuersorum operum : fugat hoc, facit illud amorem.
> Quod facit, auratum est et cuspide fulget acuta ;
> Quod fugat, obtusum est et habet sub harundine plumbum.

Guillaume de Lorris keeps this twofold division of the arrows, but he puts five in each quiver and gives each arrow a name. The good arrows are Beauté, Simplesse, Franchise, Compagnie, and Beau Semblant (Cortoisie is added in the second enumeration, v. 1775) ; the second quiver contains Orgueil, Vilenie, Honte, Desesperance, and Nouveau Penser. The god shoots the hero with each of the five good arrows in turn.

It seems more than likely that the Golden Love and Leaden Love of the English *Court of Love* are derived from this fiction of the arrows, but how the poet meant to treat them must remain uncertain until we find a complete text of the poem.

---

[1] On these characters, see G. Paris, *La littérature française au Moyen Âge*, § 111, and Langlois, *Origines*, p. 66.

[2] *Chaucerian Pieces*, p. 551, n. on v. 1315 of the *Court of Love.*

IX.   The interview with the God of Love was the central point in the group of *débats* and in the *Fablel* and its derived poem; and it is probable that it is to be so regarded in the first part of the *Roman de la Rose* also; for not only does it occupy nearly nine hundred lines (1891–2776) but it contains that exposition of the commandments, the pleasures, and the pains of love, which Guillaume must have had in mind when he said in his introduction (37–38):

> Ce est li Rommanz de la Rose,
> Ou l'art d'amors est toute enclose.

Most of that exposition belongs to the next chapter; and it is not necessary to dwell on the interview itself beyond noticing that the garden in which it takes place is not as in the other poems the property of Love, but of Deduit; and that the hero, instead of being led up to a throne on which the god is seated in state, is followed by the god, who shoots arrows at him, and finally accosts him.

X.   The distinction between Venus as the goddess of sensual love, and her son as the god of " l'amour du cœur " is paralleled by the distinction which the Greeks began to make between Aphrodite Urania and Aphrodite Pandemos after Solon had condemned the latter as the goddess of prostitution.   Eros, however, never seems to have had the higher association among the ancients; but in the Middle Ages, after Jean de Meun, at any rate, while Amour was used in both senses, Venus has, where any distinction at all is implied, uniformly the more earthly signification.

XI.   Of the allegory of warfare and the siege which occupies so large a part of Jean de Meun's share of the *Roman de la Rose* we have had examples covering the time from Prudentius and the church fathers down to the *Tornoiement d'Antéchrist*.   There is, however, nothing of this in the *Court of Love*, so that to trace it farther does not lie within our present scope.

Additional evidence of the influence of the *Roman de la Rose* will be given in those sections that deal with the allegorical literature of Italy, Germany, and England.

THIBAUT.

Closely parallel to Guillaume de Lorris's part of the *Roman de la Rose*, and belonging to the same century, is the *Roman de la Poire*[1] of a certain Messire Thibaut. The poem gets its name, which seems to be suggested by that of the *Roman de la Rose*, from a pear which the heroine eats as she sits by the poet's side under a pear tree in a beautiful garden. She shares it with the poet, on whom it works like magic, setting him on fire with love in a moment.

But this is not told at the beginning. The poem opens with a statement in eight-syllabled verses that Love has passed on the poet a sentence that can be recalled only by the lady for whom he writes the romance. Then follow twelve sections of five stanzas each, not organically connected with the Romance, but of some individual interest. The first is spoken by Love :

> Je sui li diex d'amors qui les amanz mestrai.
> As leaus faz secors et de peine les trai.
> De joie et de douçors tot ades les pestrai,
> Et les fax traïtors a grant dolor metrai.

The second group describes Fortune; the third, Cligès and Fenice :

> Je sui Cliges li amoureus et vez ci m'amie Fenice,
> Qui del dart d'Amor doucereus est navrée soz sa pelice.
> Mult en est li fers savorex et li diex ne fu mie nice
> Qui par le tret d'un dart toz seus prist sor nos .II. chastel et lice.

In the fourth Thibaut speaks of his mistress and himself; in the fifth, sixth, and seventh, Tristan tells of his love for Yseut, introducing the incident where Mark finds the lovers in the forest, and leaves his glove to shade Yseut's face from the sun. The eighth has the story of Pyramis and Thisbe, the ninth the arming for a tournament, and the tenth the tournament itself, an allegory on a small scale, which may be quoted in full :

> Li tornaiz est criez as amorex esbatre
> Vers cels qui escusez sont des amanz abatre.
> Ja les ont deffiez ; por les mesdisanz batre,
> S'i sont entrefiez. Tuit sunt prest de conbatre.

---

[1] *Li Romanz de la Poire*, ed. by Fried. Stehlich, Halle, 1881.

A cest tornoiement et vieill et jovencel
Venez isnelement! Chascuns ait panoncél!
Sor mesdisant qui ment, ferez en cel moncel,
Por l'envenimement giter de lor bocel.

Envie et Covoitise, Mesdiz et Vilanie,
Desleautez, Feintise, Cruautez, Felonie,
Chascuns le mal atise et tot bienfet renie ;
Mes d'ax prendront justise amant, ge n'en dot mie.

La bataille est fermée et d'une part et d'autre
Chascuns, la teste armée, i est, lance sor fautre.
Meinte targe entamée i ot d'or fin sanz piautre.
Amant sor gent blamée fierent con sor ors [?] viautre.

Destruit sont mesdisant et veincu en l'estor.
Bien ont li fin amant gaaignié a cest tor.
Ja mes d'or en avant en chastel, ne en tor
N'auront li souduiant garison ne retor (vv. 201–20).

The eleventh section is devoted to Paris and Helen, and, after an unimportant passage, the twelfth follows with a dedication to the mistress. At v. 284, the introduction to the romance proper begins, leading up to the episode of the pear and some disquisitions on the nature of love. At v. 771 the allegorical part opens.

The poet is besieged by Love in a tower, and is hopelessly hemmed in by the forces of the god. Biauté, Cortoisie, Noblece, and Franchise appear to treat with him, and each makes a speech. While they are still engaged in parley the god himself rides up, heralded by the singing of birds and the noise of many instruments, with " jongleurs " playing on fiddles and singing " chançons noveles." The god himself now summons him to surrender without delay, and the poet is so frightened that he surrenders at once, and swears allegiance. Love takes his heart as a pledge of good faith, and delivers a harangue on degenerate and false lovers. Then all go to Paris, which is praised as the home of all pleasant delights, and Douz Regart is sent to entrust the poet's heart to

Une dame de grant beauté,
De grant sens, de grant leauté,
De bon fet, d'enterin corage (vv. 1393–5).

The lady's charms are described at great length; but her position is too lofty for him to cherish any hopes. He longs for death, since success in love is hopeless, and all night he tosses sleepless because of her. Reason comes and argues with him on the hopelessness of his desires, and advises him to choose a place for his affections where the case will not be so desperate. Finally he determines to send a messenger to declare his love, and this romance is to be the means.

Just then Love appears, leading the lady with him. He tells the poet to take her by the hand, and says she is to free him from the prison. But soon he leads the lady away again, and shoots her through the heart with a golden-pointed arrow. Then he calls Contenence to him, and sends her to the poet to give him the lady's heart in exchange for his own. Contenence is accompanied by Sostix Penssée, Simplece, Leautez, Mensure, and Pitiez, who assure him of his good fortune. But he must have a confirmation direct from his lady before he is at ease; so the messengers return to the lady, and come back with a written message. He is to take his name (Tibaut) and read it backward, reversing the *b*, and the Latin that results (*tua sit*)[1] will show that the lady is his. Left alone with his lady's heart he asks it how he may comfort her, since she also is suffering the pangs of love. Not daring to go to her alone, he appeals to Love to give him "tres bon conduit," and the god sends a nightingale to accompany him. The nightingale goes, but the poet accompanies it only in spirit, and the lady receives the bird — which represents the romance — with great joy.

If Stehlich is right in his estimate of the date of this poem, it is probably the first important work inspired by the *Roman de la Rose.* The points of likeness are obvious enough. The god seeks the lover in both cases, but in the second poem the names of some of the arrows appear among those of the ambassadors. The lover yields and becomes the vassal of Amor in both cases, but in the latter the taking of the poet's heart in pledge is used instead of locking it with

---

[1] For a discussion of the interpretation of this passage, and the text of this poem in general, Professor Sheldon has pointed out to me the reviews of Tobler in *Litbl. f. germ. u. rom. Philol.,* II, 437, and of Mussafia in *Zt. f. d. österr. Gymn.,* XXXIII, 57–64.

a key. The pains of love are described in much the same fashion
in the two poems. Reason appears and argues with the hero against
his passion in both. The followers of Love are in part the same,
and the descriptions of feminine beauty are closely similar — a point
of more value as evidence in the thirteenth than in the sixteenth
century, when the conventions were far more hackneyed.

Attention may be drawn also to the allegory of the Tournament in
the first part of the poem, which may have been suggested by the
early forms of allegory mentioned in the last chapter, since Jean de
Meun's account of the siege and fighting in his continuation of the
Roman de la Rose was perhaps not yet written.

PHILIPPE DE REMI.

Philippe de Remi, Sire de Beaumanoir (ca. 1250–1296), is better
known as the author of an important book on the *Coutumes du
Beauvaisis* than as a poet.

In his *Salu d'Amours*[1] we have a treatment of our theme somewhat more original than that which is found in the poems of
most of his contemporaries. In the form of a letter, Philippe promises to tell his lady how Dame Amour has stolen his heart, put it in
prison, and set her on guard; and he prays her to remit to him the
ten penalties which have been inflicted on him. This was how it
happened : —

One day at a dance Philippe feels himself wounded through the
eye by Love with an arrow which reaches his heart. This arrow
figures the lady's beauty : the feather is her head, and the iron is
her glance. Amour sends Orguel, Cointise, and Traïson to summon
him to surrender, and he allows himself to be led before Amour
without resisting. Orguel accuses him of having taken the lady by
the finger. Amour promises him just judgment, and meanwhile he
leaves his heart in pledge. He is thrown into a prison called Pensée,
and guarded by the gaoler Espoir. Amour calls her vassals to the
trial, but unfortunately only the bad ones are free to come — Orguel,
Cointise, Envie, Felonie, Mesdis, and Traison. Loiauté sends his

---

[1] *Œuvres de Philippe de Remi*, ed. by H. Suchier, vol. II, Paris, 1885 (Soc.
des anc. Textes franç.), pp. 197 ff.

messenger Sens (or Sapience) to say he is delayed by urgent affairs Traïson draws up the judgment, which imposes ten penalties.[1]

No sooner is the document read than Loiauté arrives with five of his people, Franchise, Deboinaireté, Sens or Sapience, Pitié, and Esperance. Orguel, Mesdis, and Envie at once depart for the court of France. Philippe tells Loiauté and the rest what pains he is condemned to suffer, and they all kneel before Dame Amour on his behalf. She is unwilling to break the sentence of Traïson, but to alleviate it she changes it from a permanent condemnation to a merely temporary one. The limit is to be fixed according to the pleasure of his lady, to whom he is to make "ditiés et canchons." He is also to send her a rhymed account of his trial. He keeps the condition, and hence the poem.

The profession, genuine or affected, of writing a poem for the pleasure of one's lady becomes hereafter very frequent, and forms the subject of the introductory stanzas of the *Court of Love*. Before Philippe it is found in the *Roman de la Rose* where Guillaume prays

> Or doint Diex qu'en gré le reçoeve
> Cele por qui ge l'ai empris ; [2]

and in lyrical poetry — especially in Provence — it was already the custom.

The locking up of his heart in prison was probably suggested to Philippe by the passage in the *Roman de la Rose* where Love produces a key and locks the lover's heart.[3] The ten pains also doubtless are derived, in substance, from the God of Love's exposition to Guillaume de Lorris.[4]

GUILLAUME DE MACHAUT.[5]

This poet was one of the most thorough-going disciples of the school of Guillaume de Lorris. His own conception of his mission

---

[1] For details of the ten penalties, see chap. iv, below.

[2] Vv. 40–41, ed. Méon, I, 4–5.

[3] Vv. 2008 ff., ed. Méon, I, 80.

[4] Vv. 2274 ff., ed. Méon, I, 93.

[5] *Œuvres de Guillaume de Machault*, ed. P. Tarbé, Reims and Paris, 1849 Machaut died in 1377, at an advanced age. Paulin Paris thinks that he was from thirty to thirty-five years old in 1346 (*Le Livre du Voir-Dit*, Paris, 1875, p. xv).

may be drawn from the *Prologue* to his *Dit du Vergier.* Here a dialogue takes place between Nature, Love, and the author. Nature tells him that she created him to sing of Love, and gives him the assistance of three of her children, Scens, Retorique, and Musique. Love comes to him and puts at his disposal three of her children, Doux Penser, Plaisance, and Esperance, and commends to his respect the honor of ladies. His other poems lead one to believe that he faithfully lived up to his instructions.

In the *Dit du Vergier* the poet represents himself as walking in a garden one April morning. A path leads him to a beautiful orchard, full of trees, flowers, and singing birds. Lost in amorous reverie, he passes through the orchard into a meadow, where he has a vision. He seems to see six youths and six damsels:

> Et dessus le bel arbrissel,
> Qui estoit en mi le praiel,
> Se séoit une créature
> De trop merveilleuse figure.
> Car nulle goute ne veoit
> Et en sa dextre main tenoit
> Un dart qui bien estoit ferré
> De fer tranchant et acéré ;
> Et en l'autre avoit un brandon
> De feu que gettoit grant randon ;
> Et s'avoit pour voler II eles
> Si belles, qu'oncques ne vi teles.[1]

This is the God of Love. All the youths and maidens are honoring him as their sovereign lord and their god. He explains to the poet the extent of his powers in making the foolish wise and the wise foolish, the poor rich and so on, declares his name, tells why he is blind, explains the use of his arrows in causing the sweet pains of love, the use of his torch in inflaming desire, and the use of his wings in flying all over the world. The names of the youths in attendance are Voloir, Doux Penser, Doux Plaisir, Loiaüté, Celer, Desir ; of the damsels, Grace, Pitié, Esperance, Souvenir, Franchise, Atemprance. The functions of these are explained, and the names

---

[1] Ed. Tarbé, p. 15.

given of six adversaries, Dangier, Paour, Honte, Durté, Cruauté, Doutance. Then the god gives the poet advice for his own love affairs — to be loyal, secret, and afraid of displeasing his lady.

Le Dit dou Lion[1] recalls in some points the Middle English poem of the *Isle of Ladies,* usually known as *Chaucer's Dream.*

On the second of April, when the hawthorn blooms, the poet, awakened by the song of birds, goes into the country to breathe the spring air, and finds a delicious garden in an island to which he is borne in a beautiful boat. He is met by a lion and conducted to a rich pavilion, in which he finds a beautiful and noble lady. The poet, encouraged by his reception, asks where he is, and at the request of the queen one of her knights replies. Formerly this was not an isle, but only the rendezvous of all the lovers of the country (who are described in classes). The lord of the place wished to exclude those who profaned it, so he surrounded it with water and named it "l'espérance des fines amours." Only loyal and faithful lovers now can enter: all others would lose their lives there.

Le Dit de la Fontaine Amoureuse, or *Le Livre Morpheus,* is interesting not only on account of the direct influence of the *Roman de la Rose* which it shows in the association of the fountain with Narcissus, but also because of the hints which Chaucer received from it for *The Bok of the Duchesse.* The relation of Machaut to the love-lorn prince,[2] as well as the introduction of the story of Ceyx and Alcyone, is clearly paralleled by the English poet.[3] The part of the poem which is important for our present purpose is as follows:

The poet awakes to hear a sad voice singing of the pains of love. He takes his *escriptoire* and writes down the tender complaint. It includes among other things the story of Ceyx and Alcyone. Finally Machaut goes to find the singer, and learns that he is merely obey-

---

[1] The analysis follows Tarbé, p. xi. For extracts, see Tarbé, pp. 40 ff.

[2] Jean de France, duc d'Auvergne and de Berry. Machaut must have begun this poem in 1360 or 1361. See P. Paris, *Le Livre du Voir-Dit,* p. xxx.

[3] On this question see Sandras, *Étude sur G. Chaucer,* Paris, 1859, pp. 90, 291 ff. ; ten Brink, *Chaucer: Studien zur Gesch. seiner Entwicklung, u. s. w.,* Münster, 1870, I, 7 ff.; Furnivall, *Trial-Forewords,* Chaucer Society, 1871, pp. 43 ff.; M. Lange, *Untersuchungen über Chaucer's Boke of the Duchesse,* Halle, 1883, pp. 21 ff.; Skeat's *Chaucer,* I, 464.

ing the commands of his lord, whose advances had been rejected by a lady. They go to seek the unhappy lover, and find him a gentleman, handsome, amiable, and like the son of a king; and he leads the poet into a smiling garden where there is a magnificent fountain of crystal, adorned with bas-reliefs representing the stories of Narcissus and of the Rape of Helen. They sit down, and, after Machaut has received the confidences of the lover, all three fall asleep — doubtless to allow Venus to appear in a dream. This she does, and after telling them the story of the Judgment of Paris, she promises her protection to the young lord, and calls before his eyes a gracious vision of his mistress smiling and favorable. The vision vanishes; and the gentleman goes off on a long journey, accompanied by the poet.[1]

From the foregoing summaries it appears that, in spite of Guillaume de Machaut's importance on account of his influence on Chaucer, there is little or nothing in the matter of his poems which was not handed down to him by his predecessors.[2]

RAOUL DE HOUDAN.

The thirteenth century contributed several works to what we have called the Prudentius-Bunyan tradition,[3] and two of these deserve to be mentioned in the present connection also.

In *La Voie de Paradis*[4] of Raoul de Houdan, the poet, in the course of his pilgrimage, is led by Grace to the House of Love:

> Quar ele me mena tout droit
> Par dedenz la meson Amor;
> Mès ainc ne vi si grant baudor
> Ne tel joie ne tel déduit
> Que on me fit en cele nuit.[5]

---

[1] This summary follows that given by Tarbé, pp. xx, xxi. Cf. ten Brink, *Chaucer: Studien, u. s. w.*, 1870, I, 197 ff.

[2] For another work by Guillaume de Machaut, see chap. vii, p. 191, below.

[3] See p. 19, above.

[4] See *Œuvres complètes de Rutebeuf*, ed. by A. Jubinal, Paris, 1839, II, 227 ff. Another poem by R. de Houdan is treated later, pp. 191–2.

[5] Jubinal, II, 228.

The pleasures, however, were mainly of eating and drinking:

> Crémirs ert séneschaus léenz,
> Qui ne fu ne couarz ne lenz
> De nous trop doner à mangier, etc.[1]

RUSTEBEUF.

The other poem of this class, written by the author known as Rustebeuf,[2] has the same title. In it the pilgrim arrives at a House of Avarice, the description of which recalls those exceedingly metaphorical palaces of love which occur in the predecessors of the *Roman de la Rose.*

> Du fondement de la meson
> Vos dit que tel ne vit mes hom :
> Un mur i a de felonie
> Tot destrempé a vilonie ;
> Li sueil sont de desesperance
> Et li pomel de mescheance ;
> Li torcheiz est de haine,
> D'autre chose que de faine
> Fu cele meson enpalee, etc. (vv. 255 ff.).

MAHIU LE PORIIER.

Le Court d'Amours of Mahiu le Poriier is contained in a fragmentary MS. in the Bibliothèque Nationale in Paris.[3] At the point where the fragment begins a jealous husband who has been beating his wife for infidelity accuses her before the Court of Love which is assembled in the Castle of Love. The "grand Bailli" presides, assisted by twelve peers: Avisé, Perchevant, Ami, Deduiant, Maistre Connissant, Hardi, Cremu, Soutieu [or Consillier], Biau Parlier, Desirré, Profitant, and Atraiant. The author is a hidden spectator of the proceedings. The *bailli* gives judgment against the jealous

---

[1] Jubinal, II, 228.

[2] *Rustebuef's Gedichte*, ed. by A. Kressner, Wolfenbüttel, 1885, pp. 144 ff.

[3] See G. Raynaud, *Romania*, X, 519 ff., and E. Gorra, in *Tobler-Festschrift*, Halle, 1895, pp. 228 ff., both of whose accounts have been used.

husband. Other persons present cases dealing with love — a squire, a regular canon, and so on, — especially a " Roi de Frise " who wants help in the wooing of a shepherdess who persists in her preference for a shepherd. Thirty love problems are dealt with, such as, e.g., that put by a "bacheler " who asks if it be possible to love loyally against one's own will, and receives an answer in the negative ; and after eight days spent in these discussions the *bailli* puts under the ban all jealous people and all "félons d'amour." But Envy besieges and wins the castle, and forces the *bailli* and all his court to go to heaven, where alone they can be secure.

Here another piece, *Le Ju de le Capete*,[1] occurs in the MS., and then follows a sequel to the *Court d'Amours*, of uncertain authorship. This sequel is also entitled *Le Court d'Amours*.[2] When it opens, Envy is reigning in the Castle of Love, and is persecuting all true lovers, who regret the passing away of the old *régime*. The wicked are encouraged, and when rascals like the servant who betrayed his master's confidence and violated his wife, tell of their exploits, Envy laughs and applauds. The author of our poem leaves the castle in disgust and seeks the " Roi de Frise." This king, grateful to the *bailli* for helping him to win the shepherdess, collects his barons and makes an assault on the castle, and finally Envy is called upon to yield it again into the hands of the *bailli* and his court.

We to note here the substitution of the "grand Bailli " for the God or Goddess of Love; the occurrence of the *pastourelle* situation in the episode of the King of Frise ; and the predominance of the legal aspect of the Court of Love. So far, we have had no case in which the forces of the enemy so clearly organized themselves into a Court of Envy, of which the courtiers were " félons d'amour," and in which all the laws of Love were reversed. This is, of course, just the kind of elaboration to be looked for as the conception of the Court becomes more and more familiar.

---

[1] Edited by G. Raynaud, *Rom.*, X, 524–32. This poem also has personifications, such as Grace, Bonne Amour, Esperanche.

[2] Here my summary follows Raynaud (*Rom.*, X, 521). Raynaud believes that *Le Ju de le Capete* and the second *Court d'Amours* are by Mahiu, as well as the first piece in the MS.

BAUDOUIN DE CONDÉ.

Li Prisons d'Amours[1] of the elder de Condé is a long and tedious allegorical poem, describing, with frequent digressions, the Prison of Love, the way in which one gets into it, the torments of the prisoners, and five methods of escape. Though this work belongs to the general class of love-allegory, it contains little that is quite in the line of tradition which we are tracing. In the description of the foundations of the Prison d'Amour we have, however, another instance of allegorical building materials (cf. p. 28, above). These foundations are of precious stones — love-virtues :

> Car c'est biautés, sens et proëce,
> Honors, cortoizie et larguece,
> Douce raizons, parole estable,
> Simples regars et amiable,
> Nobilités sans felonnie,
> Acointance sans vilonnie,
> Biau maintien, biau fait et biel dit,
> Langue sans amer, sans mesdit,
> Cuer sans venin et sans orguel,
> De biel apiel, de biel aquel,
> Bon los qui partout muet avance,
> Entendemens et connissance (vv. 331–42).

In vv. 301–3 occur some words which seem to point to a lost poem on a kindred subject :

> Dou castiel vous ai devisé,
> Se vous i avés bien visé,
> Comment est fais ne comment siet.

According to Scheler, there is no such description to be found in any of Baudouin's extant works.[2]

---

[1] *Dits et Contes de Baudouin de Condé et de son fils Jean de Condé*, ed. by Aug. Scheler, Brussels, 1866, 3 vols., I, 267 ff.

[2] *Dits et Contes*, as above, I, 509.

JEAN DE CONDÉ.[1]

Among the works of Jean, the son of Baudouin de Condé, there is one poem of great importance in the present discussion, *La Messe des Oisiaus et li Plais des Chanonesses et des Grises Nonains.*[2]

Lying asleep one night in May, the author dreamt that he sat under a pine in a beautiful forest, and just before dawn heard the birds singing overhead. A *papegai* came flying as a messenger from the Goddess of Love, announcing her approach and calling on all the birds to prepare a joyous welcome. The tidings were received with a more than earthly chorus of joy. A gorgeous throne was set up, and here Venus took her seat to dispense justice and receive adoration. The weather was fine, and the meadows were beautiful with flowers and with clear brooks "courans sour menue graviele." Many complaints were brought before Venus, but she postponed everything till she should have dined, first giving orders that the nightingales should sing mass before her (*devant li*).

A detailed account[3] of the service follows, with a sermon by the parrot on the four virtues of lovers,[4] Obedience, Patience, Loyalty, and Hope. The sermon being ended,

> Tout li amant qui là estoient
> En genous lor coupes batoient (vv. 297–8),

when an interruption occurred. The cuckoo, who had been driven away into the forest, thought he would have his revenge, and came flying over the heads of the kneeling lovers, shouting, "Tout cuku, tout cuku!" This made everybody very angry, and a great murmur arose. The sparrow-hawk gave chase, but the cuckoo hid in a hollow tree. Then service was resumed and finished, after which all who loved "par amour" wished to go and put the cuckoo to death; but Venus forbade them, telling them of its origin, and drawing lessons of warning against villany and slander.

But now it was dinner time, and the whole company, clerks and laymen, high and low, dames and damsels, sat down on the grass

---

[1] *Floruit ca.* 1280–1345.
[2] Scheler, *Dits et Contes,* III, 1 ff.
[3] See pp. 225 ff., below.
[4] See p. 192, below.

round the throne of Venus, and each had what he wished. The
courses consisted of glances, smiles, and the like, and a great chalice was handed round, the contents of which only increased thirst
There was an *entremets* of sighs and complaints. Some drank so
much that they became excited; others fell asleep. Next came
roasted *ramprones* with sauce of jealousy, and prayers with sauce o
tears. Then were given to the ladies vessels filled with fair replies
and sweet favors, and the author knelt before one beautiful girl, who
had a full dish, praying for a portion. A fair reply he got, but no
favor. Often he asked why she was so hard as to let him die o
hunger in her presence. Then the butler came with a full cup:

> Mais k'un pou boivre n'en cuidai,
> Et le hanap tout hors widai.
> A la terre jus m'estendi,
> Que riens n'oï ne n'entendi (vv. 559–62).

Yet intoxication was no disgrace, for the ladies held those most dea
who were most drunken; so he drank till he could not hold up hi
head, and could neither hear nor see. The goddess called the vale
Souvenir, who roused him only to gaze at the girl more eagerly "
.iiii. doubles" than before. Then the servants brought in a course to
appease the fever of love, — embraces and kisses, of which man
had their fill; but the author met with an angry repulse when he
tried to steal a kiss.

The feast ended with minstrelsy, and then those who had suit
came before Venus. A company of canonesses in white, escorted b
many knights, approached to lodge a complaint against the gray
nuns for stealing their lovers. The goddess wished to hear the othe
side, and a gray nun, supported by many companions, replied tha
the lovers had been lost through the haughtiness of the canonesses
and won by the legitimate charms of the nuns. After hearing the
arguments, Venus in a long speech dwelt on the nature and power o
love, and finally gave a verdict for the nuns. Her decision wa
accepted without contest (vv. 1216–18).

In the remaining 362 verses the poet attempts to moralize the
allegory and give it a religious signification.

The Mass of the Birds and the Sermon will be dealt with in thei appropriate chapters[1]; and in the forest and meadow passages we have merely repetition of material with which we have already become familiar. But the combination of the functions of Venus in this poem is interesting. We have her first as a divine being, present in bodily form at the rites of her own worship; next she figures as a great feudal lady presiding at a feast which, apart from its metaphors, closely follows the forms of a mediæval banquet; and finally, she is a judge, listening to pleadings, giving an exposition of the law, and passing judgment. It is in the first of these three allegorical pictures, in its distinctly religious aspect, that one finds the most important contribution of Jean de Condé to the Court of Love tradition. Still, even in the more hackneyed features of the poem, Jean shows such skill in handling the allegory as to entitle him to a place far above the crowd of minor men who had dealt with the same theme. The metaphorical banquet belongs to the same kind of allegory as the palace with hedges of sighs and fountains of tears. The "plais" of the canonesses and the gray nuns obviously goes back to *débats* of the type of the *Altercatio.*[2]

NICOLE DE MARGIVAL.[3]

La Panthère d'Amours[4] introduces us to a new type.

The author follows Guillaume de Lorris and the Sire de Beaumanoir in beginning with a dedication to his lady. Then he tells that one night he dreamt that he was carried off by birds to a forest full of beasts of all kinds and colors. One of these was of surpassing beauty, and her breath so sweet that all the others, except the dragon, followed her about. The beasts departed, and the poet was left alone. Presently he heard a great sound of music, and beheld approaching a company dressed in cloth of gold and other costly materials, dancing and singing, and in the midst one of noble figure and fair countenance and gracious manner, holding a sceptre and wearing a crown of gold and jewels and a richly decorated robe. His horse had costly trap-

---

[1] Pp. 192 and 225 ff., below.   [2] See pp. 34 ff., above.   [3] *Floruit ca.* 1300.
[4] *Le Dit de la Panthère d'Amours*, ed. by H. A. Todd, Paris, 1883 (Soc. des anc. Textes franç.).

pings, and three knights acted a° bodyguard, while the birds sang
all around.   After him came a crowd of dames and damsels, knights,
squires, and clerks.   He saluted Nicole and asked him who he was and
who sent him there.   The poet told him about the beautiful beast;
and the stranger, after listening courteously, proposed that Nicole
should become his vassal.   In answer to questions, he declared himself the God of Love to whom all lovers pray.   He it was who hum-
bled the proud and exalted the lowly, emboldened the coward and
made timid the valiant, and was everywhere omnipotent.   The poet
asked pardon and swore fealty, while the god courteously reproached
him :

> Amis, tu as eü domage,
> En ce que tu as ton corage
> Vers moy si longuement celé (vv. 407–9).

Mounting a horse, the poet rode with the god in search of the
beast, who had retired to a *fosse* which was in the depths of a valley defended by a thorn-hedge.   The symbolism of the vision was explained
by the god.   The beast is a panther, the symbol of Nicole's lady ; her
sweet curative breath is her words; the dragon is Envy; the valley,
humility; the *fosse*, simplicity ; the thorns, slanderers, — and so on.
He put his horse to the hedge and rode along the valley till he
came within view of the panther.   He gazed at her, but had not
courage to speak, and when he tried to get out of the valley the
thorns of the hedge scratched him, tore his clothes, and pulled him
from his horse.   The god came to his rescue and extricated him from
his painful position, reproving him gently for not having addressed
the panther.   Esperance, Dous Penser, and Dous Souvenir then took
charge of the poet and led him to the mansion of Love, where his
wounds were cured and much advice was offered him.   In response
he composed a long *dit* (vv. 825–966).   Then the God and Goddess
of Love visited him, and told him :

> Dedans le rommant de la Rose
> Trouveras la science enclose.
> La porras, se tu veus, aprendre
> Comment vrais amans doit entendre
> A servir Amors sans meffaire,
> Si nous en pouons bien ci taire (vv. 1033–8).

Venus exhorted him to have courage, and he quoted in support of his timidity some verses by Adam [de la Halle]. The goddess advised sending the lady an emerald ring, the meaning of which, and the manner of wearing, she explained, and she gave him verses to send with it. Before he despatched it, he had a dream that on presenting the ring he had been repulsed, and awaking he told it to the goddess, and declared that he should never have courage to send the missive. Then they exchanged verses, again taken from Adam de la Halle, and after further useless exhortations to have courage, he was told that the only way was to address himself to Fortune.

So with his three companions, Esperance, Dous Penser, and Dous Souvenir, he set out for the Palace of Fortune, which is described after the model of the same mansion in the *Anticlaudianus*[1] and the *Roman de la Rose*.[2] It is built on a hill of ice, and is half-gorgeous, half-ruinous. Blind Fortune herself sits at the gate, and on her caprice it depends whether one is welcomed by Eür, who inhabits the beautiful part (called Prosperité), or by Meseür, who rules the ruins (Adversité). At the moment of Nicole's arrival the goddess happened to be angry; so he was assigned to Meseür, in whose abode (Adversité) he dwelt for a long time. But by the influence of Grace and Bone Volenté he was transferred to Prosperité, where " la douce panthère " was staying, accompanied by Merci. Even now he lost courage, but the ladies about him supported him, and finally the panther yielded to the wishes of her mother Pitié. Then he awoke and sang.

In this somewhat tedious poem of 2665 verses we find the Court of Love allegory influenced by the Bestiaries. In these characteristically mediæval productions the Panther is frequently an important animal, and in some is made the type of Christ, the breath also, as in the present form, being symbolical.[3] Nicole's treatment of his subject is rather confused. The symbolism is explained by one of the characters in the allegory while the poet is still dreaming ; we have in one instance a dream within a dream. The Panther is finally

---

[1] See p. 51, above.   [2] Vv. 5944 ff., Méon, II, 89 ff.
[3] See, for example, the Middle English *Bestiary*, 733 ff., Wright and Halliwell, *Reliquiae Antiquae*, I, 225–6; Mätzner, *Altengl. Sprachproben*, I, 73–4.

found living in the apartments of Eür, the personifications about her being figured as women. Throughout, the poet is certainly thinking more of the inner meaning of his story than of the possibility of visualizing it in the imagination.

The conception of the God of Love as riding in state, followed by a troop of lovers, suggests the procession in Andreas Capellanus, the *Lai du Trot*, the *Confessio Amantis*, and other works.[1] The author's acquaintance with the *Roman de la Rose* is made quite explicit. The valley of Humility and the *fosse* of Simplicity recall the pilgrimage type of allegory.

WATRIQUET DE COUVIN.

The poems of Watriquet de Couvin are rich in examples of the kind at present under consideration, but there is little that is new. In *Li Mireoirs as Dames*[2] (A.D. 1324–5) Dame Aventure conducts the poet to see

de biauté la fontaine,
Au chastel c'on claime Thopasse.

As they climb the thirteen steps to the castle of Beauty, he finds the first guarded by Dame Nature, and each of the other twelve by a lady representing a Virtue: Sapience, Maniere, Raison, Mesure, Pourveance, Charité, Humilité, Pitié, Debonnaireté, Courtoisie, Largesce, Souffisance (*i.e.* moderate desires). All these virtues in turn give him advice. The porter is Bonté, the *chambriere* Simplesce. Beauty is described and an account is given of the attempts made by the Virtues to keep off Forfait, Mespresure, Mot Vilain, and other vices.

The idea of the steps is found in the Provençal poem by Guiraut de Calanso already cited,[3] though in Guiraut it is the steps themselves that appear to be symbolical (see Dammann, pp. 73 ff.).

Li Dis de la Fontaine d'Amours[4] begins with the description of a walk taken by the poet on a May morning in a well-wooded garden,

---

[1] See pp. 46 ff., above. This group of poems is discussed by me in a forthcoming paper in *Romania* on *The Purgatory of Cruel Beauties.*

[2] *Dits de Watriquet de Couvin*, ed. by Aug. Scheler, Brussels, 1868, pp. 1 ff.

[3] See p. 24, above.   [4] Scheler, pp. 101 ff.

where he finds a beautiful fountain.   It is guarded from the approach
of all slanderers and liars by order of Venus, the protectors being
Celer, Loiauté, and Sens.   Three drinking cups, called Jonesce,
Proesce, and Largesce, are attached by chains, Vaillance, Cuidier,
and Courtoisie.   The cups are in the charge of Bonne Volenté,
Avis, and Plenté.   The poet drinks greedily with increasing thirst,
until, intoxicated, he stretches himself on the grass to die.   But
Venus sends Espoir, who begins to restore him.   Paour, however,
undoes the work of Espoir, but is in turn checked by Souvenir.
The poet is soothed to sleep and in a vision is summoned to the
Court of Venus.   He is to go

> Par le chemin de Verité
> Gesir droit a Humilité,
> En la maison de Charité (vv. 235–7).

Bonté, Bon Los, Biau Servir, Netteté, Maniere, Honnesté, Pitié are
to be visited on the way to the Court.   The poet sets out, " touz
dormans," and follows the route prescribed.   Arriving at the Court,
he finds an open feast spread.   The viands are lovers' glances, sighs,
dangiers roasted, sweet smiles, jealousy, gilded melancholy, sauce of
kisses, and so forth.   Then he awakes.

We find in *La Fontaine d'Amours*, as in *La Panthère d'Amours*, a
vision introduced into a situation already allegorical, though the
latter is not itself described as a dream as in the case of *La Panthère*.[1]   The *Fontaine Amoureuse* of Guillaume de Machaut and the
feast in *La Messe des Oisiaus* of Jean de Condé afford instances of
the other features of this poem.[2]   The symbolism of the cups and
chains is further elaborated by Watriquet.

Other poems by this author contain similar personifications, and
will be mentioned in the chapter on the Statutes.[8]

Here may be mentioned, in connection with these Fountain poems,
an anonymous work, of the end of the fifteenth century according
to Goujet, which is summarized in the *Bibliothèque Françoise*.[4]   It is

---

[1] See p. 71, above.   [2] See pp. 62–3, 67–8, above.   [8] See pp. 193-4, below.
[4] Goujet, *Bibliothèque Françoise*, IX (Paris, 1745), 181 ff.   Two printed editions of this poem are catalogued by Brunet (*Manuel*, 5th ed., II, 1326 ; III, 1122),

called *Le Livre de la Fontaine Périlleuse, avec la Chartre d'Amours.*
The fountain represents the passion of Love, and round it are
images of Helen, Youth, Penelope, Loyalty,. Cupid:

> Richement assis au quart lieu
>   Fut Cupido Roy d'amourettes;
> Bien ressembloit un puissant Dieu
>   Sur son trosne paint à fleurettes:
> Un arc tenoit et deux sagettes,
>   Prest de férir grands et menus:
> Ses lettres leu seines et nettes,
> C'est Cupido le fils Venus.

The plot is of the same type as that of Watriquet's *Fontaine
d'Amours.*

RAIMON VIDAL.

La Chasse aux Médisants,[1] a fourteenth-century poem by Raimon
Vidal, has more than one point of special interest. It is written in
Old French, but in the poem itself there is evidence to show —
what the similarity of the author's name to that of the troubadour
of the preceding century might lead one to suspect—that it was
written by a Provençal.[2] Its international relations are further
complicated by the fact that it is the chief example in Old French
of that form of love-allegory which is most characteristic of Middle
High German.

On the morning of the first of May, 1338, the poet meets a company of ladies and gentlemen going to hunt a boar. There were
once two lovers, it appears, who were parted by evil reports. The
youth complained to Venus and the God of Love, with the result
that the slanderer was changed into a boar; and this is the animal
they are going to hunt. The ladies and gentlemen named as engaged
in this chase are all historical personages of the fourteenth cen-

---

an earlier without date, and a later, 1572. The latter was that used by Goujet.
The poet, Goujet notes (p. 182), mentions Alain Chartier.

[1] Edited by A. Mercier, *Annales du Midi*, VI (1894), 465 ff.

[2] A. Thomas, *Annales du Midi*, VI, 493-4. The author's name (" Remon
Vidal ") occurs in v. 68; the date (1338), in vv. 12-14.

tury. Each has two dogs bearing the names of virtues. Thus Marguerite de Chauvigny is there with Belacueil and Leese as hounds; Blanche de Foys (Foix), with Beaumaintien and Dous Regart; Gensac de Musyden, with Droiture and Valour; Ysabiau de Saissac, with Humilité and Souffrance, and so on. Finally the boar is caught, slain, cut up, and the parts are distributed among the ladies.

For parallels, see the German section (*D*) of the present chapter (pp. 120 ff., below).

OTON DE GRANSON.[1]

In the *Complainte de Saint Valentin*, formerly ascribed to Alain Chartier, but certainly the work of Oton de Granson, the God of Love and St. Valentine appear to a lover who is lamenting the death of his lady, and persuade him to take another.[2]

Other poems of Granson's occasionally touch upon matters connected with the Court of Love, especially in expressing lovers' symptoms. He dwells on the lover's melancholy (Nos. 17, 20, 31)[3] and on his tendency to dream of his lady, and to brood upon her memory at all times (Nos. 12, 23, 31).[4]

EUSTACHE DESCHAMPS.[5]

Though the importance of Eustache Deschamps in the history of French literature is much greater on account of his influence on verse-forms than on account of his matter, yet there are some points worth noting in his allegorical work.

Le Lay du Desert d'Amours,[6] and No. dxxxv, a ballade (the lamentation of a woman over her lost youth, with the refrain

Lasse ! languir vois ou desert d'amours),[7]

---

[1] *Ca.* 1340–1397. (See *Romania*, XIX, 237 ff.)

[2] A. Piaget, *Romania*, XIX, 403-7. See the text in Du Chesne's edition of Chartier, 1617, pp. 759-66.

[3] Piaget, *Rom.*, XIX, 420, 424, 433-4.

[4] *Ibid.*, pp. 419, 429, 435.

[5] *Ca.* 1345–*ca.* 1405.

[6] *Œuvres complètes de Eustache Deschamps*, ed. for Soc. des anc. Textes franç. by le Marquis de Queux de Saint-Hilaire, II, 182-92.

[7] *Œuvres*, III, 373-4.

both contain descriptions of a gloomy plain with no green trees or merry songs of birds — the counterpart of the May-day meadow — which may have suggested to the author of *L'Hospital d'Amours* the grim picture of "Montjoye de Doulours." [1] The Lay mentions also the fountain of Narcissus, and the God of Love with bow and arrows.

Le Lay Amoureux [2] is Eustache's most important work from the present point of view. It opens with a buoyant spring song and an account of May-day customs, and then tells of a dream which the poet had. Walking in a wood he meets Disdain, a great *vilain* with a cudgel, and after getting past him with some difficulty, he comes into a beautiful meadow, where there is a spring, a clear stream, and a tall pine tree. Here he sees

> un seigneur tressouverain.
> Comme dieu cellui aouroie,
> Car en l'air tout seul le veoie
> Resplendissant, de douçour plain (vv. 112-15).

Under the pine are many persons kneeling and praying God

> que sa grace leur envoie
> Et s'amour au secle mondain (vv. 121-2).

The poet hides under a thorn and watches. He sees "this god" (*cilz dieux*) send down Love in the form of an hermaphrodite,

> Descendre vi celle amour digne
> En un char de feu sanz courtine.
>
> .   .   .   .   .   .
>
> Ceulx qui du recevoir indigne
> Ne furent, en eulx se bouta,
> Soutivement les embrasa.
> La fut la belle Proserpine (vv. 139-46),

as well as Medea, Theseus, Semiramis, Paris and Helen, Solomon, Ovid, Aristotle, Dido, Guinevere and Lancelot, Tristan and Yseult, and many more. Besides the famous lovers from history and legend, there are allegorical personages present, and the discussion which follows is carried on by these. Honour urges Jeunesce to love,

---

[1] See p. 87, below.　　　[2] *Œuvres*, II, 193 ff.

and promises the assistance of Vaillance and Prouesce. Poursuite, Deduis, Loyauté, Verité, Justice, Raison, Pité, and others join with Vaillance in bemoaning the power of Orgueil, Haine, Decevance, Mesdit, and the rest, Raison concluding with

> Fy d'or, d'argent, et de chevance
> Qui font toute joie cesser (vv. 273–4).

Then the famous lovers leave the place, giving thanks to the God of Love. As they pass the poet, who still lies under his thorn-tree, he feels great fear ; but the God of Love and *ses gens* (perhaps the allegorical personages) see him and the latter speak favorably to their lord :

> " Vez la Eustace
> Qui doit bien estre en vostre grace :
> Guillaume et lui noz faiz escriprent ;
> Venus et Juno les nourrirent.
> Commandez lui de ci s'en passe,
> Die tout et rien ne trespasse
> Comment ancien se maintinrent
> Aux presens." Lors s'esvannouirent (vv. 296–303),

and the poet awoke.

The most noteworthy feature of the poem is probably the description of Love as an hermaphrodite.[1] This appears to be due to an attempt to combine Venus and Cupid in one person ; but perhaps nothing more is intended than a symbol of the god's power over both sexes. The hovering in the air and the chariot of fire are also both unique, so far. The poet's spying suggests the Prologue to Chaucer's *Legend of Good Women*, and is found still later in Gavin Douglas's *Palice of Honour*.[2]

---

[1] The poem is confused. It is not quite certain how far Eustache meant to identify the resplendent figure in the air with the Love that descends in a fiery chariot ; nor is the action clear in the last part of the narrative.

[2] See pp. 160 ff., below.

JEAN FROISSART.

The great chronicler who wrote

> D'armes, d'amour, et de moralité,

left a considerable mass of poetry of the *Court of Love* type.[1]

His *Paradys d'Amour*[2] is in the form of a dream, and opens with the conventional May day, a wooded and flowery landscape, and the singing of birds. The hero, an almost despairing lover, is approached by two ladies, Plaisance and Esperance, with whom he has a long conversation. They conduct him to the pavilion of the God of Love, which stands in a *lande* in the wood (vv. 1009–16). On their way they fall in with Beau Semblant, Douls Regard, Franc Vouloir, and other huntsmen engaged in " l'amoureuse chace." The god is in his pavilion. He receives the author kindly, and commands Plaisance and Esperance to attend him. Accordingly the three continue their walk through the wood. In a meadow, by the side of a stream, they find Bel Acueil, plaiting chaplets of flowers. The poet immediately kneels down before his lady[3] and begs her to love him.

> Lors ma dame, com bien senée,
> Le chapelet qui fu estrois
> Frema elle, de ses beaus dois,
> De la flour où je me delitte,
> Que je vous nomme margherite (vv. 1669–73).

Then she makes him kiss the chaplet, kisses it herself, and places it on his head. He gives a movement of joy, and awakes.

Cupid in this poem is said to shoot his arrows through the eyes

---

[1] *Œuvres de Froissart, Poésies*, ed. by Aug. Scheler, Brussels, 1870–2, 3 vols. See also *Froissart, Étude Litteraire sur le XIVme Siècle*, by Kervyn de Lettenhove, Paris, 1857, 2 vols., and the same scholar's *Étude sur la Vie de Froissart* forming vol. I of his edition of the *Chroniques*, Brussels, 1870. The date of Froissart's birth is usually given as 1337 ; he appears not to have died before 1405.

[2] *Poésies*, ed. Scheler, I, 1 ff.

[3] " Ma dame " is now present, in an unexplained way (v. 1477). But the narrative is clear enough. The poet's discovery of Bel Acueil by the stream is equivalent to his being kindly received by his lady.

into the heart (vv. 488–92), — a detail that comes to be more and more generally adopted. The lover's associates are all old friends :

> Avec moi menrai Atemprance,
> Avis, Maniere, et Cognissance,
> Franchise et Debonnaireté,
> Sens, Pité, et Humilité,
> Qui tout soustenront ma banière (vv. 753–7).

Among the courtiers of love Froissart introduces several of the heroes of romance, Lancelot, Tristan and Iseult, Gawain, Troilus, Paris, Jason, and others. He also inserts songs, like those introduced by the author of the *Panthère d'Amours ;* as, for example, the lay which the hero sings to the God of Love.

The *Paradys d'Amour* is important also from the connection it has with English poetry. The most definite proof is the introduction of the mysterious "Eclympasteyre" of Chaucer's *Bok of the Duchesse* (v. 167), which appears in Froissart as "Enclimpostair" (v. 28).[1]

Le Joli Buisson de Jonece [2] contains some novel features. Plaisance, Desir, Humilité, Jonece, Maniere, Pité, Doulç Semblant, and Franchise engage in a literary contest, each expressing a wish in verse. The poet acts as secretary, and the prize is a chaplet. When the documents are all on record, Desir suggests the God of Love as a judge ; and the poet, his lady, and all the abstract competitors set out to find him. The journey is not finished : " on me boute ; adont je m'esveille."

In *Le Temple d'Onnour*,[3] probably written in honor of a marriage

---

[1] The question which poet was the imitator is debatable. See the references in Scheler's ed., III, xix, n. 1, and add Hales, *Folia Litteraria*, London, 1893, pp. 83–5 (from *Athenæum*, April 8, 1882); Lounsbury, *Studies in Chaucer*, Boston, 1892, I, 245 ; Skeat's *Chaucer*, I, 462, 468 ; Longnon, Introduction to *Méliador*, I, l–li (Paris, 1895); G. C. Macaulay, *Macmillan's Magazine*, LXXI, 230 (Jan., 1895); H. Bradley, *Academy*, Feb. 9, 1895, 125–6. These references I owe to Professor Kittredge, a forthcoming article by whom in *Englische Studien* may be expected to settle the question.

With the ballade refrain "Sus toutes flours j'aime la margherite" (*Paradys d'Amour*, v. 1635), cf. Chaucer, *Prologue to the Legend of Good Women*, vv. 42–3.

[2] Vv. 4602 ff., Scheler, II, 136 ff.

[3] *Poésies*, ed. Scheler, II, 162 ff. ; cf. III, xlvi–xlviii.

and containing moral instructions for a knight and his lady, the poet, following Watriquet,[1] describes the seven steps in the temple leading up to the seat of Honor as guarded by seven knightly and seven womanly virtues.

La Cour de May[2] has a repetition of many of the features of the *Paradys d'Amour*. All the month of May Amour holds his court in a *vergier*, among flowers and the joyous songs of birds (vv. 399–401). In this park the poet finds a fountain guarded by a lady in cloth of gold, Leesse, who welcomes him cordially. Doulce Pensée presents him with a portrait of his lady, and Courtoisie leads him to the dwelling of Love, which is here, as in the *Paradys*, a tent instead of a castle. But the splendor is present here too:

> Là estoit richement tendue
> Une tente sur l' erbe drue ;
> Les cordes d'or de Cypre estoient,
> Les chevilles qui les tenoient
> Estoient toutes de fin or.
> La tente valoit maint tresor,
> Le comble estoit à or batu,
> Tele richesce onques ne fu.
> De grosses perles fu brodée
> Et de pierrerie eslevée :
> Balais, rubis, saphirs, topasses,
> Gros dyamans semés par places
> Y estoient (vv. 643–55).

The enclosure is entered by means of a great portal or gate-house, on which is the warning,

> " Fuyés, fuyés, fuyés de cy,
> Mesdisans, felons, envieux,
> Hardis menteurs, faulx orguilleux,
> Parjureurs, deceveurs de dames !
> Mauvais estes de corps et d'ames.
> Amours vous fait commandement
> Que n'approuchiés aucunement
> Ce plaisant et vertueux lieu " (vv. 1440 ff.).

---

[1] See p. 72, above.   [2] *Poésies*, III, 1 ff.

Love is very friendly to the hero, and gives him much advice, which is often parallel to the Statutes (see chap. iv, below), though not put into that form.

Doubts have been thrown upon Froissart's authorship of *La Cour de May*,[1] and with regard to the next allegory to be mentioned, *Le Tresor Amoureux*,[2] there is still more uncertainty, Scheler[3] holding that it is probably not by Froissart. It is an enormous poem of over eight thousand verses, which I cannot attempt to summarize in detail. The framework is again a dream, in which the author beholds the Palace of Beauty in a great park. In the palace garden stand two magnificent tents, in one of which are

quatre dames
Belles, bonnes de corps et d'ames (vv. 121-2),—

Raison ("la bien doctrinée"), Souffisance, Congnoissance, and Lo-yauté (vv. 171-5). Congnoissance is the chief instructor of the hero. The tent is of a shining whiteness typifying purity and devotion, and is crowned with three golden *pommiaulz* symbolizing the Trinity. The other tent is occupied by Love, who is accompanied by Dame Nature.

It is evident that we have here the setting of a didactic rather than an erotic allegory, and if Froissart wrote the poem, it must have been about the time when "moralité" was supplanting "amour" as the source of his inspiration.

Some of the other details, however, are of interest in view of later features of the Court of Love. The park is guarded by eight towers, occupied by Diligence, Bonté, Beauté, Honneur, Maniere, Humilité, Atrempance, and Courtoisie (vv. 325-49). Dangier is *huissier;* Paour, *concierge;* Grace, treasurer; Hardement, constable; Deduit, grand chamberlain, and so on (vv. 303-4, 313-14, 323, 405 ff.).

In the poem as a whole there is more about Truth than about Love. There are long debates, first between the author and a squire (III, 85 ff.), and then between Congnoissance and Amour (vv. 2695 ff.), on the relation of the pursuits of Love and Arms and similar subjects.

---

[1] See *Poésies*, III, lvii–lx.   [3] *Ibid.*, III, lxii–lxvi.
[2] *Ibid.*, III, 52 ff.

It thus appears that, in spite of the considerable bulk of his poetical work, Froissart's original contributions to the love-allegory are slight. Most of these have already been remarked upon. His preference of tents to castles; his elaboration of the feudal offices; and his extensive mingling of didactic with love-allegory (if *Le Tresor* be his) are the main points.

LES ÉCHECS AMOUREUX.

The anonymous author of the poem known as *Les Échecs Amoureux* introduces an unwonted amount of classical learning into his work. The last part of it, indeed (fo. 54^b–fo. 65^b of the Dresden MS.), has been edited by Körting as a translation from Ovid.[1] The poem as a whole has not been accessible to me, but from the very full rubrics quoted at the end of Körting's extract[2] the following outline has been put together.

After a description of spring, the author tells how Nature appeared to him and advised him to see the world. Having set out with this purpose, he meets Pallas, Juno, and Venus, escorted by Mercury, who asks him to pronounce anew the Judgment of Paris.[3]

The poet decides in favor of Venus, who then talks graciously with him, especially of her sons Jocus or Deduit and Cupid, and of the "Vergier de Deduit." After Venus leaves him, he sets out for the forest of Diana. Here he meets the goddess herself, whom he describes. She has much to say against Venus and her Garden of Delight, to seek which, nevertheless, the author immediately proceeds. On arriving there, he is welcomed by Courtesy, and is allowed to go all about and see its beauty and variety. There he sees the God of Love and his retinue, and describes his beauty and rich dress and crown. Leesce and Doulz Regart are the god's constant companions. Following the *Roman de la Rose*, the author describes

---

[1] *Altfranzösische Uebersetzung der Remedia Amoris des Ovid*, ed. by G. Körting, Leipzig, 1871. The poem as a whole is contained in MS. O. 66, in the Königl. öffentliche Bibliothek in Dresden, and also in a MS. in the Library of St. Mark's, Venice; but it has never been published in full.

[2] Assisted here and there by Körting's brief summary in his *Einl.*, pp. viii–ix.

[3] Professor Kittredge draws my attention to the strong resemblance between this and Froissart's *L'Espinette Amoureuse*, vv. 396 ff., ed. Scheler, I, 98 ff.

" le rosier et les roses et le lieu ou Jalousie fist Bel-Acueil emprison-
ner," and the fountain of Narcissus.   Deduit he finds playing chess
with a damsel.   After the game is finished, the damsel, at the request
of the God of Love, plays with the author and defeats him, where-
upon Deduit presents her with a chaplet and urges the author to try
again.   The God of Love tells how he and Venus, his mother, serve
Nature, and how Deduit and Oyseuse serve them.   Diana is afterwards
discussed, and the conversation ends with the author's pretended
homage to the god.   Then the author is left to meditation.   This
results in a lamentation which causes the god to return, to talk at
length on the power of Venus, and to give some commandments.
The conversation turns on different ways of seeking satisfaction in
love, — by violence, gifts, enchantment, etc., — each method being
illustrated by examples from the classics.   The god then leaves him
alone once more, and he thinks of the lady that he loves.

Pallas now appears and presents the claims of Reason as against
love and carnal delights, enumerating the rules laid down by Ovid in his
Remedia Amoris.   She exalts the life contemplative over the life amorous, and then, following *Il Tesoro* of Brunetto Latini, she expatiates
on Paris and its University, on the King of France, on princes and
governments, on society and its origins, on virtues and vices, etc., etc.

Although the general composition of this work makes it stand out
clearly from the mass of erotic allegory, there appears from the outline to be little or nothing in it, save the game of chess from which
it takes its name, which is not to be found in Ovid, the *Roman de
la Rose*, Brunetto Latini, and the literature generally current in the
fourteenth century.   The three special sources mentioned the author
seems to have had before him as he wrote.[1]

CHRISTINE DE PISAN.

The famous controversy on the character of woman that was raised
by Jean de Meun's attacks on the sex in the second part of the *Roman
de la Rose* does not in itself concern us here.[2]   But one of the poems

---

[1] Cf. Körting's *Einl.*, pp. ix–x.
[2] For the debate on the morality of the *Roman de la Rose*, see A. Piaget, in
Études Romanes dédiées à Gaston Paris, Paris, 1891, pp. 113–20.

called forth by that controversy happens to have a framework which brings it into the Court of Love category.   *L'Epistre au Dieu d' Amours* [1] of Christine de Pisan was written, as she herself tells us in vv. 799–800, in 1399, and it is in the form of a letter from Cupid to all his subjects, reproving men for their ill-doing and ill-speaking towards women, and defending women against the charges brought by Jean de Meun and his followers.   The opening and closing verses show clearly Christine's conception of Cupido as a feudal sovereign. The poem begins thus :

> Cupido, roy par la grace de lui,
> Dieu des amans, sanz aide de nullui
> Regnant en l'air du ciel trés reluisant,
> Filz de Venus la deesse poissant,
> Sire d'amours et de tous ses obgiez,
> A tous nos vrais loiaulx servans subgiez,
> Salut, Amour, Familiarité.
> Savoir faisons en generalité
> Qu'a nostre Court sont venues complaintes
> Par devant nous et moult piteuses plaintes
> De par toutes dames et damoiselles,
> Gentilz femmes, bourgoises et pucelles, etc.

In the closing lines the legal machinery of feudalism is even more elaborately copied, though the mention of excommunication represents the religious aspect which so persistently mingles with the secular in these allegories.   The God is passing sentence on false lovers and other " vilains ":

> Si soient tuit
> De nostre Court chacié, bani, destruit,
> Et entrediz et escommenié,
> Et tous noz biens si leur soient nyé,
> C'est bien raison qu'on les escomenie.
> Et commandons de fait a no maisnie
> Generaument et a noz officiers,
> A noz sergens et a touz noz maciers,
> A noz prevoz et maires et baillis,

---

[1] *Œuvres Poétiques de Christine de Pisan*, ed. by M. Roy (Soc. des anc. Textes franç.), II, 1–27.

> Et vicaires, que tous ceulz maubaillis
> Et villennez soient trés laidement,
> Injuriez, punis honteusement,
> Pris et liez, et justice en soit faitte,
>
> .   .   .   .
>
> Donné en l'air, en nostre grant palais,
> Le jour de May la solempnée feste
> Ou les amans nous font mainte requeste,
> L'An de grace Mil trois cens quatre vins
> Et dix et neuf, present dieux et divins [1] (vv. 779–800).

Then follow the signatures.

ALAIN CHARTIER.[2]

Through his poem *La Belle Dame sans Mercy* Alain Chartier became (unintentionally, as it seems) involved in the controversy of which Christine's *Epistre* formed a part. To clear himself he wrote the *Excusation de Maistre Alain, contre ceux qui dient qu'il a parlé contre les Dames en son livre nommé* La Belle Dame sans Mercy.[3] In this poem he represents Love as appearing to him, drawn bow in hand, just before dawn, and reproaching him. Alain asserts his innocence, alleges the inoffensiveness of his book, and appeals to Love to judge the case. Love lowers his bow, puts the arrow back in the quiver, and says :

> Puis qu'à ma court tu te reclames,
> I'en suis content, et tant t'en di,
> Que ie remetz la cause aux Dames.

Then the poet awakes:

> Pour ce me rens à vostre Court,
> Mes Dames, et la foy pleuy
> D'obéir à droit sans enuy
> Ainsi qu'amours l'a commandé.

---

[1] For a comparison of this poem with Hoccleve's *Letter of Cupid*, see Furnivall's edition of Hoccleve for E. E. T. S., Lond., 1892.

[2] Chartier is said to have been born in 1386. The date of his death is uncertain. See G. Paris, *Rom.* XVI, 414; XVIII, 320; and cf. *Rom.* XXIII, 152 ff.

[3] *Œuvres*, ed. Du Chesne, Paris, 1617, pp. 525 ff.

In spite of this seeming recantation, we have a poem with full Court of Love machinery in which Alain returns to his charges against the cruel beauty. In *Le Parlement d'Amour*[1] he says that, being ordered by Love to make a new ballade in honor of his lady, he lay down on a couch, where he fell asleep and had a dream.

In the midst of the most beautiful of gardens, which was on a rock of topaz, was Love with a bow in his hand. The garden was full of cypresses and rose-trees, and was watered by a fountain "és quatre corniers." Birds sang in the trees, and the gate was guarded by Dangier. In the midst was an audience chamber (*auditoire*) of green marjoram, on which were designed in flowers the stories of Paris and Helen, and of the Chatelaine de Vergy,[2] who had loved without reproach in thought, word, or deed. It was written with marigolds on the turf that Love was going to hold his parliament in that place, to dispense justice. There were twelve presidents, of whom Franc Vouloir was the first; Espoir was "procureur des cas"; and Desir was advocate. The crowds of people who were thronging to the Parliament all seemed to be making their way towards Souvenir, the Clerk of Court. Doulx Pensier, the *huissier*, called for silence, and the Clerk bade him to call to audience

> Celle, qui outre la deffence
> D'amours, auoit cueur endurcy,
> Qu'on appella en ma presence
> La belle Dame sans mercy (p. 697).

She came, blushing like fire for shame,. and weeping for fear of Love. Then Desir gave an exposition of the prerogatives of Love, and enumerated at great length the charges against the rebel dame. He ended by advising that she be enclosed in grief and guarded by pain and sorrow and grievous languor.

The lady asked for counsel; but, though Franc Vouloir granted her request, no one dared to act for her. So she sought delay, which was permitted. Then the poet awoke and wrote his ballade.

---

[1] *Œuvres,* ed. Du Chesne, pp. 695 ff.

[2] For the form of this name see Raynaud, *Rom.* XXI, 145, 157, 158. Du Chesne's text (p. 696) has "du verger la Chastelaine."

In this poem the legal aspect of the Court is predominant throughout; but in another poem formerly ascribed to Chartier, *L'Hospital d'Amours* (*ca.* 1441)[1] we have the religious element prevailing, mixed with what might be called the pathological aspect of love, which is here elaborated for the first time.

The poet, who is enjoying himself in the Assembly of Pleasure, sits down beside his lady and begins to plead his cause ; but, being repulsed, is thrown into a deep melancholy. That night, as he lies in bed, wishing in his misery for death, he falls into a waking dream. He seemed to be walking along a thorny road called "Trop dure Responce," which led him to the bottom of a valley, where he found a great desert, "Montjoye de Doulours," a dismal place of tears. Every tree was full of "gens pendus" who had, like Phyllis, hanged themselves in despair. Under the trees flowed a river full of drowned lovers, among whom he recognized Hero and Leander. There, too, was the fatal Fountain of Narcissus. Swords he saw, stained with the blood of suicides like Pyramus and Thisbe; and a fire fed by lovers, who, like Dido, had given their bodies for fuel. In this dismal region, beyond the limits of law and nature, no creature could live : the rain was tears; the wind, sighs; the thunder, a hideous cry.

From this desert of despair he was delivered by Esperance and Sapience, who entered into him invisibly, like spirits. He was carried off, "plus que le cours" to a blessed place called the "Hospital d'Amours." The Hospital was built on a rock of ruby ; its walls were of crystal above, and of dark marble below, and it was surrounded by a flowery hedge. At the door Bel-Accueil, who bore the keys, gave him a gracious welcome, and led him to Courtoisie, the *enfermiere.* Within he found thirteen *hospitaliers :* Dame Pitié (the Prioress), Loyaulté, Simplesse, Verité, Congnoissance, Humilité, Richesse, Largesse, Maniere, Jeunesse, Liesse, Beauté, Courtoisie. There were three Counsellors, Honneur, Entendement, and Souvenir; Pitié had two servants, Regard and Humble Maintenir ; the chief physician was Espoir. Courtoisie asked his symptoms, and led him

---

[1] *Œuvres*, ed. Du Chesne, pp. 722 ff. The correctness of the ascription of this poem to Chartier was doubted by Clément Marot. See Piaget, *Romania*, XIX, 403-4.

away for treatment. They passed the *hostel* of Pitié, the Prioress, and entered a great hall full of patients, at the end of which was a glorious chapel, in which service was going on. In the chapel was an altar, on which were two images, one of Venus with firebrand and diadem, and one of Cupid with his arrows. The leader of the singing was Liesse, and the priestess Conscience, who that day was celebrating the mass of Pyramus and Thisbe. Making obeisance to the shrine as he passed, the poet came to another apartment, where he found a bed on which Courtoisie made him lie down, while she summoned the doctor. Espoir came, felt his pulse, diagnosed the case, and gave him some "eaue de gratieux penser," which put him to sleep. When he woke Pity came to comfort him, and he asked her for "ung franc baisier." She was willing to allow him this, but Love had made Dangier his gardener, and no tree was so closely guarded as "franc baisier." Yet by her urgent request Dangier was won over ; and, helped by Espoir, the sick lover staggered to the garden, where, among many ladies, he found his mistress and got the kiss, which restored his health at once.

Having offered thanks and taken his leave, he returned to the Hospital, and thence found his way to the Cemetery. There he found buried true lovers like Tristan and Lancelot; there, too, lay Alain Chartier, "saige et loyal," the victim of La Belle Dame sans Mercy.[1] Through a postern he passed into a sad valley, where lay the unburied bodies of Love's excommunicated, — among them Jason, Demophon, Æneas, Narcissus, La Belle Dame sans Mercy, and Briseyda.

Now his desire returned to him, but Dangier denied him access to his lady. The *hospitaliers* did their best for him. Espoir, the physician, recommended a sacrifice to Love, advising him to avoid thought, seek cheerful company, read pleasant stories, and above all keep him (Espoir) in mind, since he could cure all such griefs except when they were mortal. Only Love himself could melt the lady. So to

---

[1] This passage has been regarded as decisive against Chartier's authorship. See Petit de Julleville, *Hist. de la langue et de la litt. franç.*, II, 374 ; Goujet, IX, 176 ; *Catalogue Rothschild*, I, 246 ; G. Paris, *Rom.*, XVI, 413. Cf. also René of Anjou's *Le Livre du Cuer d'Amours Espris* (p. 91 and n. 1, below).

Love the poet turned his tear-blinded eyes, but could not find words, and swooned away. When he recovered consciousness, he prayed to him for mercy, recalling former miracles in the cases of Penelope, Echo, Pygmalion, and others. Then he fell asleep and dreamt that Love rose and, calling him his son, gave him encouragement, and asked why he had stopped writing songs in his honor. Had he lost his good will, or did he think the god had lost his power? He said no to both questions; he knew that only Love or death could release him from his present pain. After further reproaches on one side and professions of repentance on the other, Love took pity and told him to return to the garden, where he should find Dangier asleep. Then he awoke, went to the garden, and found Dangier asleep. Near by was his own lady. Her he told all about his case and the god's promises, and entreated her not to make Love a liar. She changed color, said she could not disobey so great a lord, and granted "ung franc baisier." He returned to the chapel to sacrifice a turtle-dove made of laurel-wood in token of gratitude. Then he thanked the ladies in the Hospital for their kindness, — after which he suddenly awoke. The poem ends with a wish that the vision may come true.

It has seemed worth while to give a somewhat full summary of this poem for several reasons. First, it is, as literature, one of the most interesting of its century. The scheme of the allegory is much more original than usual, and it is carried out with vigor and consistency. The description of the chapel of the God of Love as a part of the larger building, and as containing images of Cupid and Venus is closely paralleled in the English *Court of Love.* The conception of the Hospital and that of the cemetery were both new, and both were imitated very soon. The picture of the Valley of Despair is done with such grimness and power as to suggest the Divine Comedy.

RENE OF ANJOU.[1]

Closely associated with the foregoing, both as the friend and admirer of Alain Chartier and as the imitator of the *Hospital d'Amours*, comes King René the Good. In the whole range of the fifteenth

---

[1] A.D. 1408–80.

century there is perhaps no figure presenting more, and more varied, points of interest than this monarch. As King of Jerusalem and of Sicily, and as Duke of Bar, of Lorraine, and of Anjou, he was of the first importance socially and politically; that he was an artist of no mean skill is proved by the graceful drawings he made in illustration of his books ; he appears as a moral reformer in his substitution of the games of the Fête-Dieu [1] for the licentious " Jeux des Fous," and as a musician in composing the accompaniments for some of these ceremonies; and, finally, as a writer, he exchanged ballades with the Duke of Orléans, composed an extensive work on chivalry, and wrote a very long allegorical poem inspired by the *Roman de la Rose* and the *Hospital d'Amours*. It is to this very versatility, no doubt, that the almost complete neglect of his claims to recognition as a man of letters is due.[2]

Le Livre du Cuer d'Amours Espris [3] (A.D. 1457), as René's allegory is called, is a work, partly prose and partly verse, in the form of a vision.

One night the author dreams that his heart leaves his breast, and armed and equipped by Desir sets out to seek Doulce Mercy. His equipment includes a helmet, "timbré tout de fleurs d'amoureuses pensées," a sword, and a shield of " esperance pure " with three forget-me-nots on it. His horse is Franc Vouloir. After a long series of adventures, in which the usual personifications take part (Jalouzie, Melencolie, Bel Acueil, Tristesse, Humble Requeste, Honneur, Largesce, and many more), and in which allegorical place-names occur (such as the manor of Bon Repos, the river of Tears, the forest of Longue Actente, the bridge Pas Perilleux, and the plain of Pensée Ennuyeuse), the Heart with his two companions, Desir and Largesce, comes to the seacoast and sets sail for the Isle of the God of Love. As they approach the island they see a beautiful castle :

---

[1] For details as to the Court of Love element in this celebration, see pp. 253–4 ff., below.

[2] It has been remarked that a curiously similar oblivion obscured for centuries the literary reputation of René's princely contemporaries, Charles d'Orléans and James I. of Scotland.

[3] *Œuvres Complètes du Roi René*, ed. by le Comte de Quatrebarbes, vol. III, Angers, 1846. The date is given in the work itself (p. 195).

omewhat nearer the shore is a fine church, which forms a part of a
reat establishment called L'Ospital d'Amours. The church, with
tout le pourpris de leans," was built on a rock of diamond. The
alls were of marble and jasper, and the roof was covered with plates
f enamelled silver. The Heart and his companions are entertained
t this Hospital, of which Courtoisie is the *enfermiere* and Pitié the
rioress.

Behind the church is a cemetery, which the Heart is eager to see,
ecause he has heard that Alain Chartier and other notabilities are
uried there. On the portal of the cemetery are blazoned the arms
f many great personages, who have visited the Hospital and who
y thus, as it were, hanging up their shields have testified their sub-
ction to Love. Under each blazon is an inscription written "comme
n épitaphe," telling whose the arms are and why their owner had
ome thither. A long list of the blazons and inscriptions is given.
t includes those of David, Hercules, and Theseus, Julius Cæsar
nd Mark Antony,- Launcelot and Tristan, Charles Quint, Gaston
hébus, Comte de Foix, and King René himself. After examining
ie portal, the Heart and his companions enter the cemetery. It
ontains many tombs, six of which attract the visitor's particular
ttention. They are those of Ovid, Guillaume de Machaut, Boc-
accio, Jean de Meun, Petrarch, and Alain Chartier, and they stand
gether in an enclosure by themselves. When the Heart asks Dame
ourtoisie to whom some of the other tombs belong, she refers him
"the book of *L'Ospital d'Amours*, written by a clerk of Tournay."[1]
hen she shows him, outside the cemetery, the bodies of Love's ex-
ommunicates, unburied and frightful to see.

After hearing mass in the church for the souls of two lovers newly
ain through jealousy, the Heart visits and kisses the relics (such
ings as a vessel of the water in which Leander was drowned), and

---

[1] "Elle lui dist que s'il en vouloit savoir, qu'il lisist et regardast le livre de
spital d'Amours que jadis fist ung jeune clerc natif de Tournay et que assez lui
a deviseroit " (p. 133). This passage is valuable, not only as an acknowledg-
ent of the source of King René's description of the Hospital, etc., but as evi-
nce that he knew that *L'Hospital d'Amours* was not written by Alain Chartier.
ee p. 87, above.

Pitié takes a book and makes him swear to serve Love loyally henc
forth, and keep his commandments.

Leaving the Hospital with his two companions, Desir and La
gesce, the Heart sets out for "le beau chastel de Plaisance du die
d'Amours," while Pitié penetrates to the chamber of Doulce Merc
the object of his wanderings. This lady is shut up in the manor
Rebellion, where Dangier and Reffus hold her a close prisone
The chamber is guarded by Honte, Crainte, Jalouzie, and by tw
Mesdisans, spies of Malebouche. Pitié prepares the lady to we
come the Heart.

Meantime the hero and his comrades come in sight of the castle

Ce très bel chastel de Plaisance estoit fondé sur une roche d'esmerauc
en laquelle y avoit vaines de dyamans nayfz, foison et si grant quantité q
on y veoit presqu'autant ou plus de dyamans que d'esmerauldes. Les quat
pans des murs dudit beau chastel estoient de cristal, et y avoit à chacun pa
au bout d'une grosse tour faicte de chailloux de rubiz fins et reluisans, et
(pp. 145–6).

At the gate the wanderers are met by Bel Acueil, who consents
ask the God of Love to receive *le Cuer's* homage. Love repli
favorably and the companions enter the castle, escorted by B
Acueil. In the courtyard they find Oyseuse, who tells them that th
God of Love is "en bien estroit conseil" with his mother Venu
and must not be disturbed. She shows the new-comers the wonde
of the castle until Love is ready to receive them. When, finall
they enter the great hall, they find the god in royal raiment, "
tiroit sayettes et moult fleiches par les fenestres de la salle à
vollée hors, et pas ne lui chaloit sur qui elles cheussent." Bel Acue
presents the Heart to Love. Desir begs the god to receive th
stranger into his service and to lend him the aid of his knights
the conquest of Doulce Mercy. Love is in no hurry, and meantin
they are well entertained. After dinner Dame Venus enters,
council is held, and orders are issued for the campaign. The que
is undertaken by the Heart, Pitié, Bel Acueil, Promesse, and Hu
ble Requeste. Doulce Mercy is won and is being conducted to th
Castle of Love, when the old enemies, with Dangier at their hea
reappear and attack so violently that, in spite of the Heart's val

ιe lady is recaptured, his friends fall, and he himself is severely
ιounded. Pitié, who has been hiding in a thicket during the fight,
ιds the Heart more dead than alive. She restores him to con-
ιiousness, and takes him to the Hospital of Love, where he wishes
ι spend the rest of his days in prayer.

In this work three main streams of influence are evident. The
ɔening part, with the symbolical armor and the wandering adven-
ιres, belongs to the class of *La Voie de Paradis* and Guillaume de
ιigulleville's *Pèlerinage*.[1] The armor passage, which is frequently
ιaralleled in religious allegory, is doubtless to be traced to St. Paul[2];
om the elaboration of the same idea we have pieces like Henryson's
'arment of Good Ladies.[3] The second part is confessedly imitated
om *L'Hospital d'Amours*, even to details like Courtoisie the *enfer-
iere*, and Pitié the *prieuse*. The addition of the relics is new,
ιut is in keeping with the description of the chapel and its services
ι the earlier poem. The concluding section with the rescue and
ιss of the lady shows the influence of the *Roman de la Rose* most
ιstinctly. The work stands apart (though not quite alone) among
ιe allegories as being partly in prose and partly in verse.

CHARLES D'ORLÉANS.[4]

Charles, Duke of Orléans, father of Louis XII. of France, was a
iend of King René's, and, as has been said, joined him in the fash-
nable amusement of writing lyrics in competition. He was taken
risoner by the English at the battle of Agincourt (Oct. 25, 1415),
ιd remained in England till he was ransomed in 1440. During
ιese twenty-five years the captive duke doubtless found abundant
isure for writing poetry, and a large body of his verse has come
ɔwn to us. His extant works consist chiefly of love-poems cast
ι the elaborate verse forms that were fashionable in his time, and
ɛ poems bewailing his captivity. Among the love-poems is the

---

[1] It was also influenced by the *romans d'aventure*, as many details show.

[2] *Ephesians*, vi, 13–17.

[3] *Poems and Fables of Rob. Henryson*, ed. by D. Laing, Edinburgh, 1865, pp. 8 ff.

[4] A.D. 1391–1465.

so-called *Poème de la Prison*,[1] an allegorical piece, forming the setting for a number of ballades, rondeaux, and chansons. The arrangement of Charles's poems in the order designed by him is a task which has not yet been successfully accomplished, so that it is not possible to tell which of these short poems he intended to be contained in the whole, of which the allegory forms the framework. For our main purpose, however, the allegory alone is of first importance, and an outline of that follows.

When the poet first came into the world, he tells us, he was given in charge to a lady called Enfance and later to Dame Jeunesse. One St. Valentine's morning Jeunesse woke him and invited him to go with her to the God of Love. On arriving at the gate of a pleasant manor, they were admitted by the porter, Compaignie. Bel Acueil and Plaisance welcomed them and led them before the God of Love, who was surrounded by courtiers singing and dancing. Jeunesse presented Charles as a scion of the house of France, and Love welcomed him, saying he had known his father and others of his lineage, and asking if he had been struck by his dart yet. Then he handed him over to Plaisant Beauté, with orders to give him no rest till she had made him one of Love's vassals. She was to think of her conquests over Samson and Solomon, and keep up her reputation. When Beauté sat down beside Charles, he could not keep his eyes off her; so she sent a dart through them to his heart, which leapt for joy. He sent a thought to remove the dart, but in vain, and in great distress and deadly pale he threw himself at Love's feet. Love laughed at him and recommended a doctor, and joked him about his quick overthrow. At the instance of Beauté Charles yielded, and she then went to Love, announced his repentance, and begged mercy on his behalf. Love appointed Beauté his deputy, and she laid down four chief commandments which Charles had to swear to obey, and six minor rules which it would be well for him to follow.[2] He was then duly sworn; Bonne Foy, chief secretary of Love, made out the "lettre de retenue," Loyaulté sealed it, and it was delivered to him. This letter was a document drawn up in legal form, admit-

---

[1] *Poésies Complètes de Charles d'Orléans*, ed. by Charles d'Héricault, new ed. Paris, 1896, I, 1 ff.   [2] Cf. pp. 200-1, below.

ting Charles to the service of Cupid and Venus, granting him all the privileges of their realm and the assistance of their officers, and stating that they had received his heart in pledge as a surety for his loyalty. At this point the allegorical part of the French poem as we have it is interrupted, and the ballades begin ; but a contemporary English translation,[1] apparently made from a lost MS., carries on the narrative. The "lettre de retenue" Charles received with gratitude and humility, and promised life-long service. In exchange for his heart he asked for another — his lady's, since she had his. At this Love looked sad, and said he lacked wit in supposing his lady could give her heart to every one who asked it. She must have her choice ; and Charles's business was to devise ways of winning her in a fitting fashion. Charles turned to look at Beauty, but finding her surrounded by Disdain and cruel Danger, he was afraid to speak lest he might make his case worse, especially since Pity was asleep. So he decided to write a bill beseeching her to grant him some of her heart — were it only a piece of the size of a pin's head — to save his life. Withdrawing with Hope into an arbor, he sat down with the pen and paper which he supplied, and tried to write something pleasing. The ballades, etc., may be supposed to be the results of his efforts.

After the ballades the allegory is again taken up in the French MSS., and is continued in a series of short pieces in a variety of forms of verse. The first of these is the *Songe et Complainte.* In this Charles tells how one night in a dream there appeared to him an old man whom he thought he had seen before, but whom he failed to recognize. The visitor, however, explains that he is Aage, who had come once before from Dame Nature, bearing the letters charging Enfance to deliver the hero to Jeunesse. Raison, Aage said, had complained to Nature of the many faults committed by Jeunesse and Charles ; and he warned the poet that this was no light matter, because Vieillesse, "la mère de courrous," would soon attack him, and that, since she could not be escaped, he had better give up Folie and Love, while he still had Jeunesse. No one could serve satisfac-

---

[1] *Poems, written in English, by Charles, Duke of Orleans*, ed. for the Roxburghe Club by G. Watson Taylor, London, 1827, pp. 3–9. Cf. G. Bullrich, *Ueber Ch. d'Orléans und die ihm zugeschriebene engl. Uebersetzung seiner Gedichte*, Berlin, 1893.

torily both Amour and Vieillesse, and Amour ought to excuse him
now that his mistress was dead. Every one mocked an old man
in love; but while a man was still young he might honorably aban
don love "comme par Nonchalance," and no one could say it wa
through compulsion, but it would be clear that it was because o
faithfulness to the memory of his peerless lady. So he ought humbly
to ask the God of Love to release him from his allegiance, and
thanking him for the benefits received while in his service, retire
honorably. With his fellow-subjects, too, he should first clear al
scores, asking pardon for any offences he might have committed
against them. Such was the advice of Aage, who concluded hi
speech with a warning against Fortune, who would be certain to tr
to hinder him from the course recommended, holding up the terror
of ennui, but who should not be trusted, for she was as false as the
moon.

Trembling like a leaf the poet awoke and resolved, though much
depressed at the prospect, to follow the old man's counsel. So h
determined to write a request for an honorable discharge, which
would stop the mouths of slanderers, and to present it to Amour a
his next feast.

La Requeste follows, "aux excellens et puissans en noblesse, Die
Cupido et Venus la déesse." The petition recounts the poet's faith
ful service, and asks that on account of the death of his lady an
the impossibility of his ever loving again, he should get back hi
heart and be freed from his oath; and that Bonne Foy should b
ordered to make out a letter of quittance. If this is done, h
promises to pray for Love and to remember the favor that he ha
received and is going to receive through his "bonne mercy."

La Despartie d'Amours, which comes next, consists of nine ba
lades and two other pieces. The first ballade tells how he presente
his petition at the next parliament held by Amour, and how the go
urged him to throw aside his grief and seek another mistress. I
the second, the poet insists on the hopelessness of this, and plead
for the granting of his request. In the third the god politely regret
the poet's determination, acknowledges his faithfulness in the past
and promises to grant his wish. The fourth tells of the passin
of the quittance by the parliament, and of the replacing of his hear

n his bosom. Then follows the formal quittance, in which Amour, counselled by Franc Desir, declares Charles free from his oath, and vouches that he leaves the service of Love, not "par deffaulte, forfait ou vice," but solely because of the death of his lady, to whom he wishes to remain as faithful as the widowed turtle-dove to her mate. The letter is sealed and dated from the castle of Plaisant Recept on the day of the Feste des Mors. In the fifth ballade he is so overcome by grief that when Amour in pity offers him his assistance, he is unable to speak, and takes his leave without a word, while Amour hands him over to Confort, who, in the sixth ballade, leads him to the manor of Nonchaloir. In the seventh, Passe-Temps, the governor of this mansion, receives him, and approves of his resolve to spend the rest of his life there. Confort is sent back to report to Amour his favorable reception. The letter which Confort bore to Amour follows, and in it Charles says that he shall always be eager to hear news of Amour; that he is in good spirits in the house of Nonchaloir; that he hopes to stay there till he has to go to end his days with Vieillesse, a prospect which is gloomy enough but which is still, thank God, far off; that he sends back Confort, for whose good company he is grateful, and who will ask pardon for him if, through Non Savoir, he does not address the god properly; that he wishes now to thank Amour for all past benefits, a thing he was unable to do at the moment of parting, on account of his emotion; and that he will pray the Almighty to grant Amour honor and long life, and victory over the company of false Dangier.

In the eighth ballade Charles wishes to try whether he still possesses his old power of rhyming, and in the last he says that the plaster of Nonchaloir which he had applied to his heart has so cured him that he is now in good condition and forever proof against the "amoureuse maladie." He strains his eyes to catch a glimpse of his old enemy Plaisant Beauté, but they are "si treshastis, et trop plains de leur vouloir." The mood with which the poem closes is expressed in the last envoi:

> Quant je voy en doleur pris
> Les amoureux, je m'en ris;
> Car je tiens pour grant folie
> L'amoureuse maladie.

Though the story is told with the elegance for which Charles is famous, and without many of the crudities which disfigured most of the poems we have had to deal with, yet it cannot be claimed that he has added anything of importance to the material of love-allegory. The general scheme is very familiar, though we may perhaps discern a touch of realism in the picture of the royal court, — as, for example, when the god graciously calls to mind members of Charles's family when he is first presented. The figure is the feudal one throughout, never the religious. The "lettre de retenue" we had in germ as far back as the charter granted by the God of Love, in *De Venus la Deesse d'Amor*[1]; and the commandments have been often paralleled. The exchange of hearts is found in *Le Roman de la Poire*.[2] Samson and Solomon are stock examples of the power of woman. The conceit about Enfance, Jeunesse, and Vieillesse, and the cure at the mansion of Nonchaloir are the most individual points.

In the treatment throughout, however, it is to be remarked, Charles is less bound by convention and more alive to the psychological signification of the allegory than the great majority of the poets of his type.

JEAN DE GARENCIÈRES.[3]

René of Anjou was not the only friend with whom Charles of Orléans entered into a friendly rivalry in verse-making; and among the duke's somewhat numerous personal poems we find one ballade, entitled *Orléans contre Garencières*. In the poems of this Jean de Garencières, there occur frequent references to the God of Love in terms of the feudal allegory (phrases, for instance, in which Jean promises to serve him "ligement"), and in his *L'Enseignement du Dieu d'Amours*[4] several Court of Love features appear.

As the author rode, full of melancholy, through a meadow one beautiful May day, he heard a voice ask:

> "Que n'es tu amoureux?
> Je te promect que c'est un beau mestier!"

---

[1] See p. 43, above.   [2] See p. 58, above.

[3] On Jean de Garencières and his works, see A. Piaget, *Romania*, XXII, 422 ff. His poems fall in the first quarter of the fifteenth century.

[4] Printed by Piaget, *Romania*, XXII, 434-8. The poem consists of twenty eight-line stanzas.

The poet inquires who his adviser is :

> Il me respont : " Cellui qui a renon
> De departir de joye largement."
> " Helas ! sire, je ne sçay vraiement
> Se vous n'estes le dieu des amoureux ? "
> " Oyl," fait il : " sers moy bien loyaument,
> Je te jure de te faire joyeulx."

He is inclined to follow this advice ; but the lady on whom he
has set his heart is surrounded by admirers, some of them "plus
grans maistres" with every advantage over the poet in appearance
and accomplishments.   But the god encourages him, and, after giving him instruction, leaves him with a promise to lend assistance.

MICHAULT TAILLEVENT.

In *L'Ediffice de l'Ostel Dolloureux d'Amours*[1] of Michault Taillevent, a little poem consisting of six ballades, we find another instance
of the metaphorical building.[2]   The Ostel is the place where lovers
come to make complaints.

> Le fondement est de merancolie,
> Et les murs sont faiz de desconfiture ;
> Le mortier est d'amere confiture.
> Et puis après, afin qu'en hault se dresse,
> Il y a mis, pour la maison conclure,
> Comble de dueil et de dure destresse.

In the same MS. is another poem of Taillevent's, also consisting
of six ballades.   It is *La Resourse et Reliefvement du Dolloureux
Tostel,* a sort of counterpart of the former, showing "comment il
faudrait réparer 'l'ostel dolloureux' pour en faire 'l'ostel de paix et
d'amour glorieux, des plaisirs, des joyes, des grands soulas, de plaisance pleniere.' "[3]

---

[1] Piaget, *Romania,* XVIII, 449 ff. ; cf. Picot, *ibid.,* pp. 644–5. *Taillevent* was a
surname ; the poet's real name being Michault Le Caron. He was *valet de chambre*
to Philippe le Bon, and was dead in 1458.

[2] Cf. p. 28, above.

[3] Piaget, *Romania,* XVIII, 450.

OCTAVIEN DE SAINT-GELAIS.[1]

La Chasse d'Amours[2] of Octavien de Saint-Gelais is in the form o
a dream. The first part is chiefly political. It consists of a lamen
by La France on the state of the country, a kind of *Fall of Princ*
after Boccaccio, instructions to rulers, and other miscellaneous ma
ter. Coming at last to the love-allegory, the author imagines himse
in the Forest de Gracieux Desir, where he finds the Royne d'Amou
lamenting the injuries done her by Faux Semblant. Cupid is tryin
to console her, and Jeunesse also offers help. Beaulté is the queen
page, Plaisant Regard her "mignon de chambre," Loyaulté her se
retary, Bel Accueil her chancellor, Bonne Foy keeper of the sea
Hardiesse her counsellor, and Deduit Joyeulx her "maître-d'hôtel.
It is resolved to pursue Faux Semblant, and they get the assistanc
of the huntsman Espoyr de Joüir, with his dogs Legier Couraig
Soing, and Travail. The chase is described with many digression
and, all the company having returned to the Château de Plaisanc
"l'Amant Parfait," a young man who had rendered great service i
the Forest, is rewarded by being acknowledged a vassal of th
Royne d'Amours. Beaulté reads to him the ten statutes, Bonne F
administers the oath of allegiance, and Loyaulté reads the "lettre d
retenue." The statutes and the letter are taken from the *Poème de*
Prison with only slight alterations. Now l'Amant Parfait and Lo

---

[1] A.D. 1468–1502.

[2] This poem forms a part of *La Chasse et la Departie d'Amours*, published b
Antoine Vérard in 1533 as by Octavien de Saint-Gelais and Blaise d'Auriol. *L*
Chasse is commonly ascribed to Saint-Gelais, and *La Departie* (see p. 101, belov
to d'Auriol. Both poems have been shown by Goujet, X, 246–7, 308–9, an
Piaget (*Romania*, XXI, 584 ff.) to contain extensive plagiarisms from the *Poème d*
la Prison of Charles d'Orléans. Picot (*Romania*, XXII, 254) thinks that Véra
must be charged with this plagiarism; but see Piaget's reply (*Romania*, XXI
254 ff.). Of *La Chasse* it is the portion relating to l'Amant Parfait which com
from Charles, even the ballades, etc., being mostly copies or adaptations of h
lyrics. Piaget (*Romania*, XXII, 259, n. 3) is inclined to attribute to Blaise d'A
riol nothing but a "traité de rhétorique" contained in *La Departie*. He su
gests Simon Bourgoing as a possible author of some portion of the composit
work (*ibid.*, p. 256), and is disposed to limit the authorship of Saint-Gelais to
very small part of the whole (*ibid.*, p. 259, n. 2).

hange hearts, and when, accompanied by Jouissance, the lover
meets at the gate of the Château de Liesse the appointed lady,
mother exchange of hearts takes place. The courtship proceeds
ith extensive digressions on the praise of ladies and such topics,
nd finally the allegory ends with a multitude of rondeaux, etc.,[1] on
ll the phases and situations of love.

La Departie d'Amours, a sequel to *La Chasse*, is of uncertain
uthorship.[2] In the absence of the lover his mistress has died. He
tters many complaints, but finding these of no avail, he falls sick
nd makes his will:

> Premierement à la haultesse
> Du Dieu d'amours donne et envoye
> Mon esperit, et en humblesse
> Luy suppliant qu'il le convoye
> En son Paradis, et pourvoye ;
> Car je jure que loyaulment
> L'ay servy de veuil desireux ;
> Advoüer le puis donc vrayement
> Devant tous loyaulx amoureux.
>
> Oultre plus veuil que la richesse
> Des biens d'amours qu'Amour foulloye
> Departis soyent en grant largesse
> Aux vrais Amans.[3]

The lover then falls asleep. Age appears and gives him advice
hat leads him to go to the Chasteau de Plaisance and present to
Dame Amour and her son Cupid a request that they should give
im back his heart and release him from all his engagements. After
endeavoring in vain to make him change his resolution, Amour tells
Loyauté to make out a "lettre de quittance," which is presented to
he lover, along with his heart wrapped in black silk. This mourn-
ul sight moves the lover to tears, and Amour sends Bon Confort to
accompany him to the House of Nonchalloir, where Passe-Tems

---

[1] Mostly plagiarized from Charles d'Orléans (see p. 100, n. 2).
[2] See p. 100, n. 2, above. I follow the summary given by Goujet, X, 302 ff.
[3] Goujet, X, 305-6.

holds sway.   He is delighted with his welcome there, and sends a
letter back to Amour by Bon Confort thanking her for her many
kindnesses, and asking for news occasionally.   He continues to
dwell under the roof of Passe-Tems, writing ballades and rondeaux
to amuse himself.

A great deal of the same kind of allegory, but moralistic rather
than erotic, is to be found in *Le Sejour d'Honneur*,[1] by Octavien de
Saint-Gelais.   This work, which is partly in prose, suggests, in sev
eral respects, King René's *Livre du Cuer d'Amours Espris*, and in
the course of it the writer takes occasion to eulogize both that author
and Alain Chartier.[3]   The allegory is a slightly veiled autobiography,
the *Sejour d'Honneur* being merely an episode.   The poet falls
asleep while meditating in his chamber.   Sensuality appears to him
in the shape of a lovely woman and leads him by the roads of Fleurie
Jeunesse and Deduit Mondain to the Port de Mondaine Liesse,
whence they sail to the island of Vaine Esperance.   Leaving this
he sails, still accompanied by Sensualité, to an unknown land.   He
traverses the Forest d'Adventures and at last arrives at the Château
d'Honneur.   P. Lange[4] gives evidence to show the author's acquaintance with Chaucer's *Hous of Fame*, and believes that Saint Gelais
influenced Gavin Douglas both in the *Palace of Honour* and in *King
Hart.*[5]

MARTIN LE FRANC.[6]

Mention has been made[7] of the controversy on women that arose
in consequence of the attack made on the sex by Jean de Meun.
One of the most important books on the side of the defence was *Le
Champion des Dames*[8] of Martin le Franc.   The poem is very long,

---

[1] Goujet, X, 251–81 (from the edition of Vérard, Paris, 1519).   He dates the
poem 1489 or 1490.   [5] See pp. 160-3, below.

[2] *Ibid.*, X, 271–2.   [6] A.D. *ca.* 1410–61.

[3] *Ibid.*, IX, 160–1.   [7] See p. 83, above.

[4] *Chaucers Einfluss auf die Originaldichtungen des Schotten Douglas*, in *Anglia*,
VI, 69, 83–7.

[8] Goujet, IX, 188–214.   On Le Franc, see A. Piaget, *Martin Le Franc*,
Lausanne, 1888, and *Romania*, XVI, 382 ff., XVIII, 319 ff.   *Le Champion* dates
from *ca.* 1442.   There are two printed editions : Lyons, *ca.* 1485, and Paris, 1530.

is in five books, and is occupied with the attacks of Malebouche on women and love, and their defence by Franc Vouloir. Malebouche and his army assault the Château d'Amour, and so frighten the inhabitants that Love has to descend to restore confidence. The herald Bouche d'Or parleys with the enemy. A description is then given of Love, his followers, and his castle. This is described as a temple with altars, priests, a cemetery,[1] and so on. The priestess is Charité, the *curé* Sens Abesti, and the attendants in the refectory are Foi, Esperance, and Charité. There is a garden, too, where the retinue of the god dance and play.

Franc Vouloir, irritated by the insolence of Malebouche, goes out to defend the ladies; but the contest turns out to be legal, not military. An old "image de Verité," which had long stood neglected in a dark corner, is chosen judge, and a long argument ensues. Malebouche gets the aid of Vilain Penser, and the attack is renewed. Sacred and profane history are ransacked for instances of the infamy of women, and every conceivable charge is brought against them. The defence is conducted in a similar fashion, with digressions on such subjects as ecclesiastical politics and the Immaculate Conception. The statutes of the *Poème de la Prison* of Charles d'Orléans are quoted and commented on.[2] Franc Vouloir is victorious and Malebouche dies of chagrin.

From this very much abbreviated summary it is evident that Martin reproduced the stock material in the controversy on the morals of women, taking much from the very man whom he was especially answering, Jean de Meun. In the Court of Love frame-

---

[1] In the cemetery the poet saw the tomb

De celle qu'on va mal disant,
La belle dame sans mercy,
Et de laquelle on va lisant
Comme de dame au cœur noircy.
  Elle n'est pas en l'ospital,
Comme ne sçay qui l'a songié :
Elle est en tombeau de cristal,
Ouvré richement et forgié (15 b ff.).

Quoted by G. Paris, *Rom.*, XVI, 410. Cf. p. 88, above.

[2] For a similar poem only slightly related to the *Court of Love* type, see *Le Chevalier aux Dames*, Goujet, X, 139 ff.

work he used the *Roman de la Rose* and the erotic allegories of his own century. His conception of the sovereignty of Love is not at all consistent. At the opening of the poem the figure is military, and the God of Love descends into the besieged castle to reassure his people. But when the castle is described, it has indeed the usual pleasure grounds attached, but the building itself becomes a temple with ecclesiastical furniture and attendants, like the chapel in the *Hospital d'Amours*. Again, when Franc Vouloir champions the cause of the ladies, the dispute becomes purely legal, Truth is taken as judge, and the God of Love is lost sight of altogether. In fact, the poet too indiscriminately picked up from contemporary models fragments of different allegorical conceptions, no one of which was particularly well-fitted for his purpose of a prolonged debate, and, failing to give them any unity by a vigorous individual treatment, produced a poem which is, to an unusual extent even in the fifteenth century, an artistic monstrosity.

PIERRE MICHAULT.

La Danse des Aveugles,[1] in prose and verse, takes the form of a dialogue between Entendement and the author, but this dialogue takes place in a dream. This accords with an increasingly prevalent tendency. As the Middle Ages wore to an end and the intellectual attitude became more rationalistic, it was more and more felt as imperative to resort to some such device as a dream to· justify the fantastic machinery of the allegory. In *De Phyllide et Flora* and its French derivatives the poets frankly place the pleasure gardens of the God of Love within easy riding distance of the quite earthly and natural opening scene, while the fifteenth century *Hospital d'Amours* has a vision within a vision in its effort to avoid the palpably absurd. Yet it must be remembered that the English *Court of Love*, though dating from the sixteenth century, is not a dream ; and it is probable that in many cases this device was simply an unthinking imita-

---

[1] See Goujet, IX, 361 ff., whose analysis is here followed. Pierre Michault was a contemporary of Michault Taillevent (p. 99, above), with whom he has been often confused : see Piaget, *Romania*, XVIII, 439 ff.; Picot, *ibid.*, pp. 644–5.

tion, direct or indirect, of the *Roman de la Rose*, which in turn
derived it from the *Somnium Scipionis*.

In a dream, then, Pierre Michault is conducted into a spacious
place where there are three parks crowded with people. In each
park is enthroned one of " les Aveugles " — Love, Fortune, and
Death. In the first park, seated on a beautiful throne, is a young
prince, naked, blindfold, and holding in his hand a drawn bow. He
is accompanied by his mother Venus (for it immediately appears
that the young prince is Cupid), by Fol Appétit, and by Oiseuse.
The god explains in great detail his almost supreme power, and the
methods by which he gains his victories. Fortune and Death are
similarly treated.

SIMON BOURGOING.

This poet, *valet de chambre* to Louis XII., introduces into his book
of instructions for a young prince, *L'Espinette du Jeune Prince*,[1] an
allegory, in which the prince and his poet guide come, in the course
of their wanderings, before Venus and the God of Love. The
divinities converse with a hermit, who rails at them, and with a
young churchman, who is seduced into staying with them. The
prince has an audience in his turn. Venus and Cupid try to enlist
him under their standard ; but since, according to the title, he is
"conquerant le Royaulme de bonne Renommée," he has strength
enough to resist, and subsequently is received into the Château des
Vertus.

MARTIAL D'AUVERGNE.[2]

This poet, whose *Arrêts d'Amour* have played such an important
part in the history of the belief in the institution of the Court of
Love, has not a great deal to contribute to the history of the allegory. His *L'Amant rendu Cordelier*,[3] though in the form of a dream,
is not strictly an allegory ; yet his familiarity with such poems as we

---

[1] Goujet, X, 165 ff., who cites an edition by A. Vérard, Paris, 1508. As to the
possible connection of this poet with *La Chasse et la Departie d'Amours*, see
p. 100, n. 2, above.

[2] *Ca.*, A.D. 1440–1508.

[3] Ed. by A. de Montaiglon for Soc. des anc. Textes franç., Paris, 1881.

are investigating is shown by the recurrence of figures like Dangier,[1] Malebouche, Faulx Parlant, Faulx Semblant, Faulx Raport, and Love (as a person).

Preceding the "arrêts" themselves,[2] which are in prose, there occurs, by way of prologue, a description in verse of the Parlement d'Amours in which the decisions are rendered. Though much of the gorgeousness of the traditional Court of Love is retained, the god or king is replaced by a president, and legal imagery prevails. The parliament takes place in September, not in May.

> Le Président tout de drap d'or
> Avoit robbe fourrée d'ermines,
> Et sur le col un camail d'or,
> Tout couvert d'esméraudes fines . . .
> Plusieurs Amantz et Amoureux
> Illec vindrent de divers lieux . . .
> Les ungs de paour serroient leurs dens :
> Les aultres esmeuz et ardans,
> Tremblans comme la feuille en l'arbre.
> Nul n'est si saige, ne parfaict,
> Que quant il oit son jugement,
> Qu'il ne soit à moitié deffaict,
> Et troublé à l'entendement.

LE JARDIN DE PLAISANCE.

This anonymous compilation, the full title of which is *Le Jardin de Plaisance et Fleur de Rhétoricque,*[3] seems to have been intended as a collection of both precepts and examples in the art of poetry. It begins with a versified treatise on rhetoric, and the pieces which

---

[1] For example,

> Raison est souvent endormie,
> Mais jamais Dangier ne sommeille (vv. 345–6).

[2] For the *Arrêts* themselves see *Les Arrêts d'Amour*, etc., with commentary in Latin by Benoît de Court [ed. by Lenglet-Dufresnoy], Amsterdam, 1731. See also p. 202, below.

[3] Goujet, X, 396–408. The edition cited is *Le Jardin de Plaisance et Fleur de Rhétoricque,* "contenant plusieurs beaulx livres," etc., Paris (1547). He also cites editions, without date, at Paris and Lyons.

follow are very miscellaneous both in kind and in authorship. Some of them, such as the *Parlement d'Amours* of Alain Chartier, we have already discussed under their respective authors; others are anonymous. The fourth piece, *Le Chief de Joyeuse Destinée*, is an allegorical romance meant to show that love is the source of all good and all evil. It has the familiar figures of Doux Regard, Bon Avis, Loyauté, Soupçon, Haut Vouloir, Secret Penser, etc., and a description of the Palais d'Amours. The Jardin de Plaisance of the title is the scene in which many of the episodes, otherwise unconnected, take place. For example, there is a *morisque* in which l'Amoureux Languissant, Envieuse Jalousie, and others perform; and a number of ballades, rondeaux, and similar poems are introduced as the productions of the lovers who frequent the garden. The volume as a whole is so loosely put together that Goujet surmises that the compiler died before completing his work, and that the contents of his portfolios were published haphazard by some one who did not understand his design.

PIERRE GRINGORE.[1]

In *Le Casteau d'Amours* [2] of Pierre Gringore, the poet represents himself as meeting two young men, one downcast, coming from the Castle of Love, the other cheerful, going to it. In the conversation that ensues, the downcast youth (*le venant*) speaks from experience of the pains he has suffered there, while the cheerful one (*l'allant*) maintains that great joys are to be expected. He is not deterred by the warnings of *le venant*, but hurries off towards the castle. The poet follows. The porter, Belle Chiere, admits them to a marvellous place, whence flows

> liqueur acceptable
> Pour rauigourer ung mort monde.

In the base court they find seven men lying dead — the victims of loving madly. They are warned against such frenzy and are advised, if they desire a lady, to take the quiet and honorable way of marriage.

---

[1] *Ca.* A.D. 1475–1534.

[2] *Poésies des XVᵉ et XVIᵉ Siècles*, Paris, 1830–2, No. 2 (1830).

This last point is significant. When the inhabitants of the Casteau d'Amours begin to advise marriage we know that we are near the end of the allegorical period, and that the game of Courtly Love is almost played out. The date of the poem is unknown, but is probably about the beginning of the sixteenth century.

LE DEBAT D'UN MOINE ET D'UN GENDARME.

This section of our investigation began[1] with a group of poems whose common point was the discussion of the comparative worthiness of knights and clerks as lovers. So persistent was this motive that the last Old French work with which we have to deal before the date of the English *Court of Love* is a farce[2] upon the same subject. Cupid, seated on a throne, makes a speech about his power. A young girl comes to appeal to him for help, and is advised to take a lover rather than a husband. Two candidates, a young monk and an old *gendarme*, present themselves, and dispute for the possession of the girl. Before deciding the question, Cupid tells each of the three to sing a song. Then the *gendarme* says to the girl:

> D'ailleurs étant avec le Moine,
> Votre honneur sera déconfit.

She answers:

> Moins d'honneur et plus de profit.

The god, seeing what the girl's preference is, decides as usual in favor of the monk.

With this farce we conclude the enumeration of the poems in Old French, written before the time of the English *Court of Love*, which have the idea of the God or Goddess of Love holding a court either as their centre or as an important part of their framework. The poems which merely contain allusions to this conception, or which

---

[1] See p. 31, above.

[2] *Farce nouvelle, contenant le débat d'un jeune Moine et d'un vieil Gendarme, par devant le Dieu Cupidon, pour une fille, fort plaisante et récréative*, à 4 personnages, summarized in La Vallière, *Bibl. du Théâtre François*, Dresden, 1768, I, 10–11 (from *Recueil de plusieurs Farces*, Paris, 1612). La Vallière dates it "towards the end of the fifteenth century."

have it as only a minor part of their machinery, are so common that were they also to be included, our fifty would be more than doubled.

C. ITALIAN.

Allegory, as a special literary form, plays a very much smaller part in the literature of Italy than in that of France or England during the centuries on which we are engaged. We do indeed find allegorical figures occurring frequently enough in Italian poems, and occasionally whole works belonging to this class; but there does not seem to have been a time, like the period of French literature that we have just been dealing with, when this was the form that a poet turned to, almost as a matter of course, when he wished to use his imagination or to write of love. Dante, to be sure, used the allegorical method a great deal: the *Vita Nuova* is tinged with allegory, and the *Divine Comedy* has much in it that can be so described. But in both cases it is the detail about which this statement can be made; for the former has no plot in the sense in which the French allegorical romances have plot, and, in spite of the parabolic signification of such figures as Virgil and Beatrice, the outlines of the epic are the outlines of the poet's actual beliefs regarding the next world.

The reason for this contrast between the French and the Italian mediæval literature is not far to seek. Allegory is a characteristically mediæval form; and in Italy the Middle Ages began so late and the Renaissance came so early that that country never had the opportunity to fall completely under the spell that held France from the time of the *Roman de la Rose* till the end of the fifteenth century. Thus Petrarch, in spite of the fact that he wrote perhaps more pure allegory than any other Italian, was at the same time an enthusiast for the New Learning.

But if the more formal part of the Court of Love tradition is not prominent in Italy, many of its minor features abound. The poets of that country, with their delicate and subtle treatment of the passion of love, give us much material for the history of the growth of the chivalrous ideal. In this they show their indebtedness to Provençal sources of inspiration; and of their intimacy with French poetry generally there is abundant evidence.

SER DURANTE.

The earliest genuine specimens of love-allegory in Italy are direct borrowings from France. The *Roman de la Rose* was widely known [1]; and *Il Fiore*, [2] by a certain Ser Durante, whose identity has not yet been perfectly ascertained, though not exactly a translation, is a condensation, in two hundred and thirty-two sonnets, of the same poem. The elaborate descriptions, the mythological, philosophical, and sociological digressions are cut out, though most of the personifications, except Nature and Genius, are retained. Bel Acueil, whom the exigencies of gender led Guillaume de Lorris to make a young man, becomes here for similar reasons a girl, Bellacoglienza. This condensed version has no title in the MS., the name *Il Fiore* being chosen by M. Castets from the fact that "Fior" occurs instead of "Rose" throughout. The opening stanza will illustrate the method of treatment:

> Lo dio d'amor con su' arco mi trasse
> Perch' i' guardava un fior che m'abellia,
> Lo quale avea piantato Cortesia
> Nel giardin di Piacier; e que' vi trasse
> Sì tosto, c'a me parve che volasse;
> E disse: I' sì ti tengo in mia balia.—
> Allo[r] gli piaque, non per voglia mia,
> Che di cinque saette mi piaghesse.
> La prima à non Bieltà, per li ochi il core
> Mi passò; la seconda, Angielicanza,
> Quella mi mise sopra gran fredore;
> La terza Cortesia fu san dottanza;
> La quarta Compagnia, che fè dolore;
> La quinta apella l'uon Buona-Speranza.

---

[1] See the so-called *Detto d'Amore*, ed. by S. Morpurgo in *Propugnatore*, Nuova Serie, I, i, 18 ff. This fragment belongs to the thirteenth or fourteenth century, and is an imitation rather than a translation of the *Roman de la Rose*. Cf. also *Zt. f. rom. Phil.*, XII, 573, and *Romania*, XVII, 640, and see A. D'Ancona, *Il Romanzo della Rosa in italiano* in *Varietà storiche e letter.*, Milan, 1888, II, 1. For these references I am indebted to Professors Marsh and Sheldon.

[2] *Il Fiore, poème Italien du XIIIe siècle, en ccxxxii sonnets, imité du Roman de la Rose, par Durante*, ed. by F. Castets, Montpellier, 1881. Cf. also *Revue des Langues romanes*, XXXV, 307 f. A better edition is that by G. Mazzatinti,

BRUNETTO LATINI.

Another work which has some resemblances to the *Roman de la Rose* is *Il Tesoretto*[1] of Brunetto Latini. This poem, which is only less comprehensive than the same writer's prose *Trésor*, contains a passage in which Nature, who has been instructing the poet in all sorts of things, from the stories of Creation and Redemption to the subject of biology, directs him to a great plain[2] in which he finds emperors and kings and great lords, and above all an empress Virtue with four queenly daughters, Prudenza, Temperanza, Fortezza, and Giustizia, each in her own palace holding a court. Each has several attendant virtues, of whom only Cortesia, Larghezza, Leanza, and Prodezza are named (cap. 14, vv. 81–2).

But in the nineteenth chapter we have a much closer approach to the Court of Love scheme. In the beginning of May the poet is led to

> Un bel prato,
> Fiorito d'ongne lato,
> Lo più riccho del mondo,

and we know the God of Love is at hand.

> Io uidi dritto stante
> Ignudo un frescho fante,
> Ch' auea l'archo, e li strali,
> E auea penne, ed ali (xix, 81–4).

About him are four "donne valenti," Paura, Disianza, Amore, and Speranza.

GUIDO CAVALCANTI.

The named arrows occur also in a sonnet of Guido Cavalcanti's.[3] Love is represented as holding three arrows in his hand

> La prima dà piacere e disconforta,
> E la seconda disia la vertute
> De la gran gioia che la terza porta.

Inventario dei MSS. ital. delle Biblioteche di Francia, Rome, 1888, III, 611–730, with an introduction by E. Gorra, pp. 419–610; but this I have not seen.

[1] *Il Tesoretto e il Favoletto*, ed. by G. B. Zannoni, Florence, 1824, pp. 1–232; critical ed. by Wiese, *Zt. f. rom. Phil.*, VII, 334 ff.   [2] Chap. xiii.

[3] *Guido Cavalcanti e le sue Rime*, by P. Ercole, Leghorn, 1885, sonnet xxii, p. 307.

According to the interpretation of Rajna,[1] the first is Beauty, the second Desire, and with both of these the poet has been wounded. The third, Pity, does not reach him on account of his lady's hardness.

DANTE.

In the *Vita Nuova*, Love is often personified : as, for example, in the garment of a pilgrim,[2] or as a youth in white raiment.[3] Frequently he is described as a lord giving commands.[4]   Lovers are his liegemen ("i fedeli d'amore").[5]   Once[6] he is a lord of fearful aspect who appears holding the lady in his arms and feeding her with the burning heart of the poet.

The description of the Earthly Paradise[7] which occurs in the end of the *Purgatorio* (Cantos xxvii ff.), with its flowers and singing birds and clear stream, may be regarded as belonging to the same tradition as the landscape that we find so often in those French poems in which the Court of Love is held out of doors.

> Quelli che anticamente poetaro
>   L' età dell' oro e suo stato felice,
>   Forse in Parnaso esto loco sognaro.
> Qui fu innocente l' umana radice ;
>   Qui primavera sempre, ed ogni frutto ;
>   Nettare è questo di che ciascun dice (xxviii, 139–44).

PETRARCH.

In Petrarch's *Trionfo d'Amore*[8] we are refreshed to find some novelty in the setting, though most of the detail is familiar.

---

[1] As given by Ercole, p. 308.

[2] *Vita Nuova*, § 9, sonnet v.

[3] *Ibid.*, § 12.

[4] *Ibid.*, §§ 4, 9, etc.

[5] *Ibid.*, §§ 3, 8, etc.

[6] *Ibid.*, § 3, sonnet i.

[7] For this suggestion I am indebted to Professor Marsh.

[8] *I Trionfi di Francesco Petrarca*, ed. by C. Pasqualigo, Venice, 1874, pp. 34 ff. See also *Rime di Francesco Petrarca*, ed. by Mestica, Florence, 1896, pp. 521 ff.

One spring the poet had a vision in which he saw

> Sopr' un carro di foco un garzon crudo
> Con arco in mano e con saette a' fianchi,
>   Contra le qual non val elmo nè scudo ;
> Sopra gli omeri avea sol due grand' ali
> Di color mille, e tutto l'altro ignudo :
>   D'intorno innumerabili mortali,
> Parte presi in battaglia e parte uccisi,
> Parte feriti da pungenti strali (i, 23–30).

A certain friendly shade explained to the poet that all this came by love.[1] The shade also pointed out and named to Petrarch some of the famous lovers who followed the triumphal car of Amore (Julius Cæsar, Hercules, Demophoon, Jason, Venus and Mars, Lancelot and Guinevere, Tristan and Iseult, and others), sometimes sketching their sad history. The poet was trembling at the proofs thus given of the power of love,

> Quand' una giovinetta ebbi da lato,
> Pura assai più che candida colomba.
>   Ella mi prese ; ed io ch'avrei giurato
> Difendermi da uom coperto d'arme,
> Con parole e con cenni fui legato (ii, 89–93).

Here follows an account of his own sufferings as a lover, and many complaints against the unsatisfactoriness of the God of Love. Tamed now,[2] he looked about him to see if there were any poet there among the rout. He saw Orpheus, Pindar, Virgil, Ovid, Catullus, Propertius, Tibullus, and many others, Greek, Italian, and Provençal.

Then the whole company followed the god across country to his mother's kingdom, in a delectable isle in the Ægean which had been sacred to Venus in heathen times. Here they came into a lovely valley.

There Love celebrated his triumph, in the account of which occur a number of abstractions, hardly personified, yet treated in a manner

---

[1] "Questo per amar s'acquista," i, 42.

[2]   Ratto domesticato fui con tutti
              I miei infelici e miseri conservi (iii, 5–6).

approaching the kind of personification that we have seen in the
English *Court of Love :*

> Errori, sogni, ed immagini smorte
> Eran d'intorno al carro triunfale ;
> E false opinioni in su le porte ;
> E lubrico sperar su per le scale ;
> E dannoso guadagno, ed util danno ;
> E gradi ove più scende chi più sale ;
> Stanco riposo, e riposato affanno ;
> Chiaro disnor, e gloria oscura e nigra ;
> Perfida lealtate, e fido inganno ;
> Sollicito furore e ragion pigra (iii, 139–48).

It will be observed that the abstractions, which are almost personifications in the first of the lines quoted, run into those paradox-
ical conceits which occur all through the Middle Ages, and which
were so fashionable among the early Elizabethans.

In the isle of Venus Petrarch was brought to a wretched prison,
or Hades, in which he was confined for a long time, finding relief at
last in a consideration of the nature of Love and in pitying his
fellow-prisoners.   Some of these are represented as telling him their
tragic stories.

The *Trionfo della Castità* gives an account of the final defeat of
Love by the forces of Chastity.[1]

The "Triumph" form which Petrarch used here and in the similar
poems on Death, Fame, Time, and Divinity, was, of course, suggested
by the Roman triumphs awarded to successful generals.   Ovid had
used it in a Triumph of Love,[2] which has been already quoted.   It
was a favorite motive in mediæval art, appearing, especially in Italy,
in paintings and carvings as well as in poetry.[3]   A century after
Petrarch it was freely employed by Francesco Colonna.[4]

---

[1] The conflict reminds one of some parts of Huon de Mery's *Tornoiement de
l'Antechrist* (see pp. 48 ff., above).   [2] See p. 11, above.

[3] Another instance of the form occurs in the *Trionfo dell' amore sopra i suoi
ingrati,* by Francesco di Buonanni Malecarni (A.D. 1442).   See Veselofsky,
Novella della Figlia del Re di Dacia, p. xcv, Appendix I.

[4] See on Triumphs, Charles Ephrussi, *Étude sur le Songe de Poliphile,* Paris,
1888, pp. 49 ff.   For Colonna see p. 117, below.

The happy valley in the Isle of Venus recalls the older descriptions, such as that of the goddess's abode in Cyprus in Claudian's *De Nuptiis Honorii et Mariae.*[1]

BOCCACCIO.

In his *Amorosa Visione,*[2] which takes the form of a dream, Boccaccio tells how, following a beautiful lady, he enters a noble castle with letters of gold over the door, which read thus:

> Ricchezza, dignità, ogni tesoro,
>   Gloria mondana copiosamente,
>   Do a color che passan nel mio coro:
> Lieti li fo nel mondo, e similmente
> Do quella gioia che Amore promette
> A' cor che senton suo arco pugnente (cap. 3).

Entering, he sees a hall painted with portraits of philosophers, poets, and historians, and with the Seven Sciences and other symbolic figures. The paintings are described at great length. Among them is the picture of a most lovely woman, "La Gloria del mondo," enthroned and crowned, holding a sword and an apple of gold. Around her are a throng of mythological, scriptural, historical, and romantic figures. In a green meadow (still in the painting) the poet sees Love, a beautiful youth with golden hair, winged, clad in cloth of gold, and holding a bow and two arrows, one of gold and the other of lead. Round him are many worshippers, some gay and jocund, others sad and sighing grievously. Seated beside him in great honor is a lady like an angel, whom the poet supposes to be "her who was formerly adored in Cyprus." There are also paintings of many legendary love-episodes, from Jove and Europa to Tristram and Iseult.

The lady who is acting as guide then leads the poet into another hall, where Fortune, with her favorites and victims, is depicted on the walls. He is next conducted into a beautiful garden adorned with a wonderful fountain. Here are many lovely ladies singing,

---

[1] See p. 15, above.
[2] *Opere volgari,* vol. XIV, Florence, 1833.

dancing, and picking flowers.   With one of these he falls desperately in love.   She lends a favorable ear to his suit, but, on a sudden, he awakes, and is very sorrowful.

In *La Teseide*[1] occurs an elaborate Court of Love scene which is familiar to English readers through Chaucer's transcript of it in his *Parlement of Foules.*[2]

> Tra gli albuscelli ad una fonte allato
> Vide[3] Cupido fabbricar saette,
> Avendo egli a' suoi piè l' arco posato,
> Le qua' sua figlia Voluttade elette
> Nell' onde temperava, et assettato
> Con lor s'era Ozio, il quale ella vedette,
> Che con Memoria poi l'aste ferrava
> De' ferri ch'ella prima temperava (bk. vii, st. 54).

There were many other figures about, Leggiadria, Adornezza, Affabilitate, — represented by Plesaunce, Aray, and Lust in Chaucer, — Diletto, Gentilezza, Bellezza, Giovinezza, and others.   In the midst, raised on lofty columns, was a temple, around which danced young men and maidens, and above which doves were flying. Monna Pace sat before the door and beside her Pazienza, while within, the altar-flames were fanned by sighs caused by Gelosia. Priapus held the highest place in the temple.   There were also many relics in the sanctuary, showing the power of love, — broken bows of Diana's band, Atalanta's apples, and the like.   The walls were painted with the stories of Pyramus and Thisbe and many another lover.   In a more secret part of the temple she (*i.e.* Palemo's personified prayer) found Venus, the door guarded by Ricchezza. Inside it seemed dark at first, but presently on a great bed she saw the goddess lying with her beautiful golden hair all about her, her breasts uncovered, and a thin gauze lying over the rest of her body. Bacchus and Ceres sat on either side, and in her hand the goddess held the apple which she won in the Vale of Ida.[4]

---

[1] *Opere Volgari di Giovanni Boccaccio*, IX, 229 ff. (Florence, 1831).
[2] See p. 142, below.   Cf. Skeat's *Chaucer*, I, 67 ff.
[3] The subject is Palemo's prayer, personified.
[4] Bk. vii, sts. 55–66.

The proofs of Boccaccio's familiarity with the Court of Love tradition are so clear throughout this passage that they need hardly be pointed out. The resemblance of the stanza quoted, especially in the matter of the arrows, to the similar scene in Claudian [1] may be remarked. The temple, with love-trophies for relics, we have seen in French allegory,[2] but the instances are considerably later in date than Boccaccio. Besides the passage in the *Parlement of Foules*, the *Knightes Tale* (vv. 1918 ff.) shows some traces of Chaucer's acquaintance with the present description, though the fact of his having already used it in the *Parlement of Foules* prevented him from repeating it in full.[3]

FRANCESCO COLONNA.[4]

In the *Hypnerotomachia Poliphili*[5] of Francesco Colonna we have one of the most extraordinary documents dealt with in the whole course of our investigation. The book is the product of a man essentially mediæval in his cast of mind, but filled with an indiscriminating enthusiasm for the New Learning. Thus we have a sort of autobiographical allegory of a love affair, hopelessly confused in plan, full of absurd digressions on a variety of subjects, but especially burdened with architectural descriptions, and written in Italian disfigured by the most reckless importation of words from Latin, Greek, Hebrew — in fact from every source accessible to the author.

Finished in 1467, the volume remained unpublished till the very end of the century, when it had the good fortune to appear with the addition of a hundred and seventy-two interesting and admirable wood-cuts, by whom is uncertain. Owing largely to these illustrations, it had a great popularity in France, where it was republished (in translation) at least six times. An English translation of the first

---

[1] See p. 15, above.
[2] See p. 91, above.
[3] Cf. Skeat's *Chaucer*, V, 77.
[4] *Ca.* 1433–1527.
[5] First edition, by Aldus Manutius, Venice, 1499. The best edition of the French translation is that of Claude Popelin, Paris, 1883. See Brunet's *Manuel* (ed. of 1863), IV, 778 ; and *Supplément* (1878), p. 268.

book was made in the time of Elizabeth, and this version, if not good in itself, is at least written in a style which is wonderfully appropriate.[1]

It is fortunately not necessary to give an outline of the whole of this production ; but a few passages will show what a Renaissance treatment did for some of the commonplaces of the Court of Love.

After a variety of adventures, Poliphilus comes, led by five nymphs (his senses) to the palace of Queen Eleutherillida, whose surroundings are on the usual gorgeous scale of magnificence.   I quote from the Elizabethan translation :

In the midde prospect, opposite against our going in, upon a degreed regall throne, set full of glystering stones in a maruelous order, farre more excellent than the seat in the temple of Hercules at Tyre, of the stone Eusebes.   The Queene with an imperiall Maiestie sitting vppon it, goddesse like, and of a woonderfull magnanimitie in countenance : gorgiously apparrelled in clothe of goulde, with a sumptuous and curious attyre vpon hir head of a purple couler, with an edging of Orient Pearle, shadowing ouer hir large forhead, aunciently and princelike, euer pressing hir plemmirrulate trammels of hayre, as blacke as iet descending downe hir snowie temples, and the rest of the aboundance of hir long hayre, fastned rounde in the hinder parte of her head, and deuided into two partes or tresses, lapt about this waye and that waye, behind hir small eares, over hir streight proportioned head, and finished in the crowne with a flower of great Orient and rownd Pearles, such as be found in the Indian promontorie Perimula.[2]

There is a great deal of this kind of thing, — descriptions of banquets, ingenious fountains, a game of chess with living figures, — and then "my love Polia" comes on the scene "with a comely grace and unexcogitable elegancie."   The result is the usual one.

The archer Cupid, in my wounding heart hauing his residence, like a Lord and king, holding me tyed in the bands of Love, I found my selfe pricked and grieuously tormented, in his tyrannous and yet pleasant regiment.[3]

---

[1] *The Strife of Love in a Dream*, *being the Elizabethan version of the first book of the Hypnerotomachia*, ed. by A. Lang, London, 1890, from the edition "printed for William Holme," 1592.   The translator, " R. D.," has been thought to be one Robert Dallyngton.   I am indebted to the courtesy of Professor Charles Eliot Norton for permission to use his valuable collection of editions of Colonna.

[2] i, 9, ed. Lang, p. 117.   [3] i, 13, ed. Lang, p. 193.

In the fourteenth chapter of the first book begins a series of triumphs, in each of which the Love divinity is represented. The influence of Petrarch is marked.

Vppon the fore-ende [of the first triumphal car] I beheld Cupid, with a great number of wounded people and Nations, marueiling to see him shoote to the ayre[1] . . . [In the second car he again appears] aloft in the skyes, with the sharpe heades of his golden arrowes, wounding and making bleede the bodyes of dyuers foure-footed beastes[2] . . . [In the third, Cupid shoots into the sky, and on the other end of the car he is represented as being chastised by Venus.[3] In the fore-end of the fourth he shoots into heaven and causes Jupiter to fall in love with a mortal nymph, while] in the hinder end was Iupiter sitting in a tribunall seate as a iudge, and Cupide appearing limping before him, and making grieuous complaints against his louing mother, bicause that by hir means he had wounded himself extreemly with the loue of a faire damsell, and that his leg was burnt with a drop of a lampe, presenting also the yoong Nymph and the lampe in her hand.[4]

In another passage, in a description of tablets representing the seasons, an interesting confusion of Venus and Spring, and of their symbols, occurs.

This first was a faire goddesse, hir treces flieing abroad, girded with roses and other flowers, vpon a thin vpper garment couering her beautifull and pleasant proportion. She helde hir right hand ouer an ancient vessell, maner of a chafing-dish, called Chytropodus, sending foorth a flame of fire, into the which shee did cast roses and flowers, and in the other hand she held a branch of sweete myrtle, full of berries. By hir side stoode a little winged boy smiling, with his bowe and arrowes. Ouer hir head were two pigeons. And vnder the foote of this figure was written *Florido veri S.*[5]

But it would be disproportionate to select all the passages in this Renaissance monstrosity that are parallel to features of the Court of Love allegory. A temple of Venus, which, however, has little resemblance beyond the name to the type with which we have become familiar, occurs later, and is the scene of important events in the

---

[1] Ed. Lang, p. 202.   [2] P. 207.   [3] P. 211.

[4] P. 214. It will be observed from his treatment of the Psyche story that Colonna had not read Apuleius very carefully.

[5] i, 17, ed. Lang, pp. 242-3.

wooing of Polia. Cupid's two kinds of arrows appear again, and are distinguished in the usual way in a passage which will serve as an example of Colonna's Italian.

None palesemente sapiamo, che nella sua marauegliosa pharetra contiene due dissimile sagitte. La una di fulgoroso oro figurata. Laltra di livido & nephasto plombo. La prima di sforciato amore & uehemente, uiolentissimo gli cori ad irritabondo amare accende. Laltra in opposito intollerabile superbia & rabido & prompto odio excitante, prouoca & displicibile crudelitate.[1]

The chief importance of the *Hypnerotomachia* in this study is in the fact of its being permeated with the imagery and symbolism of love-allegory. Its original contribution is of the slightest; and there is no reason to suppose that it reached England before our *Court of Love* was written. But the work as a whole is one more proof of the prevalence of the literary forms we are studying.

D. GERMAN.

Love-allegory in Middle High German poetry grew up less completely under the influence of French literature than was the case in either Italian or English. As a result, it developed one or two characteristic forms found either not at all or to a much smaller extent in the other countries. Of such forms the most individual is the allegory of the Love-chase, where the woman is represented by the prey, and the dogs and other accompaniments of the hunt are the qualities and devices used to win her.

ALLEGORIES OF THE LOVE-CHASE.

The earliest example which I have found is the poem known as the *Königsberger Jagdallegorie*, dated by its editor " about the middle of the thirteenth century." [2] The author is unknown, but appears from his dialect to have been an Alemannian.[3]

In this work a hunter is represented as setting out after a hind

---

[1] Bk. ii, chap. 4. Cf. p. 140, below.   [3] *Ibid.*, p. 255.
[2] Ed. by K. Stejskal in *Zt. f. deutsches Alt.*, XXIV, 254–68.

with his four good hounds Trôst, Harre, Stæte, and Triuwe.   But he
has no success: the hind outstrips his dogs, and the hunter himself,
worn out and dejected, utters a long lament, throws himself down,
and is apparently about to give up the chase.   A wise man hears his
complaint and asks for details.   Learning that he has pursued this
hind for some ten years, the wise man advises him to dismiss his
hounds and set three others, Zwîfel, Wenken, and Falsch, on her
track.   The hunter rejects this counsel with contempt.   The poet,
however, who has overheard the conversation, determines to try his
luck.   He has no trouble in finding Zwîfel, Wenken, and Falsch, and
with their help he soon catches the hind.   He is leading her by a
cord when Minne and her company (*gesinde*) come up.   The poet
immediately addresses Minne, calling for judgment against the hind :
a good hunter had pursued her with good hounds for more than ten
years in vain, and now she has been taken in one day by the aid of
these false dogs.   Minne calls on her son to give judgment.

> " Mich dunket recht," sprach dô hin wider
> Ir sun, " daz man si lege nider
> Und ir breche die zen ûz " (vv. 237–9).

This opinion apparently meets with the approbation of all.

> Ez was allessamment slecht
> Die urteil dô und ôch daz recht (vv. 247–8).

Minne then departs, and the poet closes with general reflections on
the culpability of women who reject true love and accept false.

In this poem the line between the native chase-allegory and the
borrowed Court of Love is not very well concealed.   The accusing
of a hind, hunted down with hounds, of all the crimes of the cruel
beauty, before a court of human beings (or divinities in human shape),
can hardly be called artistic.   Stejskal holds that in this poem we
see in German " zum ersten male abstracte wesen personificiert."

The most famous and influential allegory of this class in Middle
High German is the *Jagd* of the Bavarian Hadamar von Laber,[1]

---

[1] *Hadamar's von Laber Jagd*, u. s. w., ed. by J. A. Schmeller, Stuttgart, 1850 ;
also ed. by Karl Stejskal, Vienna, 1880.   The *Jagd* probably dates from *ca.*
1335–40.

which, though not strictly a *Court of Love* poem, is too important in the general class of love-allegory to be disregarded here.

The hero rides out one morning to find a love, and follows his Heart, which is figured as a hound. He is also accompanied by the hounds Gelücke, Lust, Liebe, Genâde, Fröude, Wille, Wunne, Trôst, Stæte, Triuwe, and Harre, and in the course of the poem other personifications take part. He meets an experienced sportsman and gets advice. The Heart comes on the track of a splendid animal, and is wounded by it. Wolves (*i.e.* informers) appear. The hunter's horse falls lame through loss of a shoe ; so, following on foot, the hero is left behind by the dogs. An interview with a second adviser, a venerable man this time, takes place. Finally, through the efforts of Wille, Stæte, and Triuwe, and the Heart, he comes within reach of the prey. Brought so near, the hunter is somewhat abashed, and while the wolves put the hounds to flight the prey escapes, leaving the Heart more deeply wounded than ever. Further conferences with experienced persons take place, and the rest of the poem consists of complaints by the hunter about his ill-fortune, which, however, are not unmixed with expressions of hope for ultimate success.[1]

The similarity of the general plot to that of the Königsberg allegory, and the identity in name of some of the dogs, suggest a connection between the two poems. Frau Minne and her court, however do not appear in Hadamar's *Jagd*.

Die Jagd der Minne[2] is, in turn, an imitation of Hadamar. The general plan is the same, the hounds being named Wille, Liebe, Trost Haren, Stäte, Treue, Trawren, Zweifel, Mühe, Freude, and Mass Another hunter appears whose hounds are Unverschwiegen, Fälschen Triegen, Lügen, Unstät, Treulos, Wankel, Neid, Kall, Rüg, Schande Schalk, Rum, and others.

---

[1] The number and the order of the stanzas of this poem differ much in differen manuscripts, and there are frequent digressions. Schmeller (*Vorrede*, pp. xvii f.) ha taken the trouble to extract the substance of the narrative and to give it in a sum mary form, using sometimes one manuscript, sometimes another, in the arrangemer of the material. I have followed this summary, which is skilfully drawn up.

[2] Lassberg, *Lieder Saal*, II (1822), no. cxxvi, pp. 293–307. A poem calle *Der Minne Jagd*, which, if not a translation, is probably related to this school, mentioned by Goedeke in the Low German section of his *Grundriss*, I, 464.

Of the same school is *Der Minne-Falkner*,[1] in which a favorite hawk, which has run wild and taken flight, is the object of the poet's despairing pursuit. The love divinities do not take any part in the action of the allegory, but at the beginning of the second stanza occur the lines

> Venus, Amor, und Cupido
> Wenent gewalt und wunder zaigen,

which seem to imply an unexplained trinity in the godhead of Love. Still another is a fifteenth-century poem called *Die Verfolgte Hindin*.[2]

These poems have occasional details similar to those that are common in the French love-allegories, — the spring landscape and passages magnifying the power of love, for example, — but, except in the case of the *Königsberger Jagdallegorie*, the actual Court of Love does not appear in the allegories of the hunt.

DIE MINNEBURG.

This central motive, however, is by no means lacking in Middle High German literature. The inedited fourteenth-century poem known as *Die Minneburg*[3] is an important and elaborate example. The allegory — one of the most fantastic in mediæval literature — is the work of an anonymous rhetorician,[4] and is stated by Ehrismann

---

[1] Printed as *Dritter Anhang* to Schmeller's edition of *Hadamar's von Laber Jgd*, Stuttgart, 1850, pp. 171 ff. Schmeller (*Vorrede*, p. xix) remarks that the author mentions "der weise von der Laber" in st. 170, p. 205. Professor Kittredge suggests that the idea of the poem may have come from the song of the Dürenberger, "Ich zôch mir einen valken" (*Minnesangs Frühling*, 3d ed., p. 8). The editors of *Des Minnesangs Frühling* quote various parallels to this song, among them an Italian sonnet of the thirteenth century (F. Trucchi, *Poesie ital. inedite*, Prato, 1846, I, 54); cf. also Wallner, *Zt. f. d. Alt.*, XL, 290–2.

[2] Keller, *Fastnachtspiele aus dem fünfzehnten Jahrhundert*, Stuttgart, 1853, III, 892–9.

[3] Carefully studied by G. Ehrismann in Paul u. Braune's *Beiträge*, XXII, 57–341 (July, 1897). I am indebted for this reference to the courtesy of Dr. E. C. Brooks. I have followed Ehrismann's analysis, which is superior to that given by Raab, *Ueber vier allegorische Motive*, pp. 36 f.

[4] On Wilken's mistaken ascription of the *Minneburg* to Egen von Bamberg, see Ehrismann, *Beiträge*, XXII, 331.

to be, after Hadamar's *Jagd*, the most popular of the love-allegorie
of the fourteenth century. The following summary will give som
idea of its contents :

One hot day the poet comes into a wild mountain region throug
which flows a torrent. By means of a raft he reaches a beautif
meadow, and soon sees a strong castle, guarded by giants, lions, ar
dogs. These are put to sleep by a great storm, which also drives th
poet into the castle for shelter. Inside the castle is a round pilla
provided with five "spiegelfenster," and wonderfully wrought with go
and precious stones. While he is marvelling at this, the chamberla
appears and welcomes him, tells him that the castle is called Minnebur
and opens the pillar for him. Inside, behind the windows, stands th
figure of a man made of glass, and above this, the figure of a woma
made of steel. When the female figure bends, it sees in the gla
man the reflection of all that shows through the windows. On
there appears the reflection of a man, on which the woman gazes t
she becomes pregnant and bears a child,— a strong boy, knowing a
languages, but with eyesight that grows weaker as he grows olde
until he becomes quite blind.

In the second chapter the poet seeks everywhere for a wise ma
to explain to him the nature of the child. At length he finds
Alexandria one Meister Neptanaus, whom he takes back with him
the Minneburg, to interpret the mysteries. Neptanaus explains th
the child is love (Minne) ; the castle is a pure woman ; the lion[1]
her sense of honor which keeps her from shame ; the giants are h
relations ; the dogs are gossips and slanderers. When these guard
sleep the lover may enter without harm. Further, it is explaine
that the pillar also represents a pure woman : the five windows a
her five senses, the glass man her reason, the steel woman her fre
will — these last being the father and mother of love.

The third chapter is chiefly of a didactic nature, consisting of th
answers of the master to the child's questions on the nature of lov
There are also some verses about the poet's own love affairs.

In the fourth chapter the child goes to walk with his " jungfrau
Cupido or Begirde. They come to a beautiful castle, guarded in th

---

[1] In the first chapter there are several lions, but only one is here explained.

ame manner as the Minneburg. Cupido incites the child to take
his stronghold, and there follows a description of an attack on the
astle by the attendants of the child — Unmasse, Unsittigkeit, Un-
esonnenheit, and the like, and of its defence by Masse, Stärke, and
Weisheit. Negotiations follow, in which the counsels of Weisheit
revail; the child and the lady of the castle come to an understand-
ng. The result of their union is a child called Widerminne. In the
astle, which is now named " daz edel hûs zu Fröudenberc," there
is joy without end.

In the fifth chapter the child and his *amie* go out to walk one Sun-
ay before the castle, and are attacked by a great crowd of slander-
rs. On the advice of Weisheit, the child hides himself with his
ompany, and the castle-gates are opened to the assailants. They,
owever, fail to find the child; so they go away, leaving him master of
Freudenberg. Now that peace is restored, the child wishes to show
his gratitude to his attendants, Treue, Weisheit, and Gerechtigkeit,
or their help. Every true lover who has a well-founded complaint
gainst his lady may come to Minne for justice. The Court of Love
ere becomes judicial : Weisheit, Gerechtigkeit, and Treue lead their
ervants — loving knights and squires — before the judgment seat
f Love, and he gives sentence against the ladies in the case. The
oet himself is identified with one of these servants, and takes the
pportunity to pour forth endless love complaints. At this point
he manuscript mercifully breaks off. So far as the construction of
he plot is concerned, there is no reason why the poem should ever
ave stopped.

The investigation of all the sources of this conglomeration of
lidactic and lyric with the most involved allegorical material would
e a task large enough for a separate treatise. Here it must be suffi-
ient to select a few interesting points.

The account of the Minneburg in the first chapter, with the island,
he raft, the giants and lions, and the storm, suggests the machinery
f the Arthurian romances or a more direct borrowing from popular
airy-lore, rather than the scenery of the allegorical poems of France.

The doubling of many of the features in the poem is also remark-
ble. There are two symbolical representations of a pure woman ;
here are two generations of children — first Minne born of Reason

and Free-will, and then Widerminne, the child of Minne ; there are
two castles, Minneburg and Freudenberg ; two contests, one for the
taking of Freudenberg, and one with the slanderers after the lady is
won ; and finally the purely social picture of life in the feudal court
at Freudenberg gives place to a legal court where cases are tried and
judgments given.   It is in these last respects that the German poem
comes nearest to the usual Court of Love type.   The symbolism of
the pillars and windows and steel woman and glass man are more
nearly unique.   The introduction of the poet's own love affairs is, of
course, common.

DAS KLOSTER DER MINNE.

Another somewhat extensive poem of this class, but conforming
to a greater extent to the usual type, is *Das Kloster der Minne.*[1]
Here the poet wanders, on the conventional May morning, into the
depths of a forest, where he sees a lady riding alone.   She is very
beautiful and magnificently attired in green samite.   He hides behind a tree and grasps her bridle as she passes.   She threatens
him with the anger of her mistress Minne, who is a queen, and, in
answer to the poet's questions, she tells him of a magnificent Kloster
built for Minne by a wise master, where she resides, surrounded by
a multitude of her subjects.   The life of these merry devotees is
described, and the size, splendor, and arrangements of the place are
told, with directions how to get there.

The messenger then rides on and the poet sets out to find the
Kloster.   The tracks of the lady's horse guide him out of the forest,
and the rest of the way, which leads through a beautiful country, is
plain enough, and he soon comes in sight of the building.   The
gates are standing open, and at that moment a company of ladies
and gentlemen come out to dance on the green before the Kloster.
Some of these the poet recognizes as old acquaintances, but nobody
seems to know him.

---

[1] Lassberg, *Lieder Saal*, no. 124, II, 205–64.   Ehrismann mentions in Paul u
Braune's *Beiträge*, XXII, 302, a dissertation on this poem by Georg Richter
Beiträge zur interpretation des mhd. gedichtes ' Kloster der Minne,' Berliner diss
1895.   This I have not seen.

Suddenly there is heard the sound of a bell which hangs near the ate and is never sounded except by a stranger in search of some dventure.   A squire, it appears, has brought to the knights of the onvent a challenge from five hundred stranger knights to engage in great tourney.   Excitement runs high.   The poet at last musters ourage to address a lady of his acquaintance whom he sees among he throng.   She greets him well and presents him to others.   With er he passes through the gate and across the courtyard into a mag-ificent palace, which is described.   The rule of the order is ex-lained to him: Minne is over them all; it is to please her that hey have adopted this conventual life; Minne has given them an bbot, an abbess, and other officers.   The poet also sees certain ffenders who are undergoing penance: with two he holds some onversation,—a telltale (*claffer*) and a boaster (*rümser*).   From a rrace or balcony the poet and his guide look down into the court-ard, where the convent-brothers are preparing for the tournament. [ever were there monks who looked so much like knights (v. 1109). 'he tournament is then described.

After some further conversation, the lady consents, at the poet's equest, to show him Minne, whom he has long wished to behold. he accordingly conducts him to a part of the convent where he ees many ladies, knights, and squires making love.   He still in-uires for Minne, and asks if she is coming soon, but his instructress ells him that in looking at these lovers he is seeing Love.   The .dy takes this further opportunity to explain the nature of love — ow it is over all, and so on.   From this comes a familiar conversa-on, in which they grow more and more intimate, and when at last he poet is going to take his leave they agree to meet again in welve days.   So, after drinking to their speedy reunion, the poet oes off, determined to return and die in the order.

The name of this poem would lead one to expect the religious gure to be the prevalent one; but, in spite of the repeated men-on of the "Ordensregel" and the passage on penance, the picture s a whole is that of the gay life of a feudal court.   Curiously nough, the goddess herself remains in the background, and at ne point the poet refers to her as merely an abstraction; and we ave the interesting combination of the rôles of guide and mistress in the lady of his acquaintance whom the poet meets before the Kloster. The solitary maiden in the forest is a very frequent figure in German allegory, and it is a mark of the effect of physical surroundings that the forest is a much more constant element in the landscape of German poetry than in that of the other countries whose literatures we have to discuss. The allegorical signification is not pushed nearly so far in *Das Kloster der Minne* as in *Die Minneburg;* and at times it seems to be almost lost sight of while the poet is carried away by his zeal in describing the chivalrous scenes that make up the greater part of the material of the poem.[1]

FRAU VENUS UND DIE MINNENDEN.

In *Frau Venus und die Minnenden*[2] some of the characteristics of *Das Kloster der Minne* are repeated. A lover loses himself in a forest; but, following a sound of music, he comes out into an open field where he finds a great crowd of people of all nations and religions bowing before a huge pavilion. He presses through them, and, entering the tent, finds Frau Venus surrounded by a large crowd of lovers to whose complaints she is listening. Everything seems to be spoken in foreign languages, but later the lover hears a damsel present a complaint in German, and follows her example. Venus explains that the lady to whom her lover is faithless is in a far worse case than a man similarly situated. However, she promises to do justice in both cases. The poet is then carried away by the press, and goes home.

---

[1] For the religious figure Professor Sheldon draws my attention to the interesting parallelism in the *Yvain* of Chrétien de Troyes :

> Li autre parloient d'amors,
> Des angoisses et des dolors
> Et des granz biens qu' an ont sovant
> Li deciple de son covant (vv. 13–16).

See note on v. 16, p. 274, in Foerster's larger edition of *Yvain* (Halfe, 1887) and cf. Tobler in Holland's 3d edition of the *Chevalier au Lyon*, Paris, 1886, p. 3 The idea of the convent, of course, recalls the *Romaricimontis Concilium* (pp. 31 ff. above) and those other poems in which the religious figure has been prominent.

[2] Lassberg, *Lieder Saal*, no. 32, I, 233–44.

THE HÄTZLERIN MS.

Der Mynn Gericht[1] also opens with the poet's walking in a forest and hearing the birds sing. He finds a lady who has long wandered there. Her hair has been cut off; she is clad in a single garment, and her naked feet are torn and bleeding. She tells how once she had refused to listen to the wooing of a youth, and how at last the case had been brought before the Court of Love, consisting of Queen Venus and five ladies, Ehre, Treue, Stätigkeit, Sälde, and Liebe. Liebe spoke for the youth, and Stäte took the damsel's part. The decision went against the damsel, who was condemned to wander in the wood for seven years. She was now undergoing this punishment. The poem ends with her entreaty to the author to tell her story to all good women, that they may be warned in time.

Of the same type and in the same manuscript is *Ain Mynn Red von Hertzen und von Leib*.[2] The poet is out in search of adventure and comes through a forest into a flowery meadow, where, by a spring, he finds a beautiful tent. Six ladies are singing and dancing, Minne, Liebe, Stäte, Zucht, Tugend, and Scham, and "Fraw Venus sang ze tantz."[3] He presents his complaint to Venus and seeks advice, his Heart and his Body arguing the case. Venus teaches him seven virtues which are written in the Book of Love, after which the poet goes home.

In a poem *Von zwain Swestern*, also in this MS., we find Venus in the unaccustomed rôle of schoolmistress. The elder of the two daughters of a knight loves the son of a *bourgeois*. She is induced by her sister to think shame of the affair and wish to give it up. But a magnificent lady appears and announces herself:

> Ich bin fraw Mynn,
> Der lieb schulmaistrin.[4]

She then gives the faithless girl some severe blows on her snow-white hand for her want of constancy.

---

[1] *Liederbuch der Clara Hätzlerin*, ed. by Haltaus, Quedlinburg and Leipzig, 1840, no. 56, pp. 226-30. The Hätzlerin MS. is dated 1471.

[2] *Liederbuch*, no. 47, pp. 211-14.   [4] *Liederbuch*, no. 18, pp. 163 ff.

[3] Venus and Minne are the same person in this poem (see vv. 193-203).

MEISTER ALTSWERT.

In *Daz alte Swert*, the poem that gives the title to the *Altswer*
volume,[1] Venus is again instructress, though in a somewhat mor
dignified way.   She encourages the author, whose lady, he says
rejects him

> Umb daz ich mittel jare zil
> Uff mir haben und tragen
> Und sie mit sorgen beladen (p. 5).

Says Venus,

> Ein gestanden swert ist goldes wert,
> So man der niuwen niht engert (p. 7).[2]

The dream motive occurs in a long poem in the same collectio
known as *Der Kittel*.[3]   Here the poet is summoned to " Fraw Venu
lant " by the voice of an unseen messenger which comes to hin
between sleeping and waking.   He rises from his bed and seek
this unknown country.   Accompanied by his squire, he rides fa
and wide, till he loses his way in a great wood.   After five days
wandering he goes to sleep under a tree.   In a dream, the mysteri
ous messenger [4] comes and leads him into " Fraw Venus lant."

Leaving him in a beautiful garden, his guide goes to the castle c
Venus to announce him.   A damsel of surpassing beauty, clad in
silken " Kittel " (whence the name of the poem), enters the garden

> Durch die bluomen in richem schin
> Erluhten ir die füzelin (p. 25).

She has come from " Keiserin Venus " and the five queens, Ehre
Treue, Stäte, Liebe, Maze, to conduct the poet into the castle.   H
is charmed with her, and they embrace and hold a long conversa
tion.   At last she leads him into the castle, past a gigantic porte
and so into the great hall, which is adorned with all sorts of wonde

---

[1] *Meister Altswert*, ed. by W. Holland and A. Keller, Stuttgart, 1850, pp. 1–1c

[2] Cf. *Der Kittel*, in the same volume, p. 57, vv. 32–3.

[3] *Daz alte Schwert* and *Der Kittel* are probably by the same author, and dat
from the middle of the fifteenth century.

[4]
> Ein nebelkappe hat er an,
> Ich weiz, obe ez wer wip oder man (p. 18).

ıl things, including portraits of King Arthur, Wigeleis, and other
eroes. In the palace he finds Venus and the five queens, who
ıake him welcome.

Venus has sent for the poet, she tells him, to learn the truth
bout the "falsche nuwe minne" which, she has heard, prevails in
.lsace. The reply is a satire on contemporary manners. After this
ʿenus gives the poet much instruction with regard to true love.
he then takes him to her treasury and offers him rich presents, but
ıe wishes for nothing but the favor of his lady, his "G. in dem
.ittel." Venus gives him an emerald, which she declares will
ınsure the success of his suit, and he takes his leave, filled with joy.

> Do krat der han, ez was tag!

The printed collections from which have been drawn the exam-
les so far described contain several other poems with the same
ind of personifications; as, for example, *Des Spiegels Abenteuer*,[1]
ʿhich has Frau Treu and Keiserin Aventiur; and there are some
till unprinted whose titles indicate that they belong to the Court of
.ove category.[2]

DIE MINNE UND DIE EHRE.

There is still another type of Court of Love poem peculiar to Ger-
ıany, — that in which Venus appears not as judge, but as one of
ıe parties in the case. Such a poem is *Die Minne und die Ehre*.[3]

---

[1] See *Meister Altswert*, pp. 117 ff.

[2] Instances are: (1) a poem, without title, in the Heidelberg fifteenth-century MS.
ʿal. Germ. 313, fo. 409 a., described by F. Wilken, *Gesch. der Bildung, Beraubung
, Vernichtung der alten Heidelbergischen Büchersammlungen*, Heidelberg, 1817,
. 414, as "Der Frau Venus, Königin der Minne, Gericht über einer Frauen
.ertigkeit, nebst der Liebe Regeln und Orden"; see also Bartsch, *Die altdeut-
hen Handschriften der Universitäts-Bibl. in Heidelberg*, Heidelberg, 1887, no.
.8, p. 72 (also, with title *Von dem Ellenden Buoben*, in *Pal. Germ.* 344, fo. 1 a;
ee Bartsch, no. 172, p. 100; Wilken, p. 428); (2) a poem entitled *Spruchgedicht
. Pal. Germ.* 393, fo. 20, described by Wilken, p. 463, as "Klagen einer Lieben-
en und ihres Anwalds vor der Frau Minne, Stät, etc. . . . über die Untreue
.res Ritters, und Entscheid der Richterinnen"; see Bartsch, no. 215, p. 128.
ʿf. Goedeke, *Grundriss*, I, §§ 83–4.

[3] Lassberg, *Lieder Saal*, no. 205, III, 239 ff.

The author tells how one beautiful May morning he was driven b
the restlessness of love to walk in the fields.   In a wood nearby h
heard the noise of a carriage and he hastened thither to see what
meant.   The carriage was richly adorned with gold and in it sat thre
fair damsels.   The poet followed them until they came to a plac
where Frau Venus sat "an ir gericht" in a tent with her companion:
There the ladies sprang out of the carriage, and one of them, Fra
Ehre, immediately began to accuse Venus (now called Minne) to he
face as she sat there.   Ehre complained that Venus made so man
people abandon her that the number of her followers was muc
diminished, and so on.[1]   Venus said that she was sorry if there wa
any offence, but that she was only doing what she had always don
She simply made people fall in love, and if any lover abandone
Ehre it was not her fault.   This Ehre and her companions had t
grant; so the two parted in friendly fashion just as the day bega
to break.

Die Minne vor Gerichte[2] is just such another poem, Minne bein
again impeached by Gerechtigkeit, supported by Zucht, Tugen
Bescheidenheit, Mass, and Schame.   Ehre is the judge.

THOMAS MURNER.

Among the many poems inspired by the *Narrenschiff* of Sebastia
Brant, one, *Die Gäuchmatt* of Thomas Murner,[3] contains some Cou
of Love features.   The chapters *Venus Gewalt* (pp. 30–5), *Wenu
lere vnd ermanung zu allem wypplichē Geschlecht* (pp. 83–9), and th
enumeration of the usual classical and biblical love affairs, all sugge:
a knowledge of the current love-allegories.   In this book, too, ther
is a chapter *Frouw Venus berg* (pp. 186–9), which, with an accompany
ing woodcut, shows traces of the influence of the Tannhäuser legen

---

[1] Note especially vv. 130–3:

> Nu gastu an vnrechten wegen
> Vnd brichest mit gewalt für:
> Din bog, din stral, din brinent für
> Tuot mich vil kombers liden.

[2] Lassberg, *Lieder Saal*, no. 29, I, 195–208.

[3] Ed. by W. Uhl, Leipzig, 1896.   The poem was first published at Basel
1519.   For this reference I am indebted to Dr. N. C. Brooks.

THE *TANNHÄUSER* LEGEND.

The name of the Venusberg, and the points of similarity between that palace of perpetual delights and the allegorical Court of Love, make it necessary to say something of the relations of the story of Tannhäuser to the subject of the present discussion.

The points of similarity are these : the gorgeous hall; the abundance of means of sensual enjoyment; the throngs of fair women; the Queen of Love as presiding personage; and a young hero gaining admission to all this. On the other hand, let it be noted that in the Tannhäuser story there is no conscious allegory whatever; that there is no feudal figure employed; that the hero is seduced into taking part in the revels, whereas in the Court of Love poems he is usually a candidate whose admission is a matter of more or less uncertainty; and that beyond the name Venus and the fact that her attractions are those of sensual love, there is no trace of the classical in the legendary goddess.

This becomes more apparent if we strip the legend of its more modern accretions.[1] The story of Tannhäuser as it is most familiar to-day in the music-drama of Richard Wagner is a combination of several elements originally quite distinct. Two of these might at first sight seem to emphasize the relation between the legend and the Court of Love, *viz.* the Wartburg poetic contest, and the name of the minnesinger Tannhäuser. But the Wartburg contest, though going back to a thirteenth-century poem on Heinrich von Ofterdingen, was not associated with our story before the present century.

The connection with the name Tannhäuser is older, though still comparatively late. A poem by Hermann von Sachsenheim (d. 1458) represents Tannhäuser as the husband of Venus.[2] Two others of about

---

[1] See G. Paris, *La Légende du Tannhäuser*, in *Revue de Paris*, March 15, 1898 (pp. 307 ff.), and *Le Paradis de la Reine Sibylle*, in *Revue de Paris*, Dec. 15, 1897. From these articles most of the material for the analysis given here is derived. Cf. also W. Söderhjelm, *Antoine de La Sale et la légende de Tannhäuser*, in *Mémoires de la Société Néo-Philologique à Helsingfors*, II, 101 ff., Helsingfors, 1897.

[2] See Goedeke's *Grundriss*, I, 294, *Die Mörin*, in which the poet is seized by an old man and a dwarf and accused of inconstancy in love by a negress, acting for Frau Venus, before King Danhauser. Cf. *Der Schatz* in *Altswert*, pp. 70–116, in

the same date tell of the repentance of Tannhäuser after he has live some time in the mountain. The popular German ballad which i responsible for the wide circulation of the legend did not take shap till the sixteenth century. Now the dates of the minnesinger Tanr häuser are from about 1205 to about 1270, and there does not exis anything in his extant verses to connect him with the legend. Bu there was a certain rhythmical and musical form attached to one c the kinds of verse invented by him, known in its two varieties as th long and the short "ton" of Tannhäuser; and it is in the long "ton of Tannhäuser that the earliest poetic versions of the legend ar written. In this association Paris sees a probable explanation c the introduction of the minnesinger's name into a story of which th hero was previously anonymous.

The name "Venusberg" does not appear in the legend earlie than that of the minnesinger, and the supposition that it was a sut stitute for a phrase containing the name of an old Germanic divinit) Holda or Berchta, is invalidated by the facts that these names ar no more ancient than the fourteenth century, and that the person ages themselves have nothing in common with Venus. The sugges tion that Venus replaced Freya loses its force when it is pointed ou that we know nothing of Freya in a subterranean palace, allurin; mortals from the world of men. The identification of the mountai* with the Horselberg in Thuringia is a figment of the present century

Thus we have left only those elements of the story which are als* found in Italy, and found there earlier than in Germany — the tal* of a knight who is enticed into a palace of sensual delights where : queen reigns over crowds of beautiful girls, and whose remorse lead. him to abandon the palace and seek atonement.

Of this Italian story we have two main versions : one, the *Guerin* *il Meschino* of Andrea da Barberino, written in 1391 ; and the other the account given in the *Salade* of Antoine de la Sale of a visi to the *Monte della Sibilla* in the Apennines near Norcia, where th* legend had become localized. La Sale represents the story as cur rent among the peasantry of the district, and we have other evidence:

which a dwarf again conducts the poet to the Venusberg, where Frau Venus give: him a crown with twelve tines, each representing a virtue.

f the wide fame of this mountain as the abode of a supernatural
being. The journey to seek absolution from the Pope is found in
both versions, the repentant sinner being successful in the earlier,
though not in the later. In *Guerino il Meschino* the divinity still
retains much of the Sibylline character, for the hero goes to seek her
in her capacity as a revealer of the unknown. He resists her entice-
ments to remain, and absolution is granted him because he thus
overcomes temptation. In the version in the *Salade*, the Pope at
first refuses absolution in order to emphasize the greatness of the
offence, and only yields when the knight, hopeless of salvation for
his soul, has returned to the mountain to make the most of what
remains of the life of the body. The incident of the budding staff
as cause of the Pope's repentance appears first in Germany ; but all
this matter of absolution is quite clearly the result of church influence. Laying that aside, we have the legend in its original pagan
form. This form Paris is inclined to regard as of Celtic origin and
as having reached Germany from the Celtic west by way of Italy.
It belongs, he conjectures, to the group of beliefs about a happy
other-world which appear very widely in folk-tales, especially in those
countries that have come under Celtic influences.

Thus we are able to account for the quasi Court of Love elements
in the Tannhäuser story on grounds altogether remote from mediæval
love-allegory.[1]

E. English.

In England love-allegory in the vernacular began comparatively
late, and the reason is fairly obvious. The form was essentially an
artificial courtly form, meant to appeal to the cultivated if not to the
learned mind, and this kind of verse in England was written almost
entirely in French until the fourteenth century was well advanced.

---

[1] Compare with the articles by Paris (cited above, p. 133, n. 1), Erich Schmidt,
Tannhäuser in Sage und Dichtung in *Nord und Süd*, LXIII, 176 ff., Nov., 1892,
to which is appended an extensive bibliography, and J. G. T. Grässe, *Der Tannhäuser und der ewige Jude*, Dresden, 1861, especially p. 17. On Celtic beliefs
about the Happy Other-world, see Alfred Nutt's essay in K. Meyer's *Voyage of
Bran*, Lond., 1895, and cf. W. H. Schofield on the *Lay of Guingamor* in the
Harvard *Studies and Notes in Philology and Literature*, V, 221-43, Boston, 1896.

How much of the extant French poetry of this type was actually written in England it is not easy to determine; but the *Geste de Blancheflour et Florence* and *Melior et Idoine*[1] are sufficient to prove that even in the first stage of its ᵛdevelopment the Anglo-Normans were in close touch with the movement.

ROBERT GROSSETESTE.[2]

The first poem with which we have to deal in this section is in many respects typical. *Le Chasteau d'Amour*[3] of the famous Bishop of Lincoln is not properly speaking a love-allegory at all, but it contains at least one passage too closely akin to certain features of the *Court of Love* to be neglected. Grosseteste's poem was written in French, but it was translated into English as early as the beginning of the thirteenth century. Other English translations followed, and a long extract from it was incorporated into the fourteenth-century Northumbrian poem *Cursor Mundi* (vv. 9517 ff.).[4]

The other titles of Grosseteste's book, *Carmen de Creatione Mundi*, and *Vie de doux Jesus Christ*, indicate its general nature, and emphasize again the importance of the early church allegory in the derivation of some of the features of the *Court of Love*.

After an account of the Creation and the Fall, the Debate between the Four Daughters of God as to the salvation of mankind, and

---

[1] See p. 38, above.   [2] A.D. 1175(?)–1253.

[3] *R. Grossetete Carmina Anglo-Normannica. Robert Grossetete's Chasteau d'Amour,* etc., ed. by M. Cooke, Lond., 1852, for Caxton Society (containing both the French original and the English version from Egerton MS. 927); *Castel off Loue* by Robert Grossetete, ed. by R. F. Weymouth, Lond., 1864, for Philol. Soc. (containing the English version edited from the Vernon MS. and Additional MS. 22283); an English version, ed. by J. O. Halliwell, Brixton Hill, 1849, for private circulation, mainly from a fourteenth-century MS. See also *Minor Poems of the Vernon MS.,* ed. by Horstmann, E. E. T. S., 1892, pp. 355 ff., for the Vernon and the Egerton versions; the latter is also edited by Hupe, *Anglia,* XIV, 415 ff.; cf. XII, 310 ff., and XIV, 393 ff. An incomplete version in Ashmole MS. 61 is edited by Horstmann, *Altengl. Legenden,* N. F., pp. 349–54.

[4] *Cursor Mundi,* ed. for the Early Eng. Text Soc. by R. Morris, Lond., 1874–93, II, 548 ff. Haenisch (I, 23* ff.) concludes that this extract is from the French and not from any of the English versions; cf. Hupe, *Anglia,* XIV, 421.

Isaiah's prophecy of the Messiah, the author gives a description of a splendid castle — an allegorical representation of the body of the Virgin. The castle stands on a high and polished rock. It is enclosed by walls and ditches, painted with bright colors, and strengthened by towers, barbicans, and so forth. In the highest tower is a fountain whence spring four streams that fill the ditches. In this same tower is a white throne, to which seven steps lead and which is canopied with a rainbow. It is explained that this castle is our shield against our enemies. The polished rock is Mary's heart, the green color betokens her faith, the blue her hopeful and humble service, the red her holy love (*la seinte charité*). The four towers are the cardinal virtues; the seven barbicans are the seven other virtues that quell the seven deadly sins. The well is Mary's mercy, which can never be exhausted; and the brilliant throne is Mary's soul,[1] which God made his seat.

The resemblance of this castle in its situation, decorations, and fortifications, to the mansion of Venus is quite clear. The interpretation faintly suggests the other and more metaphorical type of castle.[2]

Before we come to any genuine Court of Love poem in English, we have a piece of evidence of familiarity with the conception, drawn from a non-literary source. In the *Gentleman's Magazine* for February, 1835, Sir Samuel Rush Meyrick[3] describes certain ancient carved caskets, and one of these has what is manifestly a representation of a Castle of Love. He calls it a lady's casket of ivory, of the time of Edward II. "The top contains the particulars of the siege of the Château d'Amour, or, as it was also termed, the Castle of Roses. In the left compartment is the castle, with ladies on the battlements hurling down roses on their assailants, and over the gateway an angel shooting with a longbow at the son of a knight, who has his crossbow charged with a rose. Another knight is scaling the walls with a rope ladder, while two others are employed with a trepid, loading

---

[1] The references for this passage are these: Caxton Soc. ed., French, vv. 571 ff., English, vv. 371 ff.; Philol. Soc. ed., and Horstmann, *Vernon MS.*, vv. 667 ff.; Halliwell's ed., pp. 29 ff.; *Cursor Mundi*, vv. 9877 ff.

[2] See pp. 28 ff., above.

[3] *On Ancient Caskets of Ivory and Wood*, "from *The Analyst*, a magazine published at Worcester," *Gentleman's Magazine*, New Series, III, 198 ff.

it with roses, that by the force of this projectile they may make a decisive impression on the fortress.   In the right-hand compartment the ladies are seen on the battlements, and over the gateway, welcoming the knights; while two, on horseback, in front, are about to engage two warriors completely armed, each party fighting with a bunch of roses.   The centre compartment represents a joust where one of the combatants has his shield charged with three roses." [1] The casket has also scenes from Arthurian story and other romantic material.

The so-called angel is doubtless Cupid.   In any case, the general treatment and the profusion of roses indicate that Meyrick is in the main correct in his interpretation of the scene. [2]

GOWER.

In the *Confessio Amantis* [3] of John Gower the Court of Love appears completely developed, and serves as the framework for the whole poem.

In the month of May the poet goes out to walk in the woods, and, coming to a green plain "the wood amiddes" he begins to bewail his love pains.   In answer to his moans there appear both the King and the Queen of Love.

The king is wroth at him, and departs with a frown, but before going,

> A firy dart me thought he hente
> And threwe it through min herte rote (I, 46).

But Venus asks who he is and what is his malady.   He replies that he is

> "a man of thine
> That in thy court have longe served
> And axe that I have deserved
> Some wele after my longe wo " (I, 47).

---

[1] *Gentleman's Magazine*, New Series, III, 199–200.

[2] But compare with festivals described on pp. 255 ff., below.

[3] *Confessio Amantis of John Gower*, ed. by Reinhold Pauli, 3 vols., London, 1857.

She says that there are many "faitours" such as he may prove to be, but asks for more detail. This he promises if his life lasts, and she recommends that he confess himself to Genius, her own Clerk. Genius appears with a "benedicite," and in order to make the confession exhaustive he begins to go over the seven deadly sins, with illustrative stories.

Having exhausted the sins and all their subdivisions, the confessor (bk. viii) advises Gower to give up love; but the poet says this is not possible and asks for the good offices of Genius with Venus and Cupid. After debate Genius agrees to carry a letter written with the tears of the lover. The letter despatched, the poet awaits the result. Suddenly Venus appears and asks his name, but does not encourage him,

> For loves lust and lockes hore
> In chambre accorden never more (III, 356),

and advises him to make "beau retrete." At this rebuff he swoons, and thinks he sees

> Cupide with his bowe bent;
> And, like unto a parlement
> Which were ordeined for the nones,
> With him cam all the world atones
> Of gentil folke, that whilom were
> Lovers, I sigh hem alle there (III, 357–8).[1]

There is great noise of music, and in the company Gower sees Tristram and Isolde, Lancelot and Gunnor, Galahot and his lady, Jason and Creüsa, and many others. Elde comes towards Venus with slow music, followed by David with Bersabee, Solomon with more than a hundred wives and concubines, Samson, Aristotle, Virgil, and other old men. These aged lovers pray to Venus for him. Finally Cupid comes and withdraws his "firy lancegay" (III, 369); Venus applies a cooling ointment to the poet's wounded heart, his temples, and his reins, and shows him his wrinkled face in a mirror. Genius bestows absolution, and Venus, having pre-

---

[1] Pauli's erroneous punctuation of the passage has been corrected.

sented Gower with "a paire of bedes blacke as sable" and some parting advice to "tarry in her court no more," vanishes (III, 375).

Significant details, especially with reference to Cupid's arrows, occur frequently throughout the intermediate books. For example,

> Cupide which hath every chaunce
> Of love under his governaunce,
> Sigh Phebus hasten him so sore,
> And for he shulde him haste more
> And yet nought speden ate laste
> A dart throughout his hert he caste,
> Which was of golde and all a-fire,
> That made him many fold desire
> Of love more than he dede.
> To Daphne eke in the same stede
> A dart of led he caste and smote,
> Which was all colde and nothing hote.[1]

Gower is here borrowing directly from Ovid, and as this passage in the *Metamorphoses* is the source of so many similar references (as, for example, that quoted from the *Hypnerotomachia*)[2] it may be as well to give the most important lines :

> Dixit, et eliso percussis aere pennis
> Inpiger umbrosa Parnasi constitit arce
> Eque sagittifera prompsit duo tela pharetra
> Diuersorum operum : fugat hoc, facit illud amorem.
> Quod facit, auratum est et cuspide fulget acuta ;
> Quod fugat, obtusum est et habet sub harundine plumbum.
> Hoc deus in nympha Peneide fixit ; at illo
> Laesit Apollineas traiecta per ossa medullas.
> Protinus alter amat, fugit altera nomen amantis.[3]

But the greater part of the ideas in the framework of the *Confessio Amantis* as it has been sketched above come not directly from the classics, but from the French models that have been already

---

1 *Confessio Amantis*, Bk. iii, Pauli, I, 336.

2 See p. 120, above.

3 *Met.* i, 466–74. Cf. also Gower, *Confessio Amantis*, ed. Pauli, II, 44, and III, 351, etc.

fully exhibited. The personal application to Gower's own old age has already been paralleled[1]; but the other features are easily recognized. Genius is borrowed from the *Roman de la Rose*, and the idea of using the form of a Confession might easily be suggested by any of the poems where Venus's temple figures prominently.

CHAUCER.

The poems of Chaucer which were written during the periods when he was strongly influenced by French and Italian models so abound in the conventions of the Court of Love allegory that it is not at all wonderful that an uncritical age should have attributed the English *Court of Love* to him. The single fact of most importance in considering his relation to love-allegory in general, is his translating the *Roman de la Rose*. This gave him at the outset of his poetical career a profound and apparently a sympathetic acquaintance with the most prolific love poem of the Middle Ages; and traces of its influence are easily found throughout most of his works written before 1386, and occasionally even after he had begun the *Canterbury Tales*.

The *Book of the Duchesse*, though not an allegorical poem in any strict sense, has several of the stock features of that class. There is a description of the dwelling of Morpheus (vv. 153–71); the birds are jubilant on May morning; the setting is a dream; Fortune is personified:

> The dispitouse debonaire
> That scorneth many a creature (vv. 624–5);

there is a list of famous lovers, — Medea and Jason, Phyllis and Demophon, Dido and Æneas, Echo and Narcissus, Delilah and Samson (vv. 725–39); and the description of the Duchess, though more elaborate than usual and with more emphasis on character, is yet distinctly of the regular type that prevails from the *Roman de la Rose* to the English *Court of Love*.

Mention has already been made of Chaucer's debt in this poem

---

[1] See, e.g., pp. 95 ff., above.

to *Le Dit de la Fontaine Amoureuse* of Guillaume de Machaut,[1] and of his borrowing from Froissart.[2] The lines,

> For that tyme Youthe, my maistresse,
> Governed me in ydelnesse (vv. 797-8),

may possibly have suggested to Charles d'Orléans the character and office of Jeunesse in the *Poème de la Prison.*

In the *Compleynt of Mars, Compleynt to his Lady, Compleynt of Venus*, and others, we have examples of a form of poem that occurs as part of the *Court of Love* and often also in other allegories.[3]

The *Parlement of Foules* shows close relations to the Court of Love convention, though its main situation is that borrowed from the *Anticlaudianus*, in which Nature is the presiding goddess.[4] The form is again that of a dream, and the debt to the *Somnium Scipionis* and the commentary of Macrobius is not only openly acknowledged, but Africanus himself acts as guide to the hero as he enters the " parke, walled with grene stoon." This park is the regular Court of Love meadow, the description being characterized by the tendency towards lists, as of trees and beasts, which seems especially common in Middle English poetry. The descriptions of Cupid and the Temple of Venus which follow are translated, as has already been noted,[5] from the *Teseide* of Boccaccio. The courtiers are Plesaunce, Aray, Lust, Curtesye, Craft, Delyt, Gentilnesse, Beautee, Youthe, Fool-hardinesse, Flaterye, Desyr, Messagerye, Mede, and others. The temple is of brass, founded upon great pillars of jasper, and its ministers and altars, its representations of Priapus, Venus, Bacchus, and Ceres, and its wall-paintings of famous love-stories are just as in Boccaccio.

The *Consolation* of Boethius, translated by Chaucer, contains several personifications such as Philosophy, Fortune, Rhetoric, and Music, belonging naturally to the type of the abstractions in Claudian and Martianus Capella. The picture of Philosophy (Prose i) has much in common with Virgil's Fame,[6] the main features of which

---

[1] See p. 62, above.
[2] See p. 79, above.
[3] *The Compleynte to Pity* is dealt with in chap. vii.
[4] See p. 50, above.
[5] See pp. 116-17, above.
[6] See p. 10, n. 3, above, and cf. passage from Ovid quoted on p. 13.

occur in the *Hous of Fame.* In Boethius, too, occurs a passage on
Love which may not be without significance in connection with the
frequent outbursts on the sovereignty of Venus or Cupid.[1] The
same passage is imitated in the *Troilus.*[2]

The rest of *Troilus*, though dealing with the same natural phenomena as the love-allegories, has wonderfully few parallels to show.
The description of the heroine conforms to the type in some degree,
and Troilus finally gains his end by swooning (iii, 1092), just as
Philogenet and many other heroes do. His sleeplessness and the
other indications of his distressful condition are similar to the symptoms that will be remarked upon among the statutes in the next
chapter. But it is to be observed that these are all points where
the allegories approach realism, not where the *Troilus* approaches
allegory. Had it been the other way, *Troilus and Criseyde* would
not stand out in such magnificent contrast as it now does, against
the mass of barren and characterless production for which the muse
of allegory is responsible.

The *Hous of Fame* has a double claim to be mentioned in an
account of the growth of the type of allegory which we are studying.

First, the main part of the poem, dealing with the House of Fame
proper, belongs to the genus of descriptions of divine habitations, —
a genus of which the Palace of Love is a species. The House of
Fame stands on the summit of a hill difficult of access. This feature
is paralleled in Claudian[3] and in Alanus de Insulis,[4] and its origin
is probably to be found in the classical conception of the top of
Olympus as the dwelling-place of the gods. In Chaucer, the mountain is of ice, and on it are inscribed many names of famous men,
though on the south side these names have been thawed almost to
illegibility. The building itself is of "stone of beryle" (v. 1184),
and in this respect may be compared with the gorgeous descriptions
of the Castle of Love already cited, which appear as early as Ovid.[5]
In some instances the costly material is used also for the rock on

---

[1] Boethius, *De Consolatione*, Bk. ii, metre 8.

[2] iii, 1744–57; see Skeat's *Chaucer*, II, 483. With this may be compared
Court of Love, vv. 591–5.   [4] See p. 50, above.

[3] See pp. 16, 17, above.   [5] See p. 12, above.

which the palace is built, as in the case of the rock of diamond in
King René's poem.[1]   The gorgeousness of the interior, the music,
the pomp of the feudal court, the statues of famous men, the crowds
of suitors, the dream-setting — all these are familiar features in
Court of Love poems.

   Secondly, there is an actual Temple of Venus in Book ii of the
Hous of Fame.   This building is of glass, splendid with jewelled
pinnacles, "curious portreytures," golden images, and "riche taber-
nacles."   Within is a picture of the goddess

> Naked fletinge in a see.
> And also on hir head, pardee,
> Hir rose-garlond whyt and reed,
> And hir comb to kembe hir heed,
> Hir dowves, and daun Cupido,
> Hir blinde sone, and Vulcano,
> That in his face was ful broun (i, 133–9).

The walls are decorated with scenes from the first book of the Aeneid.[2]

   The *Prologue* to *The Legend of Good Women* is of still greater
importance for our purpose, on account of its relations to the English *Court of Love.*   The dream-setting and the " jolly tyme of May "
both reappear ; Daunger and Pitee are personified[3]; and the Daisy
makes its first important appearance in literature.   Its praises had
already been sung by Guillaume de Machaut in his *Dit de la Fleur
de lis et de la Marguerite,*[4] and this Chaucer doubtless knew; but
there seems reason to believe that Chaucer had a special personal
liking for the flower that thenceforth was to have so honorable a
place in English poetry, and that his affectionate treatment of it
here is the result of his own feeling rather than merely an imitation
of Machaut.   Froissart's *Dittié de la flour de la Margherite*[5] may also
have been known to Chaucer.

---

   [1] See p. 91, above; but cf. Garrett, *Studies on Chaucer's House of Fame,* II, in
Studies and Notes in Philology and Literature, Boston, 1896, V, 157–75, for
similar instances from folk-tales.

   [2] For a discussion of the sources of this poem see Rambeau, *Englische Studien,* III, 209 ff.   [3] Text B, vv. 160–1.

   [4] Ed. Tarbé, p. 123.   See also Skeat's *Chaucer,* III, xxxi–xxxii.

   [5] *Poésies,* ed. Scheler, II, 209 ff.   See also p. 79, above.

In the *Legend* the God of Love appears in a meadow, not in a castle. He is gorgeously arrayed

> In silke, enbrouded ful of grene greves,
> In-with a fret of rede rose-leves,
> The fresshest sin the world was first bigonne.
> His gilte heer was corouned with a sonne,
> In-stede of gold, for hevinesse and wighte;
> Therewith me thoughte his face shoon so brighte
> That wel unnethes mighte I him beholde;
> And in his hand me thoughte I saugh him holde
> Two fyry dartes, as the gledes rede;
> And aungellyke his winges saugh I sprede (B, vv. 227–36).

This is the first passage in which I have noted the God of Love wearing a halo, and this feature, along with the title "Seyntes Legende of Cupyde"[1] applied to the whole poem, and the phrase 'Seynt Venus" (B, 338), suggests strongly the religious figure which we have found alternating with the feudal. The picture of Cupid strolling in the flowery meadow with his queen and train is, of course, very close to the situation in the *Roman de la Rose*, and even in the earlier poems of the *Altercatio* group.

The function of Alcestis as the queen of the God of Love, as well as her transformation into a daisy, is original with Chaucer, and forms the clearest proof of the acquaintance of the English *Court of Love* poet with his works. The description of the lady is individualized in Chaucer by the device of making her dress represent the different parts of the daisy.

The anger of the God of Love and expiation by the writing of poetry are frequent motives.

In the *Knightes Tale* Chaucer again draws the main features of his Temple of Venus from Boccaccio, but his treatment of the original is much freer than in the *Parlement of Foules*. The personified abstractions, instead of being represented as walking about, take their place along with sighs and tears as mere wall paintings (vv. 1060–76). There are pictures also of the "Mount of Citheroun," the garden with the porter Idleness, Narcissus, Solomon, and the rest.

---

[1] Introd. to *Man of Lawe's Prologue, C. T.,* B, 61.

The statue of Venus is like that in the *Hous of Fame*, — "naked fleting in the large see," and

> Biforn hir stood hir sone Cupido,
> Up-on his shuldres winges hadde he two ;
> And blind he was, as it is ofte sene ;
> A bowe he bar and arwes brighte and kene (vv. 1105–8).

The temples of Mars and Diana are of a similar type.[1]

LYDGATE.

The influence of Chaucer's allegorical poems upon the works of his successors down to the date of the *Court of Love* was very strong ; and in no one is it more clearly evident than in John Lydgate (1370?– 1450?). If we accept the chronology outlined by Schick in the Introduction to his edition of Lydgate's *Temple of Glas*, this influence is most apparent in the disciple's early and most imaginative period, about 1400–12.

The first poem of Lydgate which approaches the Court of Love type is the *Flour of Curtesye*,[2] which shows especially the influence of the *Parlement of Foules*. We have the St. Valentine's Day setting, with the prominence of birds; but the main part of the poem is devoted to the praise of the lady in whose honor it is named. Personifications such as Malebouche, Envy, and False Suspicion occur.

The Complaint of the Black Knight[3] begins with a description of May and has an elaborate landscape of the familiar type. Personifications like those in the preceding poem are more frequent.

The Assembly of the Gods[4] has descriptions of Venus and Cupid which are worth noting :

> By him sate Dame Venus with colour crystallyne,
> Whoos long here shone as wyre of goold bryght.

---

[1] The discussion of the actual relation of Chaucer to the English *Court of Love* is held over for chap. vii.

[2] Skeat, *Chaucerian Pieces*, pp. 266–74.

[3] *Ibid.*, pp. 245–65.

[4] Ed. O. L. Triggs, Chicago, 1895 (*Univ. of Chicago, English Studies*, I; also E. E. T. S.). On conventional materials in this poem, see the editor's *Introduction*, pp. l ff. In the quotations that follow I have made some changes in punctuation.

Cryspe was her skyn ; her eyen columbyne
Rauysshed myn hert, her chere was so lyght.
Patronesse of plesaunce be named well she myght.[1]
A smokke was her wede, garnysshed curyously.
And aboue all other she had a wanton ey.

. . . .

On her hede she weryd a rede copyr crowne.
A nosegay she had made full pleasauntly (sts. 54–5).

Then was there set the god Cupido,
All fresshe and galaunt and costlew in aray,
With ouches and ryngs he was beset so
The paleys therof shone as though it had be day.
A kerchyef of plesaunce stood over hys helme ay.
The goddesse Ceres he lookyd in the face
And with oon arme he hyr dyd embrace (st. 43).

This same collocation of Cupid and Ceres is found in Boccaccio, *Teseide*, vii, 66, where Bacchus also is of the company; and Boccaccio is imitated by Chaucer, *Parlement of Foules*, v. 276.   The jewels and other features of both descriptions are, of course, familiar enough.

The Temple of Glas,[2] however, is the poem of Lydgate's which is of the highest importance for the present study.   The plot is as follows:

One winter night the author went to bed sad at heart, and dreamed of being carried in spirit to a Temple of Glass on a rock of ice. He entered and found the walls painted with the portraits of many famous lovers, kneeling as they presented "bills" to Venus.   Dido was there and Medea, Penelope, Alcestis, "who was turnyd to a daiesie," and many another.   He saw also thousands of lovers complaining to the gods of hindrances such as envy, jealousy, slander, "daunger," poverty, and the like.   But last of all he saw a peerless lady, whose beauty and character are described in great detail, kneeling before the statue of Venus and holding in her hand a bill to the effect that she was dying for love and prayed for help.   Venus answered favorably, promising to send joy after pain.   The maiden was grateful and promised faithful service.

---

[1] Triggs prints "he named well se myght."
[2] Ed. for E. E. T. S. by J. Schick, Lond., 1891.

Apart from the crowd of worshippers who were thronging round the altar was a love-sick knight, torn between Hope and Dread, who, after a long soliloquy, approached the oratory and prayed for aid in the wooing of his lady. She, it appeared, was the one who had just been seen in the pains of love for this same knight. So Venus smilingly gave him hope, and laid down a long series of rules for his observance, finally sending him forth to seek an interview with the lady. In fear and trembling he went and presented his complaint, which the lady received blushingly, but which she referred to Venus. Together they went before the goddess, who bound them with a golden chain heart to heart, and added further instructions.

Now all the people in the temple joined in singing praises to Venus, and in offering prayers for the happiness of these two. The poet was awakened by the music, and ends with a dedication to his lady.

Borrowings from Chaucer appear throughout this poem with great frequency. The Temple of Glass itself on the rock of ice is, of course, taken directly from the *Hous of Fame;* Alcestis and the Chaucerian story of her transformation into a daisy appear both in the allegory itself and in the *Complaint*[1] which in some manuscripts is appended to it; references to the Tales of the Knight, the Squire, and the Merchant occur; and minor allusions are scattered through the whole poem. Lydgate also shows an acquaintance with the Ovidian form of the story of Phœbus and Daphne already quoted[2]:

> I saw3 hov Phebus with an arow of gold
> Iwoundid was, þuru3 oute in his side,
> Only bi envie of þe god Cupide,
> And hou þat Daphne vnto a laurer tre
> Iturned was, when she did[e] fle (vv. 111–15).

Mention is made of the *De Nuptiis Mercurii et Philologiae* of Martianus Capella,[3] and other instances of Lydgate's proverbially famous learning abound.

Further details of this poem will be found in the next chapter,[4]

---

[1] See Schick's edition, pp. 59–67.
[2] See p. 140, above.
[3] See p. 16, above.
[4] See pp. 208–9, below.

and its special relation to the English *Court of Love* will be discussed in chap. vii.

HOCCLEVE AND SIR R. ROS.

Contemporary with these poems of Lydgate's is Thomas Hoccleve's *Letter of Cupid*,[1] translated in 1402 from Christine de Pisan's *Epistre au Dieu d'Amours* which was written in 1399, and which has already been examined.[2] Hoccleve rearranges the matter of the poem and makes some additions which need not be discussed here. Another translation may be mentioned at this point, though it was probably made nearly fifty years later, that by Sir Richard Ros, of Alain Chartier's *La Belle Dame sans Mercy*.[3] Nothing of importance for our present purpose is added in the English version.

THE FLOWER AND THE LEAF.

The Flower and the Leaf,[4] long attributed to Chaucer, and modernized by Dryden, is an anonymous poem of the fifteenth century. The God of Love does not appear in it; but it has several important details linking it to the Court of Love class.   It begins with a May morning, and the description of a walk in a grove where the heroine (for it purports to be written, or at least told, by a woman) finds an arbor in which she sits down to listen to the song of the birds. Presently there comes from the grove a procession of gorgeously arrayed ladies, all clad in white, laden with jewels, and wearing garlands of green leaves of laurel, *agnus-castus*, and woodbine.   These are followed by a crowd of knights correspondingly apparelled, who engage in jousts, those wearing laurel proving the victors.   Then they join the ladies in dancing under a great laurel tree.

Next appear another company of knights and ladies clad in green and garlanded with flowers, who do reverence to a flowery

---

[1] *Hoccleve's Minor Poems*, ed. Furnivall for E. E. T. S., 1892, I, 72 ff.; Skeat, *Chaucerian Pieces*, pp. 217–32; cf. pp. 499–501.

[2] See p. 84.

[3] Furnivall, *Political, Religious, and Love Poems*, E. E. T. S., 1866, pp. 52–80; also in Skeat, *Chaucerian Pieces*, pp. 299–326.

[4] *Chaucerian Pieces*, pp. 361–79.

"tuft," while one of them sings "a bargaret in praising the daisy,'
with the refrain, "Si douce est la margarete." But as the sun
rises high their flowers wither, and shortly a storm comes and
drenches them with rain, while those who are crowned with leaves
are safe under the laurel from both rain and sun.

Now the queen of the fortunate band comes forward to offer help.
Her followers make fires and dry the drenched ones and anoint
their sunburnt faces. Finally both companies ride away together.

The speaker now leaves the arbor and meets a solitary lady in
white, who explains that the first group were the Ladies of the Leaf,
and their queen was Diana. Those of them who bore *agnus-castus*
had remained virgins; those with laurel had made "victorious
name"; those with woodbine had never been untrue in love. The
knights were the Nine Worthies, the Knights of the Round Table,
the Twelve Peers of Charlemagne, and the Knights of the Garter.
The Ladies of the Flower had been led by Flora, and her followers
were such as loved idleness, hunting and hawking, playing in meads,
"and many other such lyk idle dedes." The writer decides to
choose the Leaf for her own allegiance.

The fact that the procession and the different degrees of merit
among the ladies bear a slight similarity to the scene described in
Andreas Capellanus[1] has led Professor Morley[2] to mention this
poem as merely a variant of the *Lai du Trot* story. That tradition
may have influenced the form of *The Flower and the Leaf*, but this is
the most that can be said.

The landscape, the costuming, and the rôle of the queens are
the main points connecting this poem with the *Court of Love*. The
influence of Chaucer and probably of Lydgate worked on the
authoress.

THE ASSEMBLY OF LADIES.

The same lady, according to Professor Skeat,[3] wrote some years
later *The Assembly of Ladies*,[4] a poem still more nearly approaching

---

[1] See pp. 46 ff., above.   [4] *Ibid.*, pp. 380–404.
[2] *English Writers*, Lond., 1887–95, IV, 221.
[3] *Chaucerian Pieces*, pp. lxii–lxx.

he Court of Love model, and important also as helping to show the
ontinuity of the tradition from Chaucer and Lydgate to the time of
he English *Court of Love.*

In this work the allegory takes the form of a dream which a lady
elates to a knight. She dreamed that a lady in blue, called Perse-
eraunce, summoned her to the house of Loyalte, called Plesaunt
Regard. Diligence served as guide; a robe of blue was provided
or the heroine also; Discrecioun, the chief purveyor, was met near
he gate; the porter, Countenaunce, admitted them; the steward was
Largesse, the marshal of the ball was Bel Chere, the chamberlain
Remembraunce, the secretary Avysenesse; and every one was clad
n blue. A great number of ladies soon arrived, and after some
delay all were led into a great hall of the usual type, with walls of
beryl and crystal, on which were engraved stories of Phyllis and
Demophoon, Pyramus and Thisbe, Antony and Cleopatra, the love-
orn Anelida, and many more. On a platform was set a throne en-
rusted with jewels, on which presently the lady of the palace took
her seat and received the "bills" of the throng. Each petition had
French motto, "Sans que jamais," "Entierment vostre," and the
like, and they complained of the faithlessness and instability of
overs, and so on. The bills were handed over to the secretary, and
he lady announced that

> Within short tyme our court of parliment
> Here shal be holde, in our palays present (vv. 720-1),

then redress should be given to all. So the crowd departed and
he dreamer awoke.

Here it will be observed that the regular function of the Queen of
Love is performed by a lady whose name is not given after she
appears, but who is once mentioned at the beginning as Loyalte.
The attendant figures are familiar, as is the use of blue as the color
f constancy. The poem is peculiar in having no male figures in it,
except the man to whom the dream is related and his companions.
The allegory proper is purely an "assembly of ladies."

The presumption arising from the fact that the narrator repre-
ents herself as a woman seems neither to require nor to receive
much strengthening from the stress which Professor Skeat lays on

the elaborate descriptions of costume.   I cannot think his argumen
for the identification of the authoress with the writer of the *Flowe
and the Leaf* at all conclusive.   The parallelisms quoted are extremel
frequent commonplaces, and the attributing of the different trea‑
ment of the final *e* to a later period in the lady's life[1] is too eas
to be convincing.   The movement of the verse of the two poem
seems to my ear very different.   Professor Skeat has himself notice
the frequency of run-on stanzas in the *Flower and the Leaf*, and th
absence of them in the *Assembly*.   A similar statement can be mad
about the lines; for in the former poem full stops and semicolon
are much more frequent in the middle of lines, and run-on line
also occur oftener.   The common authorship must be regarded a
at least not proved.

JAMES I. OF SCOTS.

The attempts that have been made to establish an immediat
connection between the *Kingis Quair*[2] of James I. of Scots and th
English *Court of Love* make it necessary to analyze the former i
some detail.

The poem begins with the account of a sleepless night and c
the impulse that led the author to write the book.   This forms
kind of prologue (sts. 1–13).

After an apostrophe to his unripe youth and an invocation of th
Muses, the poet tells how one spring, when he was about ten year
old,[3] he was put on board ship to be taken abroad.   But the shi
was captured by enemies, and he was thrown into prison, where h
had to remain nearly eighteen years.   There he used to complai
bitterly against Fortune's cruel treatment of him; and once, gettin
up early to seek comfort, he went to the window and looked dow
into the garden, where the nightingales were singing love-songs.   A
he stood watching them he began to wonder how true all the tal
about the rapture of love might be; and, looking down into the ga‑

---

[1] *Chaucerian Pieces*, p. lxvi.

[2] Ed. by Skeat for the Scottish Text Society, Edinburgh, 1884.

[3]   Noȝt fer passit the state of innocence,
              But nere about the nowmer of ȝeris thre (st. 22).

den again, he saw the fairest woman his eyes had ever rested on, and suddenly his heart

> became hir thrall
> For euer, of free-wyll (st. 41).

As he watched her, he speculated on whether she was a goddess or a woman; and, concluding that she was human, he offered thanks to Venus for receiving him into her service, and prayed for mercy. Looking down once more at the lady, he envied her little dog, and began to reproach the nightingale for having fallen silent when

> Here is the tyme to syng, or ellis neuer (st. 59).

He was at his wit's end to know how to rouse the nightingale to a sense of the occasion without scaring her away, when she burst into song again, to the melody of which he made a prayer to the lady. Then all the birds took up their song in praise of Love and May, and again he gave it words.

But now the lady turned and passed out of the garden, and the lover was left to bewail his plight. Worn out at length with weeping and complaining, he threw himself on his knees at the window, and, with his head on the stone, dreamt.

Suddenly, it seemed to him, a great light blinded him, and a voice said :

> I bring confort and hele, be noʒt affrayde (st. 74).

At once he was caught up through the air and came to the great crystal Palace of Venus, which he found thronged with lovers, some of whom had died in Love's service after a long life, and now, with the heroes of romance, and love-poets such as Ovid and Homer, were attended by Good Will. Others, young people who had been true lovers but had been cut off in middle age, were attended by Courage. A third group, people of religion, who had forsworn Love, and repented afterwards, but had not had courage to serve him openly, were attended by Repentance. All this a voice explained to him. Beyond a curtain stood a multitude who came to present complaints, some because they had been shut up in cloisters in their youth, some about unhappy marriages, some of being cruelly parted from their true lovers.

In a chair of state sat Cupid with a bent bow in his hand. B
him hung, "in a case," three arrows, headed with gold, silver, an
steel, respectively, and fit to inflict wounds of greater or less severity
the last being the worst.   In an alcove lay Venus, attended by Fai
Calling and Secrecy.   Her the poet saluted, and prayed for merc
and for help in his suit.   Venus answered favorably, but said tha
on account of his imprisonment the matter was not altogether in he
hands.   She dwelt on his inferiority to his lady, and sent him t
Minerva for counsel, with Good Hope as his guide.   She also tol
him to remonstrate with men for their neglect of her laws, —
neglect that she felt so deeply that she wept.   (Her tears are th
rain which causes the flowers to spring to pray men to be true i
love; in proof of which it may be noted that the birds cease fror
song when it rains.)

The poet thanked Venus, and set off for the palace of Minerv
to which he was admitted by Patience.   Minerva received hi
graciously, and gave him much moral advice, quoting *Ecclesiaste*
to induce him to bide his time, and promising him aid if his inter
tions were strictly honorable.   Having been assured on this poin
she said she would use her influence with Fortune in his beha
The mention of this goddess leads to a digression on chance an
necessity.

Returning to earth, the lover found himself in a fair plain beside
river, and there he saw all manner of beasts (which are enumerate
each with an epithet, in the manner of the lists of trees, etc., alread
noticed).[1]   Within a "round, walled place" he found Fortune, an
before her feet was her wheel, on which a multitude of people wer
clambering, some of them falling into a dreadful pit below, whenc
they never came up.   When he called for Fortune's help she admitte
that hitherto he had had bad luck, but said it was going to tur
now.   With this he was led to the wheel, stepped upon it, and, ju
as Fortune, telling him to hold on, took him by the ear to say far
well, he awoke.

His distress was not at all abated when he came to his sense
and he prayed for some token of assurance that his dream bode

---

[1] See p. 142, above.

good. He went to the window, and there alighted on his hand a white dove bearing a branch of red gillyflower, on the "lists" of which was written in gold a message bidding him be of good cheer, for his cure was decreed in heaven. This he read again and again, and pinned it above his bed. Gradually his pain died away, and Fortune so well fulfilled her promise that he gained both his freedom and his love.

With thanks and rejoicings and apologies, and a dedication to Chaucer and Gower, the poem closes.

The relation of this poem to Lydgate's works on the one hand and the *Court of Love* on the other will be discussed in a later chapter.[1] At present we may note that there are here all the most important Court of Love features: the abundance of flowers and birds and their use as erotic symbols; the courts of Venus, Minerva, and Fortune with the allegorical figures and the shades of departed lovers in attendance; the palace of crystal and the meadow watered by a river; the instructions to the true lover, and the binding together of the whole by the thread of the hero's love-story. The most striking thing about the poem as a whole is the extent to which this mass of convention is vitalized, every detail being given a signification for the individual case, so that we are left with an impression of reality such as we get from no other poem of the type. Even if the arguments [2] recently put forth against King James's authorship of the *Kingis Quair* had not been met on technical grounds of language and history, they would not have been convincing. It would still have remained well-nigh impossible to believe that there existed in the fifteenth century a poet, anonymous and hitherto unsuspected, with sufficient dramatic capacity to produce a work bearing throughout the marks of emotion which should appear profoundly personal but which should yet in fact be only imagined. Such an achievement as the writing of this poem by any one but the hero of it would imply not only the use, but the mastery, of a form of art utterly unknown in the Middle Ages; and the *Kingis Quair*, whatever we may assert about its freshness and vitality, remains in form an essentially mediæval production.

---

[1] See pp. 232 ff., below.   [2] See pp. 235 ff., below.

THE ISLE OF LADIES.

This poem, more commonly known as *Chaucer's Dream*,[1] is far from being a pure Court of Love poem. It is a mixture of the allegorical type with the supernatural romance, and it abounds in features characteristic of those mediæval productions which drew their materials from popular fairy-lore.

The *Dream* is the vision of a May night.

> Within an yle me thought I was,
> Where wall and yate was all of glasse (vv. 71–2).

This island was peopled with beautiful ladies, all young but one, and she was still lusty. To her the author had to give an account of himself; but before she passed judgment the queen arrived, and with her a strange knight and the poet's lady. This knight had seized the queen on the rock whither she had gone to gather the apples of perpetual youth, health, and pleasure for her maidens; and the poet's lady had come to her rescue, after which all three came to the isle. When the knight was asked his intentions he swooned, but was brought back to consciousness after many tender attentions from the queen.

Just then the God of Love arrived with a fleet of 10,000 ships, all about which birds

> Sate and song with voice full out,
> Ballades and layes right joyously (vv. 716–17).

The walls of glass and gates of gold were of no avail in keeping out the mighty lord who came with bow in hand. Approaching th

---

[1] Aldine *Chaucer*, ed. by R. Morris, Lond., 1891, V, 86–154. Brandl, *Engl. Stud.*, XII, 175 ff., interprets this poem as an allegorical account of the match between Henry V. and the fair Katherine of France; see also W. Hagedorn *Ueber d. Sprache einiger nördlicher Chaucerschüler*, Göttingen, 1892, p. 20. B cf. *Engl. Stud.*, XIII, 24. On the resemblance of the poem to *Le Dit dou Lic* of Guillaume de Machaut, I have already commented (p. 62, above).

queen he reproved her for having so long refused to serve him and so long neglected his laws :

> And bent his bow and forth he goth
> A pace or two, and even there
> A large draught, up to his eare,
> He drew, and with an arrowe grounde
> Sharpe and new, the queene a wounde
> He gave, that piersed unto the hearte,
> Which afterward full sore gan smarte,
> And was not whole of many yeare (vv. 786–93).

The god then prophesied to the knight a speedy recovery, and addressing the poet's lady he recommended the poet as a faithful servant. The lady was well-disposed towards him. The queen now came and presented a bill to Cupid in which she promised life-long devotion. The god read it with a smile and called a council for the next day.

The next day arrived, and the god was seated in state in the midst of the throng. A long speech was made by "a counsayler, servant of Love," the conclusion of which was a promise from the god to put all parties in accord before he left the island. Another swooning scene took place. The poet's lady set sail, and the poet, running into the water after her ship, was almost drowned and was taken on board unconscious. Vitality returned only with the gift from his lady of one of the magic apples.

The rest of the poem does not bear on the present inquiry.

The two elements already referred to (p. 156) are easily detected here. The meadow, the walls of glass and gates of gold, the throngs of fair ladies, the God of Love with attendant birds, the arrows, the reproving of the stubborn beauty, the swooning lovers, the throne of state and the council—all this is familiar Court of Love machinery. On the other hand, the part played by boats, the magic apples, the seizure and rescue of the queen, are clear traces of the supernatural romance. The ballade with which the poem closes contains some statutes which will be discussed in the next chapter.

THE PARLIAMENT OF LOVE

MS. Ff. I. 6, fol. 51, in the Cambridge University Library, written in a fifteenth-century hand, contains a short poem called *The Parliament of Love.*[1]

Draw near, says the poet, all ye that will learn of love, and hear

> Houth loue made late his parleament,
> And sent for ladyes of every londe . . .
> And al tho men that lovers were . . .
> Within a castell feyre ande stronge.

A company of gentlewomen sang a ballade instead of the mass, and after the song all the ladies went into a chamber and took their places according to rank, the Goddess of Love being enthroned above them. But one lady so smote the poet with her beauty that he retired to a corner

> A litle bill for to compile,
> Vntoo thys lady wych was soo faire.

The text of this "bill" ends the poem.

This short work contains nothing new, and is only one more proof of the familiarity of the Court of Love tradition in the fifteenth century.

LANCELOT OF THE LAIK.

Romance and allegory come together in another fifteenth-century poem, — the Scottish *Lancelot.*[2] The romance proper is introduced by a kind of prologue.

One April morning when the poet was walking in a beautiful garden full of flowers that represented to him his lady, he fell into a sleep or ecstasy and had a vision.

A bird appears, sent by the God of Love, to reprove him for his witless complaining. Any one who does nothing to move his lady

---

[1] Ed. by F. J. Furnivall, for E. E. T. S., in *Political, Religious, and Love Poems,* Lond., 1866, pp. 48–51.

[2] *Lancelot of the Laik,* ed. for E. E. T. S. by W. W. Skeat, Lond., 1865. Written *ca.* 1490–1500.

ot even by telling his love, deserves to suffer. Ovid is quoted
gainst the policy of concealing one's feelings. But it is useless to
ry to escape love: the poet must either seek the remedy or continue
o suffer. He replies to all this that it is useless for the servant to
lispute with the lord: Love knows why he smote him with this
opeless passion. "Fool," says the bird, "there is no woman so
igh as to despise or hate a man who is worthy to be of Love's court,
nd shows her faithful service." The poet is charged either to speak
ut to the lady, or to write a complaint and make a treatise

> Of love, ore armys, or of sum othir thing (v. 147).

o with a farewell the bird flies off, and the poet awakes, and deter-
iines to write of Lancelot. The romance follows.

ROBERT HENRYSON.

In Henryson's *Testament of Cresseid*[1] are to be found several of
ie Court of Love features.

Calchas, the father of Cresseid,

> Wes keeper of the tempill, as ane preist,
> In quhilk Venus and hir son Cupido
> War honourit (vv. 107–9).

fter Cresseid was cast off by Diomede, she came back to her father.
ne day, entering an oratory in the temple, she reproached Venus
nd Cupid with such vehemence that she fell into an ecstasy, and
.w a vision. She heard Cupid the king ring a bell that summoned
ie seven planets from their spheres. First came Saturn, described
s a personification of winter; then Jupiter, amiable and garlanded
as it had been in May"; Mars, armed and foaming at the mouth;
hœbus, riding in his chariot of the sun; Venus, who "with ane
/e lauch, and with the uther weip"; Mercury, with book in hand
id carrying a box of drugs; and last Cynthia, with the man-in-the-
oon painted on her breast. Mercury is chosen "to be foir-speikar
. the parliament," and Cupid charges Cresseid with having slandered

---

[1] *Poems and Fables of R. Henryson*, ed. by D. Laing, Edinburgh, 1865, pp. 75–
. Also in Skeat, *Chaucerian Pieces*, pp. 327–46.

his mother and himself.   It is agreed to leave the sentence to Saturn and Cynthia, who condemn her to the loathsome life of a leper (The rest of the poem does not concern us here.)

This "parliament" is, to be sure, not strictly a Court of Venus but it is a court of the gods on a question to which Venus and Cupid are parties, and in which love is the principal matter.   The description of Venus departs entirely from the tradition, all the stress being laid on her character :

> Richt unstabill, and full of variance,
> Mingit with cairfull joy, and fals plesance (vv. 235–6),

while Jupiter has the hair like gold wire and the May garland (vv. 174–5, 177).

GAVIN DOUGLAS.

The list of Court of Love poems in the sixteenth century opens with Gavin Douglas's *Palice of Honour*[1] (1501).   Here we have not only a picture of the Court of Venus on the march, but in the Palace of Honor itself a mansion which conforms closely to the type of building usually inhabited by the God or Goddess of Love, but which we have before found used for other divinities, as, e.g., in Chaucer's *Hous of Fame*.

After a Prologue in praise of May, the poet describes a vision in which he finds himself in a desert place through which runs a hideous torrent.   As he is complaining against the instability of Fortune, he perceives approaching a cavalcade of ladies and gentlemen, in the midst of whom there sits in a jewelled chariot a magnificently beautiful queen, in purple and gold, attended by twelve damsels and a "lustie rout" of lords and ladies.   After they pass, two wretches, who turn out to be Achitophel and Sinon, ride up and explain that it is Minerva, Queen of Sapience, who has just gone by, and that the twelve damsels are the sibyls,

> Cassandra eik Delbora and Circes,
> The fatall sisters twynand our weirdis out,
> Judith, Jael, and mony a Prophetis (i, st. 13).

---

[1] *Poetical Works of Gavin Douglas*, ed. by John Small, Edinburgh, 1874, I, 1–8.

The crowd, he continues, includes many famous wise men ; and the whole procession, which is to be followed by the courts of Diana and Venus, are going to the Palace of Honor. The two caitiffs then move on, and the poet is left alone.

Soon, however, he sees Actæon, in the form of a stag, torn by hounds, and immediately there follows Diana riding on an elephant and attended by a scanty train, including Jephtha's daughter, Virginia, and other famous virgins. Next he hears a sound of music, and in a car of a degree of gorgeousness extraordinary even for a Court of Love poem, Venus appears, drawn by twelve coursers trapped in green velvet, with golden harness. Beside the goddess sat her son :

> He bair a bow with dartis haw as leid,
> His cleithing was als grene as ane huntair,
> Bot he forsuith had na eine in his heid (i, st. 39).

The account of the music which accompanies this car gives the poet an opportunity to display his knowledge of musical terms and the names of instruments. Mars rides on horseback beside Venus, and in the account of those who follow her chariot Douglas shows his familiarity with Chaucer by his choice of such lovers as Arcite, Palamon, and Emily, Troilus and Cressida, Ceyx and Alcyone, Alcestis, and Griselda. As they ride past, the poet, who is watching all from a hiding-place in the tree, is moved to sing " a ballet of inconstant love," in which he insults Venus and Cupid. The goddess hears and is wroth, and he is dragged before Mars, Cupid, and Venus to answer the charge of blasphemy brought by a clerk called Varius. In reply he denies her jurisdiction, first, because " ladyis may be judges in na place," and, second, because he is a " spirituall man." Naturally this does not pacify the goddess, and when the First Part of the poem ends the poet is trembling lest she condemn him to death or transform him into a beast.

In the Second Part, however, an interruption is caused by the arrival of the Court of the Muses, attended by a great crowd of poets, ancient and modern. To Calliope Venus submits the case, and at her suggestion the author is pardoned on condition that he " say sum breif or schort ballat " in praise of Venus, and promise not to refuse the next reasonable request which she shall make of him.

He recites the "ballat" on the spot, and is set free. He gives
thanks to Calliope, who places him under the charge of a sweet
nymph, and he sets off with the Muses on a tour about the world, in
the course of which they come to the "Musis caballine fontane."
There a scene after the style of the Court of Love meadow is
described, and in a tent the Muses have a banquet, while Ovid and
other poets recite their verses to them.

In the Third Part the poet and his guide finally arrive at the
Palace of Honour, situated on the summit of a "roche of slid hard
marbell stone," which shines like glass. The top of·this hill the poet
reaches only by the aid of the nymph, who takes him by the hair and
carries him up. On the top of the hill is a lovely meadow, in the
midst of which stands the palace. This is most imposing, with lordly
towers and carvings and precious stones. Here the poet again finds
Venus enthroned, and before her

> Stude emerant stages twelf, grene precious greis,
> Quhairon thair grew thre curious goldin treis (iii, st. 21).

By her side is blind Cupid. Facing her is a mirror, more wonderful
than Canace's,[1] in which all the events of history are to be seen. The
goddess recognizes her quondam prisoner, and after some conversation gives him a book[2] to put in rhyme. More details about the palace
are given: Lawtie (Loyalty) is the keeper and Patience the porter,
Charity master of the household, Constance the king's secretary,
Liberality treasurer, Innocence and Devotion "clerkis of closet and
cubiculairis," and so on. The hall of Prince Honor is described
in the traditional fashion with decorations from natural phenomena
and classical story, and the magnificence of it all, and finally of its
lord, is such as to cause the poet to swoon. His nymph restores
him, preaches him a sermon on honor, and finally leads him out to
show him the garden. But as he crosses the moat he falls off the
tree which serves as a bridge, plunges "over the head" into the
water and awakes.

Nearly all the forms of the Court of Love are represented here:
the form with a procession found earliest in Ovid's *Triumph of Cupid*

---

[1] In Chaucer's *Squire's Tale*.

[2] "By thys boke," says the marginal comment, "he menis Virgil."

nd later in Andreas,[1] Nicole de Margivale,[2] and Petrarch[3]; the
ourt in the meadow, represented here by the trial-scene of the poet
nd the feast of the Muses by the Castalian spring; and the court
1 the palace, represented by the Mansion of Honor itself. The
:gal aspect appears in the trial-scene just referred to. The allegor-
:al courtiers are found in the officers of the household, and the
epresentative figures from history and romance occur half a dozen
imes. Douglas seems to have been very well read in this class of
oetry as well as in the classics; and suggestions must have been
athered from many sources. Chaucer's *Hous of Fame*[4] is the work
ɔ which he seems to owe most.

The Palice of Honour so thoroughly represents Douglas's allegor-
:al powers that it is hardly necessary to dwell on his other poem of
his class, *King Hart.*[5] This is an allegory on the life of man and
elongs rather to the didactic than to the erotic type. It is full of
ersonifications, and there are descriptions (for example, that of the
astle of Dame Plesance) which resemble the familiar Castle of
,ove.

WILLIAM DUNBAR.

The Golden Targe[6] of Dunbar is an allegory of the assault of Love
n the heart of the poet and its defence by the golden shield of
Reason.

Beginning with a description of the song of birds and the bloom-
1g of the flowers on a May morning, the poet tells how in a dream
e saw Nature, Venus, Aurora, Flora, and many another divinity
ome by ship into a beautiful meadow. They danced and sang by
1e river, and the poet crept through the leaves to see. But the
Queen of Love saw him and bade her archers come against him.

---

[1] See p. 46, above.   [2] See pp. 69 ff., above.   [3] See pp. 112 ff., above.

[4] Cf. P. Lange, *Chaucer's Einfluss auf die Originaldichtungen des Schotten
avin Douglas*, Halle, 1882.

[5] *Poetical Works*, ed. Small, I, 85-120.

[6] *Poems of William Dunbar*, ed. by J. Small for the Scottish Text Society,
:dinburgh, 1889-93, II, 1-10, and by J. Schipper in *Denkschriften der kais. Akad.
'. Wissenschaften zu Wien, Phil.-hist. Classe*, XL, iv, 10-23.

And now a whole army of personified feminine attractions, Fa
Having, Fyne Portrature, Lusty Chere, Womanhood, Youth, ar
many others, headed by Beauty, attacked him, but

> Resoun, with schelde of gold so clere —
> In plate and maille, as Mars armypotent,
> Defendit me, that nobil cheuallere (vv. 151–3).

At first Reason succeeded in repulsing the assailants; but Ven
sent Dissymilance, with the pick of her army, including Presenc
and Presence cast dust in Reason's eyes so that he was befoole
Then the poet, wounded almost to death, yielded to Beauty. Ve
soon, however, the whole company re-embarked, and with the noi
of their parting salute the poet awoke. He concludes with a loy
apostrophe to his masters, — Chaucer, Gower, and Lydgate.

The idea of collecting all the divinities in the Court of Lo
meadow has not occurred in any previous example; and Dunbar
personifications, though familiar enough, are handled with a goc
deal of vigor.

The Thrissil and the Rois[1] is a poem after the model of the *Par*
ment of Foules, Dame Nature being the presiding deity. She mak
the Lion King of Beasts, the Eagle of Birds, and the Thistle
Flowers, crowning the Rose as his queen while all the surroundir
creatures rejoice. The occasion of Dunbar's poem (the marriage
the king) was similar to that of Chaucer's. Both in this poem ar
in *The Golden Targe* we have May personified as a fresh maiden "
brycht atteir of flouris forgit new,"[2] — a point which seems origin
with Dunbar.

In *Bewty and the Presoneir*[3] we have another allegorical love-co
test, which, though not properly a Court of Love, has yet so many
its features as to deserve mention. The lover gazes on his lady t
he has no power to resist, and Fresche Bewty shuts him up in th
castle of Penance, where Strangenes is porter, Comparison captai
Languor warden, and Scorn jester. At the suggestion of Gud Hou

---

[1] Schipper's edition, in *Denkschriften*, XL, iv, 2–10; Small's edition, II, 183–18
[2] *The Thrissil and the Rois*, vv. 15 ff. ; *The Golden Targe*, vv. 82 ff.
[3] Schipper, XL, iv, 23–26; Small, II, 164 ff.

e writes a "bill," which Lawlines bears, along with Fair Scherwice.
hese enlist Petie, the castle is assaulted, and, with the help of Lust,
hocht, and Bissines, is taken. Strangenes is burnt in the lodge;
korne has his nose pierced and is banished; Comparisone is burned
ive, and Sklander, who had appeared as soon as victory was assured,
chased away by King Matremony.

STEPHEN HAWES.

The Pastime of Pleasure[1] (*ca.* 1506), the latest English allegory
efore the *Court of Love* which we shall discuss, is too long to be
ealt with in detail; and in the following analysis many parts that
re not strictly in the line of the investigation will be very slightly
dicated.

The hero, La Grande Amour, meets Fame as a lady on horseback,
rrounded with tongues of fire and accompanied by the hounds
overnaunce and Grace. (This is the only instance of allegorical
ounds I have met with outside of German literature.) She tells him
f the great beauty of La Bell Pucell, directs him to the tower of
)octrine, and departs, leaving the greyhounds with him. He finds
e tower, which is of copper, and which stands on the summit of a
raggy rock. Its turrets gleam with images of gold. Within, the
alls are draped with arras, on which is pictured a foreshadowing of
is own adventures. The officers of the household are named in the
shion just noted in the *Palice of Honour.* Countenance is the
orter, the marshal is dame Reason, the butler Curteis Continuance,
e chief cook Temperance, the chamberlain Fidelity, and the high
eward Liberality. Dame Doctrine sends the hero to Grammar,
ogic, Rhetoric, Arithmetic, and Music, who all have quarters in the
stablishment. At the tower of Music he meets La Bell Pucell,
ances with her, and falls deeply in love. He also gets acquainted
ith Counsel, who gives him much good advice. On further inter-
iews with La Bell Pucell, the hero wins her favor; but their union
postponed. After visits to Geometry and Astronomy, he goes to

---

[1] *The Pastime of Pleasure, reprinted from edition of 1555*, Percy Society, Lond.,
845.

the Tower of Chivalry, where he offers prayer in the temple of Mars
Mars advises him to make oblation to Venus, but Fortune stands b
and mocks.   Minerva leads him to King Melyzyus, who knights him
and he gets armor :

> For fyrst, good-hope his legge harneys sholde be ;
> His habergion of perfyte ryghtwysenes ;
> Gyrde faste wyth the gyrdle of chastite,
> His riche placarde should be good besines,
> Brandred with almes so full of larges ;
> The helmet mekenes, and the shelde good fayth ;
> His swerde Goddes worde, as saynt Poule sayth (chap. 28).

Thus accoutred, he rides forth with Sir Truth, Sir Fidelity, Sir For
titude, Sir Consuetude, Sir Justice, Sir Misericord, Sir Sapience, Si
Curteysy, Sir Nurture, and Sir Concord, who escort him for som
distance.   After an encounter with False Report, he comes to th
temple of Venus.

> There sate dame Venus and Cupide her sonne,
> Which had their parliament ryght newly begone.
> To redresse lovers of their payne and wo,
> Whiche in the temple did walke to and fro.
> And every one his byll did present
> Before Venus in her hyghe parliament (chap. 29).

The temple is walled about with ivory and is all of gold.   Dame
Sapience is secretary, and to her the lover makes appeal, and she
consents to draw up a "Complaynt to Venus" for him.   This sup
plication, which contains a summary of his previous adventures
requests that Venus send Cupid to let the lady know what he i
suffering for her.   Venus gives him hope, and instructs him to b
patient and faithful, while she tells Sapience to write a letter exhort
ing La Bell Pucell to show favor to La Grande Amour.   This lette
is given

> Under our signet, in our court ryall,
> Of September, the two and twenty day (chap. 31),

and is sent by Cupid.   The lover offers a turtle dove to Venus and
departs. . . .

Later he meets, and with his sword Clara Prudence overcomes, a
giant with three heads (Falsehood, Imagination, and Perjury), where-
upon Verity, Good Operation, and Fidelity congratulate him. Per-
severance, meeting him, tells of La Bell Pucell's favorable reception
of the letter from Venus and her resistance to Disdain and Strange-
ness. After more fights with giants and other adventures, he
finally arrives at the mansion of La Bell Pucell, who, with Peace,
Mercy, Justice, Reason, Pleasaunce, Grace, and Memory, receives
him graciously into her gorgeous house. Suddenly Venus and Cupid
arrive to hasten the marriage, which takes place next day, Lex
Ecclesiae officiating.

Grande Amour and La Bell Pucell live together for many years;
but at last Age comes and arrests the hero. He has interviews with
Confession, Contrition, Satisfaction, and Conscience, then dies,
and Remembrance writes his epitaph. The temple where he is
buried is visited by Fame, by Time, and finally by Eternity.

In spite of the enormous length of this work, it will be seen from
the outline that the material and the general treatment are far from
novel. The poem is excessively diffuse and wearisome, so much so
that one suspects irony in the title.

Yet the allegory of Stephen Hawes suggests considerations of
some importance. It is about three hundred years later than the
Fablel dou Dieu d'Amours and *Venus la Deesse ;* and from these three
hundred years we have found still extant so many examples of
the Court of Love type that we are justified in saying that, even if
one is lost, there was produced on an average one every three years
or three centuries. Yet the development of the characteristic ideas
in the interval has been extremely small. The personification of
the sciences is as old as Martianus Capella ; the allegorical armor
is taken from St. Paul ; the gleaming palaces are found in Ovid ; the
fights with the many-headed giants are only a slight step beyond
Prudentius. The combination of these things, digressions on natural
phenomena and all, was already familiar in the thirteenth century;
and, indeed, Hawes's poem is very close in parts to *Li Fablel* and
the *Roman de la Rose.* Here and there we may find points taken
from men nearer his own day; but the advance from the poems we

have just mentioned is no greater than we might expect to be made
in one generation by a single man of genius. Yet Boccaccio, Petrarch, and Chaucer, to mention only three, had used the form.
There could hardly be a more striking evidence of the barrennes
and perniciousness of allegory.

CHAPTER IV.

THE STATUTES OF LOVE.

In the summary of the plot of the English *Court of Love* in the
first chapter, mention was made of certain statutes which Philogene
had to sign.[1] From the manner in which they are introduced, these
commandments might be expected to be in the form of laws for the
regulation of the conduct of the subjects of the Lord of Love; and
to some extent this is the case. The first one of the twenty, for
example, demands loyalty to the King and Queen of Love; while
with a transference to the religious figure, the fourth exhorts subject
to seek to extend the kingdom of Love, to

> Stiren folk to love, and beten fyr
> On Venus awter (vv. 324–5).

But in the great majority of the statutes, the God of Love and his
kingdom or court are quite lost sight of, and the rules become statements of the ideal of conduct for the mediæval gentleman, of the
traditional symptoms of lovers, or of precepts for seduction. The
task of classification is not an easy one; for in addition to the fact
that these divisions, from the very nature of the subject-matter, run
into one another, the poet occasionally found a difficulty in making
his exposition of a particular principle end with the end of a stanza
and, in order to complete the stanza, threw in an additional precept
having no close connection with that contained in the former part.
As, however, these addenda are usually repeated in the principal

---

[1] See p. 3, above.

part of another statute, we can afford in most cases to ignore them without neglecting any point of importance.

The following classification is made merely for working purposes, and it should be understood that the groups are by no means mutually exclusive.

THE TWENTY STATUTES.

A. LAWS OF THE KINGDOM OF LOVE.

i.	To be true to the King and Queen of Love.
iv.	To stir up others to love.
xix.	" Ech other day see that thou fast for love."

B. RULES OF CHIVALROUS LOVE.

ii.	" Secretly to keep councell of love."
iii.	To be constant to one's lady.
vii.	To be patient.]
ix.	To be meek and afraid of being over-bold.
x.	To be conscious of inferiority to one's lady.
xii.	To think nothing of pain for her sake.
xiii.	To be thoughtful to please her.
xiv (b).	To believe no evil of her.
xv (a).	To defend her honor and reputation at all costs.
xviii.	To keep one's person and dress neat and clean.

C. LOVERS' SYMPTOMS.

v.	To be sleepless when the lady is cruel.
vi.	To wander alone musing on her.
xiv (a).	To dream of enjoying her love.
xvii.	To be interested in love even when one is old.
xx.	To be wretched in her absence.

D. PRECEPTS OF SEDUCTION.

viii.	To be persistent in one's suit.
xi.	To know how to make love by coughs, smiles, sighs, etc.
xv (b).	" Her appetyt folow in all degree."
xvi.	" Seven sith at night thy lady for to plese, And seven at midnight, seven at morow-day."

Group *A* seems the natural result of the Court of Love conception, but plays a very small part in the development of the code.

Group *B* is a collection of the principles which pervade the literature, as they must have pervaded the society, of the chivalrous epoch, and the ideas represented will be found abundantly, both formally drawn up, as here, and informally expressed or implied, in the material collected in this chapter.

Group *C* consists of ideas which are naturally to be found with great frequency in love-poetry whether allegorical or not, but which are more rarely drawn up in lists.

Group *D*, which is less fully represented in the present poem, is still important, since in some of the earlier poems it includes the greater number of the rules. Statute xvi is not properly a statute of seduction, of course, but is placed here for convenience as belonging to that side of the subject which deals with the more sensual aspect of love. It seems to be quite original with the author of the English *Court of Love.*

A. The Ovidian Tradition.

A complete discussion of the ideas represented by these statutes is quite impossible here. It would imply not only the tracing of the development of the erotic precepts of Ovid as they spread through mediæval Europe, but also a study of the growth of the whole chivalrous ideal and its expression in lyric, in romance, and in books of conduct and courtesy, as well as in allegory. The present chapter must be regarded as little more than a collection of material for such a study from the particular part of the field represented by the class of works treated in the previous chapter.

Even for this limited purpose, however, it is necessary to go back to the *Ars Amatoria.* The advice given by Ovid in this poem belongs as a whole to Group *D* ; yet in some of its precepts we find the beginnings of rules belonging in their later associations to other groups.

Thus Statute xiii of the *Court of Love,* which

Whylom is to thinke
What thing may best thy lady lyke and plese (vv. 393–4),

goes on to recommend the lover to devise something,

> Some hert, or ring, or lettre, or device,
> Or precious stone ; but spare not for no price (vv. 398-9).

So in Ovid, *Ars Amatoria*, ii, 163 :

> Secum habet ingenium, qui, cum libet, ' Accipe ' dicit.

And here it may be said once for all, that in each case the spirit of the entire poem determines into which group a rule should be put. In Ovid the whole matter of winning the lady's good-will, of which the giving of presents is a detail, is simply a basely conceived means to an immoral end. Thus, if a rule retained this character, it would belong to Group *D*. But in the Middle Ages, in that part of the literature inspired by the finer side of courtly love, the spending of thought, pains, or money to please one's lady is part of the quasi-religious worship offered her ; and, to whatever extent this had a sensual basis, it was still one side of knightliness.

Again, Statute xviii is

> That thou eschewe
> With sluttishness thyself for to offend ;
> Be jolif, fresh, and fete, with thinges new, etc. (vv. 471 ff.).

Cf. *Ars Amatoria*, i, 513 ff. :

> Munditie placeant, fuscentur corpora Campo ;
> Sit bene conueniens et sine labe toga ;
> Lingua ne rigeat ; careant rubigine dentes ;
> Nec uagus in laxa pes tibi pelle natet :
> Nec male deformet rigidos tonsura capillos :
> Sit coma, sit trita barba resecta manu.
> Et nihil emineant et sint sine sordibus ungues,
> Inque caua nullus stet tibi nare pilus.

The rule for complaisance in Statute ix and in the latter part of xv —

> And ay what thing that she thee will forbede,
> Eschew all that, and give her sovereintee,
> Her appetyt folow in all degree (vv. 432-4) —

finds its counterpart in *Ars Amatoria*, ii, 197 ff. :

> Cede repugnanti : cedendo uictor abibis ;
>   Fac modo quas partis illa iubebit agas.
> Arguet : arguito ; quicquid probat illa, probato.
>   Quod dicet, dicas ; quod negat illa, neges.
> Riserit : adride ; si flebit, flere memento.
>   Imponat leges uultibus illa tuis.

Recommendations to concealment are frequent in Ovid ; but here again the lower ethical level is apparent, for while in the chivalrous codes consideration for the lady is the motive insisted on, in Ovid it is fear of the husband or the desire to carry on more intrigues than one without exciting the suspicions of the different mistresses. |

The same thing holds of the rules in Group *C.* The paleness and sleeplessness of lovers, instead of being the genuine symptoms of the passion-struck youth, appear in Ovid as shams assumed for the purpose of working on the feelings of the intended victim. Take, for example, *Ars Amatoria*, i, 729 ff. :

> Palleat omnis amans ; hic est color aptus amanti.
>   Hoc decet, hoc stulti non ualuisse putent.
>
> .   .   .   .
>
> Arguat et macies animum ; nec turpe putaris
>   Palliolum nitidis imposuisse comis.
> Attenuant iuuenum uigilatae corpora noctes
>   Curaque et in magno qui fit amore dolor.
> Ut uoto potiare tuo, miserabilis esto ;
>   Ut qui te uideat, dicere possit ' amas.'

Of Group *D* it is hardly necessary to quote particular instances from Ovid, since, as has already been said, the *Ars Amatoria* as a whole might be placed in this category. The eleventh Statute is closely paralleled in the fourth elegy of the first Book of the *Amores :*

> Me specta nutusque meos uultumque loquacem ;
>   Excipe furtiuas et refer ipsa notas.
> Verba superciliis sine uoce loquentia dicam :
>   Verba leges digitis, uerba notata mero, etc. (vv. 17–20).

The *Court of Love* has :

> Thy signes for to con
> With y and finger, and with smyles soft,
> And low to cough, and alway for to shon,
> For dred of spyes, for to winken oft :
> But secretly to bring a sigh a-loft (vv. 379–83).

IMITATIONS AND TRANSLATIONS OF OVID.

In forming an opinion about the erotic literature and the literary tastes of the Middle Ages, we must not regard Ovid merely as a classic whose reputation was known to all while his books were read only by the few. The number of translations, paraphrases, adaptations, and moralizations of his works which were current throughout Western Europe, but especially in France, prove him to have been popular in a sense in which this word can be used of very few classical writers.[1]

One of the earliest mediæval works to show Ovid's influence is the Latin " comedy " (of about the twelfth century), known as *Pamphilus de Amore*.[2] The plot of the piece consists in the seduction of a girl, Galatea, by a young man Pamphilus, with the aid of an unscrupulous old woman. It opens with a soliloquy on the pains of love by the young man. He appeals to Venus, and in answer to his reproachful prayers the goddess appears and gives him counsel as to how to obtain his desires. It is in this speech by Venus, and afterwards in some of the instructions of the old woman that the parallels to our statutes occur. Naturally most of them fall in Group *D*. Much stress, for example, is laid on Persistence :

> Tunc illam multo temptamine saepe fatiga (v. 131).

> Ergo tuis primum si non fauet illa querelis,
> Arte uel officio fac tamen ut faueat (vv. 81–2).

---

[1] See G. Paris, *Hist. Lit.*, XXIX, 455 ff., and *La Poésie du Moyen Âge*, Paris, 1885, pp. 189–209, for French versions of Ovid in the Middle Ages, and cf. *Rom.*, XXII, 271 ff. Cf., also, Legrand d'Aussy, *Fabliaux ou Contes*, Paris, 1879, II, 265, 270, 274.

[2] *Pamphile, ou l'art d'être aimé*, ed. by A. Baudouin, Paris, 1874.

The duty of being merry is also insisted on :

> Gaudia semper amat et ludicra laeta iuuentus
> Et iuuenum mentes hoc in amore ligat.
> Laetum semper ei te laetis uultibus offer :
> Est cum laeticia pulcrior omnis homo (vv. 101–4).

Advice to bribe the lady's servants (vv. 125 ff.) and many other points show the author's indebtedness to Ovid.

Baudouin gives a list of no fewer than sixteen editions of this work from about 1470 to an uncertain date, probably in the seventeenth century. This includes two French paraphrases and an Italian version. Besides these closer imitations, we have proof of the influence of the *Pamphilus* in the character of the procuress in the famous fifteenth-century Spanish tragi-comedy *Celestina*,[1] which in turn was translated and imitated very widely throughout Europe.

Much closer to Ovid is Maistre Elie's version of the *Ars Amatoria*,[2] the chief departure from the original being in the substitution of Paris for Rome, and the consequent adaptation of the passages dealing with the customs of classical times to suit the French life of the thirteenth century.

A similar adaptation forms the main part of *La Clef d'Amors*,[3] in which the God of Love appears to the poet in a dream and asks him to draw up the rules of the doctrine of love for the guidance of lovers. This exists in a fourteenth-century MS.

L'Art d'Amors,[4] by a certain Jacques d'Amiens, is a free translation from Ovid with the insertion (vv. 466–1035) of specimen conversations between a lover and his lady, after the manner of Andreas Capellanus.[5]

---

[1] *Celestina*, by Fernando de Rojas, Barcelona, 1886. English Elizabethan translation, *Calista and Meliboea* by James Mabbe, ed. by Fitzmaurice Kelly, Lond., 1894. The Archpriest of Hita also shows the influence of the *Pamphilus*: see his *Poesías* in Sanchez, *Colección de Poesías Castellanas*, Madrid, 1790, vol. IV, especially pp. 135–9. I owe this last reference to Professor Marsh.

[2] *Maître Elie's Ueberarbeitung der ältesten franz. Uebertragung von Ovid's Ars Amatoria*, ed. by H. Kühne and E. Stengel in *Ausg. und Abhandl.*, No. 47, Marburg, 1886; see especially Kühne's *Prolegomena*.

[3] Ed. by E. Tross and H. Michelant, Lyons, 1866; and also by A. Doutrepont in Suchier's *Bibliotheca Normannica*, Halle, 1890.

[4] Ed. by G. Körting, Leipzig, 1868.   [5] See p. 177, below.

Paris mentions also *L'Art d'aimer* by one Guiart, and a fourteenth-century prose translation with a commentary, fragments of which are preserved.

The Latin manual of conduct known as *Facetus*[1] (*i.e.* "courteous") is also indebted to Ovid. After some generalities, advice on education and the choice of a career, matters of dress and the care of the person, the author goes into an Art of Love, which takes up vv. 131–384 (out of a total of 510), after which he returns to general advice on conduct. A Catalan version from the second half of the fourteenth century expands the amatory part and follows it up with a diatribe against women. In both versions the moral tone remains Ovidian in the parts dealing with love.[2]

As a further evidence of the popularity of the *Ars Amatoria* may be quoted a passage from Marie de France,[3] describing a wall decoration.

> La chambre ert peinte tute entur.
> Venus, la deuesse d'amur
> Fu tres bien mise en la peinture ;
> Les traiz mustrë e la nature
> Cument hom deit amur tenir
> E leialment e bien servir.
> Le livre Ovide, u il enseigne
> Coment chascuns s'amur estreigne,
> En un fu ardant le gettout,
> E tuz icels escumenjout,
> Ki ja mais cel livre lirreient
> Ne sun enseignement fereient (vv. 233–44).

The Goliardic authors of the *Carmina Burana* knew Ovid well. Sometimes they quote him exactly, as in a precept of secrecy (cf. *Court of Love*, Statute ii) :

> Praecipue Cytherea jubet sua sacra taceri[4] ;

---

[1] The work begins with the verse, " Moribus et vita quisquis vult esse *facetus*." There is a second Latin poem entitled *Facetus*, and a third called *Fay-* or *Fagi-facetus:* see Hauréau, in *Notices et Extraits*, XXVII, ii, 15–20.

[2] Both the Latin poem and the Catalan version are edited by Morel-Fatio, *Romania*, XV, 192–235.   [4] *Carmina Burana*, p. 222; *Ars Amatoria*, ii, 607.

[3] *Lai de Guigemar*, in *Die Lais der Marie de France*, ed. by K. Warnke, Halle, 1885, p. 14. I owe this reference to the courtesy of Mr. W. D. Howe.

more frequently we have merely similarity of idea, as in the version of the same commandment which occurs in the poem called by Langlois *Carmen de Rosa* [1]:

> Pange lingua igitur
> Causas et causatum
> Nomen tamen dominae
> Serva palliatum,
> Ut non sit in populo
> Illud diuulgatum,
> Quod secretum gentibus
> Extat et celatum.

ANDREAS CAPELLANUS.

The *De Arte Honeste Amandi* of Andreas Capellanus is by far the most important and interesting Ovidian document of the Middle Ages.

Whatever may be finally proved concerning the personality of the author or the date of the work, there can be no doubt that it is a product of the courtly society of the time of Eleanor of Aquitaine and her daughter Marie de Champagne, and that its author was a person who had full opportunity to observe the workings of the social code to which these ladies gave their sanction. The book of Andreas gives us the theory of that system the practice of which is concretely presented in the romances of Chrétien de Troyes; and for scientific purposes the abstract statement is more illuminating than the concrete, for the elements of the new code are more easily analyzed in it.

The ascetic ideal upheld by the mediæval church could not in the nature of things appeal permanently to a fashionable society, so that, when the reaction came, the pendulum not only swung away from celibacy, but, passing the point of married chastity, went to the other extreme, and a system of conduct grew up in which the central point was adulterous love. | But to social anarchy the human spirit is always in the long run averse; and no sooner had the revolt to license taken place than there began to grow up round the new immorality a system of checks and restrictions, perhaps

---

[1] *Carmina Burana*, p. 141.

less burdensome but no less elaborate than those which surrounded the old ecclesiastical code. It is of this immorality, with its checks and restrictions, its conventions and traditions, that the work of Andreas is a manual.

The plan of the work is taken from Ovid, who thus lays down the scheme of the *Ars Amatoria :*

> Principio, quod amare uelis, reperire labora,
> Qui noua nunc primum miles in arma uenis.
> Proximus huic labor est placitam exorare puellam :
> Tertius, ut longo tempore duret amor.[1]

The same threefold division may be detected in the opening sentence of Andreas :

> Est igitur primo uidere, quid sit amor, et unde dicatur amor, et quis sit effectus amoris, et *inter quos possit esse amor, qualiter acquiratur amor, retineatur,* augmentetur, minuatur, finiatur, et de notitia amoris mutui, et quid unus amantium agere debeat altero fidem fallente.

The italicized phrases which correspond to the three things stated as aims in Ovid, — whom to love, how to win her, how to keep her, — form the kernel of Andreas's book. In chap. vi of bk. i, which includes more than half the work, there are given imaginary conversations between lovers of various ranks, as, for example, *plebeius ad plebeiam, plebeius nobili, nobilis plebeiae, nobilior nobiliori,* and so on. It is in one of these, that in which *loquitur nobilis nobili,* that the account of the palace of love and the procession of lovers already quoted [2] occurs. Other chapters deal with the love of clerks, nuns, rustics, and courtesans ; another with twenty-one love decisions, and still another with the rules of love. A third book has been added on the model of the *Remedia Amoris,* and it is devoted chiefly to the vices of women. There is no attempt made in this last part to be consistent with the first two.

There are two sets of rules given in the Chaplain's book. The first and shorter [3] is that given by the God of Love to the knight

---

[1] *Ars Amatoria*, i, 35–8.   [2] See p. 46, above.
[3] See Trojel's edition of Andreas, p. 106.

who sees the vision of the Palace and Purgatory of Love. These are on the whole moral rules, all coming under Group *B*, and in some cases corresponding to the statutes of the *Court of Love*. There are twelve in all, commending the virtues of Generosity (i), Constancy to one only (ii), Truthfulness (v), Secrecy (vi), Obedience (vii), Modesty (viii), Courtesy (xi), Moderation (xii), and forbidding slander (ix), babbling (x), the seducing of another man's mistress (iii), and the holding of intrigues with a woman whom one would be ashamed to marry (iv).

The longer set of thirty-one rules[1] is not so high in moral tone. These also profess to have high authority. The story is told of a British knight whose lady refused to grant him her love unless he brought her the hawk which perched in Arthur's hall. After many adventures and contests, and with much machinery of magic banquets and gorgeous castles and terrible giants, the knight achieves his quest, and at the same time finds attached to the hawk's perch a " chartula, in qua regulae scribuntur amoris, quas ipse amoris rex ore proprio amatoribus edidit."

These *regulae*, however, are laws rather than commandments, statements of what naturally occurs in matters of love rather than rules to be obeyed. This distinction appears even when the subject-matter is the same as in the direct commands of the statutes of the *Court of Love*. Thus, corresponding to the rule of Secrecy, we have :

Qui non celat, amare non potest (ii),

and

Amor raro consueuit durare uulgatus (xiii).

So Constancy is represented by

Nemo duplici potest amore ligari (iii) ;

and

Verus amans alterius, nisi sui [var. sue = suae] coamantis ex affectu, non cupit amplexus (xii),

is modified in

Biennalis uiduitas pro amante defuncto superstiti prescribitur amanti (vii),

---

[1] Ed. Trojel, pp. 295-312.

and apparently contradicted in

Unam feminam nil prohibet a duobus amari et a duabus mulieribus unum (xxxi).

Similarly Generosity is not commanded, but it is stated that

Amor semper consueuit ab auaritiae domiciliis exsulare (x).

Other laws coming under Group *B* are:

Probitas sola quemque dignum facit amore (xviii),
Amor nil posset amori denegare (xxvi),

and

Non decet amare quarum pudor est nuptias affectare (xi).

Group *C*, of the Symptoms of Lovers, is represented by several items :

Omnis consueuit amans in coamantis aspectu pallescere (xv) ;
In repentina coamantis uisione cor contremescit amantis (xvi) ;
Amorosus semper est timorosus (xx) ;
Minus dormit et edit, quem amoris cogitatio uexat (xxiii) ;
Quilibet amantis actus in coamantis cogitatione finitur (xxiv) ;
Verus amans assidua, sine intermissione, coamantis imagine detinetur (xxx).

But many of the sections of this code cannot be included in any one of the four groups into which the statutes of the *Court of Love* fell. The first one, for instance, is a frank statement of the place of marriage in this discussion of love :

Causa coniugii ab amore non est excusatio recta.

Most of the others are observations on what one might call the natural history of love, — bits of love-lore, some of which were doubtless traditional sayings, and others evolved by the author in the scholastic spirit of elaboration of detail. Such are these:

Semper amorem crescere uel minui constat (iv) ;
Non est sapidum quod amans ab inuito sumit coamante (v) ;
Masculus non solet, nisi plena pubertate, amare (vi) ;
Nemo, sine rationis excessu, suo debet amore priuari (viii) ;
Amare nemo potest, nisi qui amoris suasione compellitur (ix) ;
Facilis perceptio contemptibilem reddit amorem, difficilis eum carum facit haberi (xiv) ;

Nouus amor ueterem compellit abire (xvii) ;
Si amor minuatur, cito deficit et raro conualescit (xix) ;
Ex uera zelotypia affectus semper crescit amandi (xxi) ;
De coamante suspicione percepta zelus et affectus crescit amandi (xxii) ;
Amans coamantis solatiis satiari non potest (xxvii) ;
Modica praesumptio cogit amantem de coamante suspicari sinistra (xxviii) ;
Non solet amare quem nimia uoluptatis abundantia uexat (xxix).

The wide circulation and influence of Andreas are well proved. Twelve manuscripts of the Latin version, the earliest (Vaticanus, coll. Ottobonianae No. 1463) being probably of the thirteenth century, are extant. In the thirteenth century it was twice translated into French; in the fourteenth, twice into Italian; and in the fifteenth, twice into German. Mention of the book occurs several times in the thirteenth century, and traces of its influence, even where no name is mentioned, are not infrequent.

About the author, the date, and possible earlier forms of the book many questions still remain unsettled.[1] That parts of the book were in circulation before it took the shape in which it has come down to us seems to be proved by the fact that it quotes itself: as, for example, when the knight who describes the palace of love ends his list of precepts with the words:

Sunt et alia amoris praecepta minora, quorum tibi non expediret auditus, quae etiam in libro ad Gualterium scripto reperies,[2]

where the words "libro ad Gualterium" agree with a description of the work of Andreas frequently found in manuscripts of the book itself and in allusions to it elsewhere.

It further appears that lists of rules of love other than those given by Andreas were known to the society which he describes. The

---

[1] For the state of the question down to 1892 see the introduction to Trojel's edition. See also G. Paris, *Journal des Savants*, 1888, pp. 664–75, 727–36, and *Romania*, XIX, 372 ; F. X. Wöber, *Der Minne Regel von Eberhardus von Cersne aus Minden, 1404*, Vienna, 1861 ; and cf. F. Bech, *Germania*, VII, 481, and VIII 268–70, *Litterarisches Centralblatt*, 1893, col. 288–9, and *Rom.*, XXVIII, 119–20.

[2] Ed. Trojel, p. 106. For other instances see pp. 283 ("capellani doctrina") and 148.

ule quoted in the following passage does not occur in either of the odes already described:

> Verus amans nunquam potest amorem exoptare nouitium, nisi primitus b certam iustamque causam prioris cognouerit aduenisse defectum. Quam *egulam* nostri quidem experimento cognoscimus esse uerissimam.[1]

Neither do we find elsewhere the rule condemned here:

> Non est igitur amoris regula, quam dixistis, quum falsa reperiatur et allax, scilicet ut amantium rarus aspectus amoris faciat attenuari poten- iam — [2]

he reference being to a speech by the lady who held that

> Regula nobis demonstrat amoris, quod amantium quotidianus aspectus rescere facit amorem.[3]

The fact pointed to by these allusions was one to be looked for. The practice of discussing fine points in love was a fashionable amusement before the earliest date possible for Andreas's book; he substance of his codes must have been drawn from these dis- cussions, and it was natural that the principles involved should sooner or later take the form of laws.

B. Provençal.

The troubadours draw up no formal codes like those in the *Court f Love* and Andreas. They constantly refer, however, to the vir- ues which are required by the statutes, and in some of these refer- ences different virtues are grouped together. Thus in the *A leis cui im de cor e de saber* by Guiraut de Calanso[4] there are four steps eading up to the door which Guiraut Riquier explains thus:

> Le premiers es onrars,
> El segon es selars,
> El ters es gen servirs,
> El quartz es bos sufrirs.

---

[1] Ed. Trojel, p. 263.   [2] *Ibid.*, p. 140.   [3] *Ibid.*, p. 139.
[4] See p. 24, above. But on the meaning of the steps, see also Dammann, pp. 73 ff.

Again in Gaucelm Faidit[1] several statutes can be recognized in th
lines :

> Chant e deport, joy, domney e solatz,
> Ensenhamen, largueza e cortezia,
> Honor e pretz e leyal drudaria.

But more frequently the virtues are mentioned singly.   In Be
nart de Ventadorn the obligation to secrecy is thus acknowledged :

> Mas s'a lieys plazia
> Que m fezes qualque be,
> Ieu li juraria,
> Per lieys e per ma fe,
> Qu'el bes que m faria
> No fos saubutz per me.[2]

In the same poet we find constancy represented :

> E vos etz lo meus jois premiers,
> E si seretz vos lo derriers,
> Tan quant la vida m'er durans.[3]

The determination to do or suffer anything to give his lady pleasur
is also found in Bernart :

> Re mais non am ni sai temer,
> Ni ja re no m seri' afans,
> Sol mi dons vengues a plazer[4] ;

and again :

> En son plazer sia,
> Qu'ieu sui en sa merce ;
> S'il platz que m'aucia
> Ieu no m'en clam de re.[5]

---

[1] Raynouard, *Lexique Roman*, I, 373.
[2] Mahn, *Werke der Troubadours*, Berlin, 1846–82, I, 15.
[3] *Ibid.*, I, 21.
[4] *Ibid.*, I, 34.
[5] *Ibid.*, I, 15.

The second part of the fourteenth statute of the *Court of Love*, ommanding the lover to believe no evil, appears in Peire Rogier [1]:

> Bos drutz non deu creire auctors
> Ni so que veiran sey huelh
> De neguna forfaitura
> Don sap que sa domna 'l trays ;
> So que dis qu'a fait alhors
> Creza, sitot non lo jura,
> E so qu'en vi dezacuelha. [2]

The examples just given all belong to Group *B*. Lovers' symp-oms are even more frequent. Sleeplessness is particularly common :

> Ben sai la nueg quan mi despuelh
> El lieg que no i dormirai re ;
> Lo dormir pert, quar ieu lo m tuelh,
> Domna, quan de vos mi sove. [3]

This same kind of thing is exemplified rather frequently in the *Jlamenca*. The following lines describing the love-anguish of Guillem re typical :

> Apres manjar Guillems intret
> En sa cambra, lai si pauset,
> Si pausar pot hom appellar
> Tremblar d'angoissa ni sudar,
> Estendillar e trassallir,
> E badaillar e sanglotir,
> Planer, sospirar e plorar,
> Estavanir et ablesmar [4] (vv. 3306-13).

---

[1] Professor Sheldon draws my attention to a striking group of instructions in other poem by this poet, *Ges en bon vers non posc falhir*, especially the last two anzas. See Bartsch, *Chrest. Prov.*, 4th ed., 1880, col. 81-4; and Mahn, *Werke*, 123-4.   [2] Mahn, *Werke*, I, 119.

[3] Bernart de Ventadorn in Mahn, *Werke*, etc., I, 19. For other instances see rnaut de Marueil in Mahn, I, 153; Bernart, *ibid.*, I, 24; I, 38, etc. On the gen-al theme see Diez, *Die Poesie der Troubadours*, 2d ed. by Bartsch, Leipzig, 1883, eben u. *Werke der Troubadours*, 2d ed. by Bartsch, Leipzig, 1882; Stimming, art. 1 *Provenzalische Litt.* in Gröber's *Grundriss*, II, Abt. 2, pp. 1-69; and L. F. Iott, *The System of Courtly Love*, Boston, 1896. To this last work I am debted for several of the references just given.

[4] *Roman de Flamenca*, ed. by P. Meyer, Paris, 1865. Cf. vv. 2999 ff.

In the Provençal *Cour d'Amour* already described,[1] the names Love's barons show the same group of ideas that we find in Grou *B* of the statutes — Joi, Solatz, Ardiment, Cortesia, Bon' Esperanz Paor, Largueza, Domnei, Celament, and Dolsa Companhia.

Finally in the *Breviari d'Amor*, a manual of conduct begun b Matfre Ermengaud in 1288, these ideas, found scattered through th writings of the troubadours, are collected and arranged. The auth himself describes the part dealing with love as "le perilhos tract d'amor de donas segon que han tractat li antic trobador en lors ca sos."[2] Rules are laid down for ladies[3] as well as for their lover They are instructed to be neat, to have good manners both in th house and in the street, to be gay and courteous, to keep good co pany, and not to stop to speak on their way from church. If an one seeks their love they are not to shriek or complain to their hu bands, for such as make most noise are not the most careful guar ians of their honor. A lady should be sweet and gracious, y dignified and reserved, and ought to snub sharply all coarse and di courteous lovers. A specimen dialogue after the fashion of those i Andreas is given.[4]

C. French.

In this matter of the Statutes of Love, as in the case of the centr conception of the Court, Old French literature furnishes the large contribution. Incidental allusions in narrative poems and form

---

[1] See p. 30, above.

[2] *Le Breviari d'Amor de Matfre Ermengaud,* ed. by Gabriel Azaïs, Béziers a Paris, 1862–81, II, 430. Cf. Raimon Vidal, *So fo el temps c'om era iays,* ed. Max Cornicelius, Berlin, 1888, which I have not seen, but which, from the descri tion given by Stimming, Gröber's *Grundriss,* II, Abt. 2, p. 12, seems to deal in comprehensive way with much of the same material as Matfre.

[3] *Ibid., Cosselh a las donas,* II, 522.

[4] The main points in the *Cosselh als Amadors* are these: Larguesza (vv. 31,9 ff.); Ardimen (vv. 32,125 ff.); Cortezia (vv. 32,191 ff.); Umilitat (vv. 32,270 ff Domney, "l'art de courtiser les dames d'après les règles de la chevalerie" (v 32,327 ff.); Alegransa (vv. 32,378 ff.); Retenemen, *i.e.* restraint, moderati (vv. 32,430 ff.); Ensenhamen (vv. 32,499 ff.); Proeza (vv. 32,568 ff.). The e position of each virtue is supported by quotations from the troubadours.

lists in didactic and allegorical works combine to form a plentiful stream from the twelfth century downwards.

It is in the first of these ways, *i.e.,* incidentally, that the story-tellers of the time of Queen Eleanor and her daughter contribute. In Marie de France the qualities of knighthood are those implied in the constant approving use of the adjectives *pruz, curteis, vaillant, hardi, fier, franc, large,* and *sage.*[1] In Chrétien de Troyes the same virtues are emphasized, and in the *Cligès*[2] especially several of the traditional symptoms recur frequently.

> Vos qui d'amor vos feites sage,
> Qui les costumes et l'usage
> De sa cort maintenez a foi,
> N'onques ne faussastes sa loi,
> Que qu'il vos an deüst cheoir,
> Dites moi, se l'an puet veoir
> Rien qui por amor abelisse,
> Que l'an n'an tressaille et palisse?   (vv. 3865-72.)

The necessity for secrecy is also fully recognized, and the heroes ive up to the requirements of such theoretical passages as this in natters of paleness, fainting, and sleeplessness.

In *Venus la Deesse d'Amors,*[3] when the lover lies listening to the ongs of the nightingale, the bird shows an intimate knowledge of he tradition:

> Hom qui bien aime doit auoir cuer ioli
> Et souent tristre et irie et mari.
> Si doit trambler mainte fois san froidor
> Et doit suer mante fois sans chalor
> Et sospirer et cangier sa color
> Et de pensees languir et nuit et ior.

ROMAN DE LA ROSE.

The commandments laid down by the God of Love in the work f Guillaume de Lorris are not numbered, but otherwise they are

---

[1] See E. Schiött, *L'Amour et les Amoureux dans les Lais de Marie de France,* und, 1889.   [3] See p. 42, above.
[2] Ed. W. Foerster, Halle, 1888.

clearly conceived as statutes to be observed by all true lovers. They
almost all come under Groups *B* and *C*, and are on the whole elevated
in tone.

The main points, severely condensed, are these [1]:

GROUP *B*. — To leave villany and act as a gentleman (English
vv. 2175–2222 ; French, vv. 2159–94).

To avoid ribaldry ; to serve and honor women, defend them against
slander, and endeavor to please them and get their good-will (English, vv. 2223 ff.; French, vv. 2195 ff.).

To avoid pride, and yet to be careful and neat in dress and person (English, vv. 2239 ff.; French, vv. 2211 ff.).

To be always cheerful (under which come more detailed instructions : as, to use one's accomplishments to entertain people
by making mirth, by feats of horsemanship, by singing, playing,
dancing, and composing songs) (English, vv. 2290 ff.; French,
vv. 2261 ff.).

To be liberal in gifts (English, vv. 2328 ff.; French, vv.
2297 ff.).

Then, more concisely, the requirements are summed up in the
English version, vv. 2342 ff. and the French text, vv. 2310 ff., as
follows : to be courteous, void of pride, merry, liberal ; to love without repentance; to dwell in thought on coming meetings; to give the
heart entirely, and to one only.

GROUP *C*. — The main symptoms are given in the passage immediately following the foregoing, thus: solitariness, alternations
heat and cold, absent-mindedness, restlessness in absence, insatiable
desire to look on the lady, bashfulness, secret haunting of her neighborhood, dumbness in her presence, sleeplessness, dreaming of her
and waking to disappointment, humility, rising before dawn and
going to her house in all weathers, and leanness.

GROUP *D*. — The clearest trace of the *Ars Amatoria* is found in
the instructions to give presents to the maid and other servant
(English, v. 2720; French, v. 2668).[2]

---

[1] References to the English version are to Skeat's text, and references to
French version are to the edition of P. Marteau, 5 vols., Orléans, 1878–80.

[2] But see notes in Marteau's edition, *passim*.

In Jean de Meun's part of the *Roman de la Rose* a short passage occurs in which the principal points are gathered into a few lines:

> Vilenie
> Doi foïr, et que ne mesdie ;
> Salus doi tost donner et rendre ;
> A dire ordure ne doi tendre ;
> A toutes femmes honorer
> M'estuet en tous tens laborer ;
> Orgoil foïr ; cointe me tiengne,
> Jolis et renvoisiés deviengne ;
> A larges estre m'abandoingne ;
> En ung seul leu tout mon cuer doingne (vv. 10,768–77).[1]

From this point on, though differences of phrasing and differences of stress occur, the general character of these statutes is fairly constant.

HUON DE MERY.

Huon de Mery (*ca.* 1235), in *Le Tornoiement d'Antéchrist,*[2] makes Prowess, Courtesy, and Largesse the attendants of Love.

THIBAUT.

Li Romanz de la Poire[3] of Thibaut is full of allusions to the qualities of knightly lovers. The ambassadors sent by Love to the hero have each certain lessons to inculcate, Franchise especially insisting on the lover's being "douz et franz et afetiez" (v. 1074), on the importance of *cortoisie* (v. 1081), on absence of pride (v. 1092), on courage (v. 1114), and on his obligation to serve, fear, and honor his lady (v. 1091). The speech of Love himself (vv. 1234 ff.) on the degeneracy of the lovers of the time continually lays stress on the same qualities, and the passage in which the lover describes his agony of despair abounds in the usual symptoms (see especially vv. 1986 ff.).

---

[1] Ed. Marteau, III, 26. It should be said also that the directions for personal cleanliness follow Ovid closely.

[2] Ed. Tarbé, p. 51. See p. 48, above.

[3] See p. 56, above.

Similar symptoms are alluded to in an anonymous *Lai d'Amours*[1]
(*ca.* 1250), in which Love's arrow is called

> Li darz qui fait muer colors,
> Li darz qui ocit et refride, . . .
> Li darz qui les dormanz esveille, etc. (vv. 408 ff.).

RICHARD DE FOURNIVAL.

La Puissance d'Amour[2] of Richard de Fournival (d. before 1260)
is a prose Art of Love in which instructions are given for choosing
and winning a lady. Four kinds of love are distinguished, and
appropriate methods of procedure are recommended for each.

1. He who loves "pour honneur et pour miex valoir" should have
agreeable speech, generosity, courtesy, and diligence in seeking to
please his lady.

2. He who loves with a view to marriage should be gentle, kindly,
and desirous of a good reputation.

3. He who loves for solace and companionship "doit estre baus et
jolis en point et en saison," ought to get the lady's confidence, never
to bore her, and ought to induce her to accept gifts.

4. He who loves for profit also receives appropriate instructions.

The *Conseils d'Amour* of the same author is a book of directions for
conduct in love affairs written for a "sister."[3]   These do not touch
the statutes at many points or closely, being much taken up with
advice against arrogance on the one hand and too ready yielding on
the other.   It is with reference to the first of these points that an
adaptation of the story of the *Lai du Trot* from Andreas Capellanus
is introduced.

DOTRINE D'AMOR.

From a MS. dated 1287, F. Wolf has printed a *Dotrine d'Amor*
the chief part of which is taken from Andreas Capellanus, som

---

[1] Ed. by G. Paris, *Romania*, VII, 407–15.

[2] Analyzed by P. Paris in *Bibliothèque de l'École des Chartes*, 1e sér., II, 43–7

[3] See P. Paris, *ibid.*, pp. 47 ff.

[4] F. Wolf, *Ueber einige altfranz. Doctrinen und Allegorien von der Minne,*
Denkschriften der kais. Akad. d. Wissenschaften zu Wien, Phil.-hist. Classe, 186
XIII, 178 ff.

assages being literally translated.   It contains *Li comandemenz 'amors:* "donques chascuns qui viaut amer, covient savoir huit rincipax comandemenz d'amor, se il viaut joir de lui":

1. Cortoisie sanz aucune vilenie.
2. Largece sanz avarice.
3. Non amer fame d'autrui.
4. Non amer fame de religion.
5. Non eschafer-soi de celi que no covient d'amor.
6. Estre creenter d'amor.
7. Honorer les fames an totes guises.
8. Ardimanz sanz coardise.

ROBERT DE BLOIS.

Le Chastiement des Dames[1] of Robert de Blois consists of instruc- ons to ladies on their relations to men and on behavior generally. ome of these coincide with the statutes, and still further resem- lances, treating of love less specifically, occur in the passage which illows the *Chastiement* proper.   Secrecy is thus commanded:

> S'aucuns de vostre amor vous prie,
> Gardez ne vous en vantez mie;
> C'est vilonie de vanter (vv. 163–5).

eatness of person:

> Voz mains moult netement gardez,
> Sovent les ongles recopez,
> Ne doivent pas la char passer,
> C'ordure n'i puist amasser (vv. 463–6).

hen more concisely:

> Amors essauce cortoisie,
> Amors het toute vilonie,
> Amors contrueve les chançons,
> Amors fet doner les biaus dons.
> Amors ne set rien de perece,
> Amors est mere de larguece (vv. 910–15).

---

[1] Barbazan and Méon, *Fabliaux et Contes*, Paris, 1808, II, 184–219.   See also Meyer, *Romania*, XVI, 25 ff., XVII, 282 ff.; and *Robert von Blois sämmtliche* 'erke, ed. by J. Ulrich, Berlin, 1889–95, III, 62, 70, II, 120.

The symptoms of love are also given:

> Tout lor solaz, toute lor vie,
> Et main et soir est de muser
> Privéement, et de pensser (vv. 957–9).

> La dolors que li amanz sent,
> C'est souspirer et baailler,
> Petit dormir et moult veillier,
> Sanz froidure sentir, trambler,
> Et sanz trop chaut avoir suer,
> Mangier petit et boivre mains,
> Estendre, pleindre et estre sains ;
> Descolorer et amaigrir,
> Et mas et pales devenir (vv. 1039–47).

PHILIPPE DE REMI.

The ten pains inflicted by Trahison on the lover in Philippe de Remi's *Salu d'Amours*[1] turn out to be merely symptoms of love-sickness. They are the following: (1) to remain always in the prison of Pensée ; (2) to sigh ; (3) to doubt ; (4) to be wakeful ; (5) "d'estendillier"[2]; (6) to burn with desire ; (7) to carry always in his heart the image of his lady ; (8) to be jealous ; (9) to be alternately hot and cold ; (10) to despair.

GUILLAUME DE MACHAUT.

In Guillaume de Machaut's *Dit du Vergier*[3] the same symptoms of fever, change of color, and sighing are found,[4] and the god, advising the poet about his love affairs, tells him to be loyal, secret, and diligent in pleasing the lady.[5]

RAOUL DE HOUDAN.

Li Romans des Eles[6] of Raoul de Houdan is a didactic allegory designed to teach knights true courtesy. There is a kind of knight

---

[1] See pp. 59–60, above.   [4] Ed. Tarbé, p. 27.

[2] For the sense cf. *Rom.* XXIII, 130, n. 2, and Suchier's ed., II, 379.

[3] See p. 61, above.   [5] *Ibid.*, pp. 37–38.

[6] Ed. by Aug. Scheler, Brussels, 1868. See also F. Wolf, *Ueber Raoul de Houdenc* in *Denkscriften der kais. Akad.*, Vienna, 1865, XIV, 153 ff.

ys Raoul, who so prides himself on his valorous deeds that he
inks he can dispense with the more elegant virtues. But "la
rouesse est vaine et ne confère aucun titre à l'estime, si elle n'est
ɔurvue de deux ailes, qui sont Largece et Cortoisie." Each of
ese wings is composed of seven feathers, Largece, the right wing,
ɔntaining (1) Hardement, the mother of Largece; (2) freedom
ɔm petty economies; (3) lack of ulterior motives in giving; (4)
ithfulness in keeping promises; (5) giving quickly; (6) giving
ɛnerously; (7) "bel doner à mangier."

Cortoisie, the left wing, consists of (1) honor to Holy Church;
) absence of pride; (3) absence of boasting; (4) joyfulness and
spectful treatment of women; (5) absence of envy; (6) guarding
ɛe tongue from slander and ribaldry; (7) being a lover and a
ɑtient one.

Though this poem is not strictly a Court of Love poem at all, and
ɪough the precepts are meant to direct chivalrous conduct gener-
ly, yet it is to be noted how close the list comes to the usual com-
ɑndments of love.

BAUDOUIN DE CONDÉ.

A novel way of indicating the qualities of the true lover appears
ɪ the *Prison d'Amours* of Baudouin de Condé.[1] Here the Prison
described as founded on precious stones:

> Car c'est biautés, sens et proëce,
> Honors, cortoizie et larguece,
> Douce raizons, parole estable,
> Simples regars et amiable,
> Nobilités sans felonnie,
> Acointance sans vilonnie,
> Biau maintien, biau fait et biel dit,
> Langue sans amer, sans mesdit, etc. (vv. 331–8).

JEAN DE CONDÉ.

Jean de Condé's *La Messe des Oisiaus*[2] has a unique importance.
'he religious type of the Court of Love allegory so predominates

---

[1] See p. 66, above.   [2] See pp. 67 ff., above.

over the feudal that the commandments, instead of taking a legal form, are thrown into a sermon delivered by the Parrot.

Four virtues, the preacher says, must be cultivated by all lovers.

1. Obedience. — The lover must obey his lady in everything that may please her, in word and deed.

2. Patience. — He must willingly suffer the grief, pain, evil fatigue, and labor that come from loving, and must never complain If he is slandered, he must suffer in silence and not give place to anger that might bring on annoyance.

3. Loyalty. — He is no lover who is not loyal. He must keep secret all his trysts, bring peace and honor to his lady, and never wish to change her for a richer or more beautiful one.

4. Hope. — He must joyfully live in hope to attain his desires and must " son cors tenir joliement."

It is hardly necessary to point out that though the form of statement is changed here, the subject-matter is simply that of the usual statutes.

CHASTEL DE LEAL AMOUR.

Another novel form of the statutes, probably also showing ecclesiastical influence, is found in the *Chastel de leal Amour*,[1] where they appear as the answers to questions in a kind of catechism.

1. Du chastel d'amours vous demeauns
   Dunt est li primer fundement?
   > D'amer lealment.

2. Or me nomez le mestre moeurs
   Qe plus li fet fort et seürs?
   > Celer sagement.

3. Dites moi qy sunt kernels,
   Les siates et les quariaus?
   > Regard atreiaunt.

4. Només moi ly porter et ly gaite
   Qe l'entrer deferme et gayte.
   > D'amy danger.

---

[1] MS. of the fifteenth century, formerly no. 8336 in Sir T. Phillipps's library at Cheltenham. See P. Meyer in *Romania*, XIII, 503–5, whose text I follow. He mentions five other MSS. of the same work: *Bulletin de la Soc. des anc. Textes franç.*, 1875, pp. 26 and 30.

5. Q'est la clef, saver m'estoet,
   Qe la porte defermer poet?
      Continuelment prier.
6. Nomez la sale & le manoir
   La ou poet primes joye avoir.
      Doucement dalier.
7. Après la garde me nomez
   Par quels le chastel est gardez.
      Par contenyr nettement,
      Par honorer tote gent,
      Par vestir corteisement,
      Par tenyr simplement.
8. Dites, sire, q'est la dart d'amour vileyn
   Qe come pys me fet joe le plus eym?
      Faus semblaunt.

  . . . .

21. Quele chose est que les amauns plus alleve
   & que prymes les fet joye avoyr,
   E memes cele chose plus les greve,
   E les fet mettre en nounchaloyr?
      Richesse.

WATRIQUET DE COUVIN.

In the poems by Watriquet de Couvin already described there are
abundant allusions to the virtues prescribed by the statutes, Cour-
oisie, Largesse, Netteté, and so on.[1] Somewhat more explicit is
the *Dis du Preu Chevalier*,[2] in which the knight is instructed as to
the way to "haute prouesce" by the stages of Vigour (whence he
sets out), Renommée, the hostel of Courtoisie and Largesce, Valour,
and Hardement, to Prouesce, Science, Loiauté and Vraie Amour.[3]
The same author's *Dit des huit Couleurs*[4] represents Venus as direct-
ing young bachelors in the ways of "prouesce" and love. The
instruction is given by way of interpreting the "eight colors" of a

---

[1] See pp. 72, ff., above.
[2] *Dits de Watriquet de Couvin*, ed. by Aug. Scheler, Brussels, 1868, pp. 187 ff.
[3] Prouesce and the three other virtues live together (vv. 252–5).
[4] Ed. Scheler, pp. 311 ff.

marvellous peacock. *Li Dis de l'Escole d'Amours*[1] is of the same
class and puts emphasis

> En beau priant en temps et liex,
> Et que li cors est gais et liez (vv. 113–14).

Other works of Watriquet de Couvin abound in similar impli-
cations.

JEAN FROISSART.

The close resemblance between Froissart and Watriquet de Couvin has already been pointed out.[2] In *Le Temple d'Onnour* (*ca*
1386) the figure of the steps, which we found in Guiraut de Calanso
and also in Watriquet, is elaborated as follows: the knights guarding the steps by which the bridegroom ascends represent the virtues
of Avis, Hardement, Emprise, Atemprance, Justice, Loyauté, Largece; and the ladies guarding the steps at the bride's entrance are
called Maniere, Humilité, Francise, Courtoisie, Carité, Pité, and
Fois. This poem contains also a sermon bidding the knight honor
the church and be to his friends

> Debonnaires, courtois et gens
> Et douls com pucelete en feste (422–3),

and to his enemies

> Fel, outrageus, hardis et fiers (v. 425).

The instructions given by Love in *La Cour de May*[3] are directed
against lying, boasting, and "tristesse," and consideration for ladies
is strongly insisted on. The inscription over the portico, against
liars and deceivers, has already been quoted.[4] In the same poem
Congnoissance also dwells on "leauté en couraige," "verité en
langaige," and "honnesté en usage" (vv. 76 ff.).

The statutes of Group *A* are also represented by the God of
Love's commandment:

> De moy tousjours servir et craindre,

and in the advice of Courtoisie:

> Tenir vers amours leaulté
> Puisqu'il lui a fait feaulté (vv. 1481–2).

---

[1] Ed. Scheler, pp. 355 ff.		[2] See p. 80, above.		[3] *Ibid.*		[4] *Ibid.*

LES ÉCHECS AMOUREUX.

The rubrics of *Les Échecs Amoureux*[1] indicate that in this poem Venus gives commandments, and three of the virtues which she inculcates are mentioned: Loyalty, Secrecy, and Diligence.

LA PUISSANCE D'AMOUR.

An unpublished MS. of the second half of the fourteenth century contains another *Puissance d'Amour*• (to be distinguished from Richard de Fournival's), called also *Consaus d'Amours*.[2] It is a dialogue in prose between the author and the Duke of Brabant, and the first part is after the manner of Andreas Capellanus. The five qualities of a lover are thus stated: (1) qu'il soit discret; (2) qu'il soit boins; (3) qu'il ne soit ireux; (4) qu'il ne soit orghilleus; (5) qu'il soit loiaus.

CHRISTINE DE PISAN.

The conception of the Statutes of Love was familiar enough to Christine de Pisan. They are given, for example, in *L'Epistre au Dieu d'Amours*[3]:

> Et ceulz tienent mes vrais commandemens,
> Justes, loiaulz, et bons enseignemens ;
> Si leur deffens villenie et meffait,
> Et leur commans poursuivre honneur de fait,
> Estre loiaulz, secrez et voir disans,
> Larges, courtois, et fuïr mesdisans,
> Humbles et doulz, jolis et assesmés,
> Fermes et frans, poursuivre a estre amez,
> Armes suïr a ceulx qu'il apartient
> Loz acquerir.   Qui en ce point se tient,
> Sache pour vray que ne lui fauldray mie
> A lui donner dame belle et amie (vv. 73-84).

---

[1] See pp. 82 ff., above.

[2] F. Wolf, *Ueber einige altfranz. Doctrinen*, etc., in *Denkschriften der kais. kad. d. Wissenschaften zu Wien, Phil.-hist. Classe*, 1864, XIII, 135 ff.

[3] *Œuvres Poétiques*, ed. by M. Roy, Paris, 1886-96 (*Soc. des anc. Textes franç.*), , 3 ; and see p. 84, above.

Several of Christine's ballades are devoted to describing the ideal knight and lover. No. lxiv [1] of her *Cent Balades*, beginning

> Sages et bons, gracieux et courtois,
> Doivent estre par droit tous chevaliers,

is an excellent example.

LE LIVRE DES CENT BALLADES.

One of the most interesting as well as one of the most exhaustive treatments of the character of the true lover in mediæval literature is to be found in *Le Livre des Cent Ballades*,[2] which may have been written by the famous Maréchal Bouciquaut and his companions. The editor dates it between 1386 and 1392. The instructions for knightly conduct are fitted into the following framework:

The young man who tells the story represents himself as meeting, on the road between Pont de Cé and Angers, an old knight who guesses from his appearance that he is in love. This conjecture turning out to be correct, it gives the veteran an excuse for explaining in a long series of ballades the rules of loyal and honorable love, which Amour had given him when he was in the same case. These rules are in substance as follows.

To be joyous day and night, to be envious of no one, to love God, to destroy no good man's reputation, to support no bad cause, to love his lady, to praise " ses faiz, ses riz, ses jeux," and to be curious to find things to please her (v, xxiv, etc.).

To be "gent," "doulz et plaisant," not to be too silent but to speak seasonably and graciously, to clothe himself neatly, not to slander any one (vi, vii, etc.).

To be generous in giving, to be secret, not to be proud, to sing, dance, joust, and fight well (vii, ix).

If one's own country is at peace, to get the lady's consent to go abroad to war; to discipline one's followers (viii).

To spare no pain, peril, or labor to win honor (ix).

By following these commands, the old knight says he had won the

---

[1] *Œuvres*, I, 65; cf. also I, 55.

[2] *Le Livre des Cent Ballades*, ed. by De Queux de Saint-Hilaire, Paris, 1868. For authorship, etc., see the editor's Introduction and *Rom.*, I, 370.

love of the loveliest of all ladies, and life had been paradise to him. The youth declares his resolve to follow the same path (li), and after expatiating further on the beauty of loyalty and the misery of falseness, the old knight takes his leave (lii).

The youth next finds himself in the midst of a joyous company disporting themselves on the banks of the Loire. But he strays off alone to gaze on the water and think of his mistress, when a lady, observing his lovesick appearance, comes to him with advice. She is surprised at his determination to be loyal, and prophesies great dejection for him if his mistress should turn out to be unkind to him. The instructions she offers are on a much lower plane than those of the old knight, though some are naturally the same. Thus she too tells him to be "gracieux, secret, débonnaire, joieux, plaisant, . . . lié, gent, joliz, et gaillart" (lxii, lxxviii, xcii). But the burden of her discourse is not to be too discriminating, to be pleasing to all women, and to take what favors they offer him. Persistency is especially recommended:

> Mais les belles que prierez,
> Poursuivez-les jusques en fin
> Humblement . . . simplement,

without long speeches but also without long intervals, and "main, soir, nuit, et jour" (lxiii). Flattery is to be used. She dwells at great length on the risks he runs by placing his love entirely on one woman, and displays great ingenuity in her casuistry.

But the youth remains unconvinced, and they agree to refer the question to some knights of renown in love and war. The lady refuses to defend sheer unfaithfulness, but wants to know whether

> Qu'estre secret et plaisant,
> Pourchaçant
> En mains lieux joie pleniere,
> Ne soit fait de vray amant.

Thirteen ballades [1] in reply are given, the great majority favoring the position of the old knight. See especially the eleventh:

> J'aray Dame et Seigneur
> En ciel un Dieu, en terre une Déesse.

---

[1] For the 12th and 13th see L. Pannier, *Rom.*, I, 367–73.

In this book we have very clearly opposed two different ideals of love, of both of which we have had abundant indications in the two preceding centuries, though we have not before found them thus clearly contrasted. That of the lady is the old attitude which is most clearly represented by Ovid and his mediæval imitators, with some of the grossness left out, but with an essentially immoral element at the heart of it. It is lower than the usual troubadour ideal, inasmuch as that made much of the virtue of loyalty to one woman at a time. That of the old knight, on the other hand, is loftier than the troubadour's, since it is clearly honorable love with a view to marriage which he recommends and praises. It includes all the nobler attributes of the mediæval " gentle " knight, and all the reverential devotion to woman which characterizes the chivalrous youth of all times. It is, on the whole, the finest ideal to be found in the field which we are at present attempting to cover, in the twelfth, thirteenth, or fourteenth century. In the fifteenth, parallels are more easily discovered.

A very delightful picture of the realization of this ideal is to be found in the life of the famous chevalier who is supposed to be one of the authors of *Le Livre des Cent Ballades.* In *Le Livre des Faits du Maréchal Bouciquaut,*[1] we read that when the "gracieux jouvencel" began to feel the arrows of love he became more pleasant and gracious than ever. He made poetry, was more careful about his dress, and constantly sought to distinguish himself in arms to win his lady's favor. If she was present no one surpassed him "en gracieuseté et courtoisie, en chanter, en danser, en rire, en parler, et en tou. ses maintiens." He wrote chansons and rondeaux, and recited them in such a way as to convey secretly to his lady their application to her

Ains devant elle et entre toutes dames estoit plus doux et benigne qu' une pucelle. Toutes servoit, toutes honoroit, pour l'amour d'une. So parler estoit gracieux, courtois, et craintif devant sa Dame. Si celoit s. pensée à toute gent, et sagement savoit jecter son regard et ses semblan que nul n'apperceust où son cuer estoit. Humblement et douteusemer servoit Amour et sa Dame, car il lui sembloit qu'il n'avoit mie assez faic de bien pour si haute chose requerre et demander comme l'amour de dame

Here surely was the knight without reproach !

---

[1] See Appendix to Saint-Hilaire's edition of *Le Livre des Cent Ballades.*

THE WOLFENBÜTTEL MS.

More formally stated, but somewhat similar in spirit to the rules of the old knight in *Le Livre des Cent Ballades* are ten commandments "moult honnêtes" drawn up by an unknown author, which "fait Amours à ses sergens, auxquels tous cœurs loiaulx doibvent doulcement et sans contredit obéir." [1]   The statutes are these :

    I. C'est que d'orgueil et d'envye soit exempt en tous temps.
    II. La parole ne dye qui a nulley puist estre nuisans.
    III. A toute gent soit acquointable en parlers plaisans.
    IV. E toutes villonies soit par tout eschievans.
    V. D'estre faitis et quointes doibt tousjours estre en grans.
    VI. De honnourer toutes femmes ne soit ja recreans.
    VII. En toutes compaignies sois et lyes et ioians.
    VIII. Nulx [2] villains mots ne soit hors de sa bouche partans.
    IX. Soit larges aux petis, aux moyens et aux grans.
    X. En ung tout seul lieu soit son cœur perseverant.

> Qui ces commans ne garde
> Secret et obéissant,
> Aux biens d'amours qu'on garde,
> Ne soit participant.

ALAIN CHARTIER.

In the works of Alain Chartier the statutes are nowhere formally drawn up, though the traditional qualities are often mentioned. Thus in *La Belle Dame sans Mercy* Secrecy is commanded :

> Nul ne se doit enamourer,
> S'il n'a cueur de celer l'emprise :
> Car vanteur n'est à honnorer,
> Puis que sa langue le desprise. [3]

---

[1] Quoted by De Roisin in his translation of Diez (*Essai sur les Cours d'Amour*), Paris, 1842, p. 81, note, from a XV century MS. in the library at Wolfenbüttel.

[2] Printed *Aulx*.

[3] *Œuvres*, ed. Du Chesne, 1617, p. 521 ; cf. the Middle English translation by Sir Richard Ros, vv. 737-40, Skeat, *Chaucerian Pieces*, p. 322.

The names of the "Hospitaliers" in the *Hospital d'Amour*[1] are almost all names of qualities required by the statutes.

CHARLES D'ORLÉANS.

The statutes[2] in the *Poème de la Prison* of the Duke of Orléans are divided into two groups : (1) four commandments which every subject of the God of Love must swear to observe; (2) six rules to which the lover takes no oath, but which are recommended as likely to be of service. Beauté it is who, under instructions from the god himself, draws up these rules and administers the oath.

The four imperative precepts are these: (1) to hold the God of Love as "seigneur and souverain," to be a faithful subject, and to spare no pains in his service; (2) to love in one place only; (3) to keep counsel, and not to give slanderers occasion to talk, by foolish words and glances; (4) not to boast of ladies' favors. In these we have, as it were, the binding rules of the game, the first being, like the first in the English *Court of Love*, a formal statute in keeping with the feudal situation, and the others the points which were absolutely essential if the practice of courtly love was to go on at all.

Most of the six minor rules ought to come under Group *B*, as simply regulations for gentlemanly conduct; but they are stated with the proviso that no lover is bound to keep them "se son prouffit n'y voit." The poet, then, regarded them rather as devices to help in winning the lady (a sort of elevated version of the Ovidian precepts), and so they may be referred to Group *D*.

> Le premier est qu'il se tiengne jolis,
> Car les dames le tiennent à grant pris.
> Le second est que tres courtoisement
> Soy maintendra et gracieusement.
> Le tiers point est que, selon sa puissance,
> Querra honneur et poursuivra vaillance.

---

[1] See pp. 87 ff., above. The poem is no longer ascribed to Chartier.

[2] *Poésies complètes de Ch. d'Orléans*, ed. by Charles d'Héricault, Paris, 1896, I 10–12.

> Le quatriesme qu'il soit plain de largesse,
> Car c'est chose qui avance noblesse.
> Le cinquiesme qu'il suivra compaignie
> Amant honneur et fuiant villenie.
>
> Le sixiesme point et le derrenier
> Est qu'il sera diligent escollier,
> En aprenant tous les gracieux tours,
> A son povoir, qui servent en amours.
> C'est assavoir à chanter et dansser,
> Faire chançons et balades rimer,
> Et tous autres joyeux esbatemens (sts. 37–8).

These commandments will be discussed further in the chapter on
e immediate sources of the English *Court of Love*.[1]

LAWS OF THE ROUND TABLE.

It will be remembered that in the account of the longer *Code
Amour* in Andreas Capellanus a legend was told connecting it
th the court of King Arthur. This association appears again in
me of the later prose romances, where there are to be found lists
Laws of the Round Table, giving the qualities requisite before a
ight was admitted to fellowship in Arthur's hall. The following
oup is representative, though much longer codes occur.

1. All knights must give proof of extraordinary prowess.
2. They must have shown honor and respect to ladies, and, at
me time, love.
3. One knight must not try to gain another's lady.
4. A knight must not take love favors from a damsel if she
iously resists.
5. A knight must never refuse a lady's request, and must be pre-
red to undertake battle for her, especially if it is to save her honor.
6. A knight must observe strict silence about favors granted him
a lady, and about this only may lie.[2]

---

[1] See chap. vii, below.
[2] I follow the account in *Bibl. Univers. des Romans*, Paris, July, 1776, pp. 100–2,
ich cites *Le Roman du Roi Artus et des Compagnons de la Table Ronde*, Paris,
8, 3 vols. See also *Hist. Univ. des Théâtres*, IX, 229 ff., Paris, 1780.

MARTIAL D'AUVERGNE.

The lover's symptoms appear again in *L'Amant rendu Cordelier*
Martial d'Auvergne (vv. 161–214).[1] The insistence on cheerfulnes
which occurs so often elsewhere, appears in an amusing form in t
fortieth of the same author's *Arrêts d'Amours* [2] in which

> Une dame contre son amy demande qu'il soit condemné à fuyr co
> paignies melancholieuses, et que la court meist telle provision en sa p
> sonne, qu'il deveinst joyeux, comme il avoit esté.

D. ITALIAN.

Formal codes of love occur very seldom in Italian literature.
the Sicilian school we naturally find, as we found in the Provenç
troubadours, single statutes, especially belonging to Group *C*, sca
tered through the lyrics. Thus, for example, we have the palene
of the lover mentioned by Re Enzo (A.D. 1225–72):

> Ed in tanti tormenti
> Abbondo in mala guisa,
> Che'l natural colore
> Tutto perdo, sì'l cor si sbatte e lagna.[3]

Later, in Guittone d'Arezzo, we have a series of twenty-four so
nets[4] which Goldschmidt takes together as forming a kind of *A
Amandi*. These consist chiefly of the commonplaces of the tro
badours, but show also the influence of Andreas Capellanus a
Ovid. Thus sonnets 406–8 define Love; 409 advises the lover
declare his passion; 410 suggests different courses according
the lady's attitude; 411 shows that too much responsiveness mu
not be looked for at once; 412 provides for the lady's coldness; 4
interprets her glances; 414 shows how further behavior must
determined by the relative social positions of the lovers. It is cle

---

[1] Ed. by A. de Montaiglon, Paris, 1881, for *Soc. des anc. Textes franç.*, p. 12.

[2] For an account of these *Arrêts*, see p. 243, below.

[3] Nannucci, *Manuale della Letteratura italiana del Primo Secolo*, 3d ed., Fl
ence, 1874, I, 69; D'Ancona e Bacci, *Manuale della Lett. ital.*, I, 37.

[4] D'Ancona and Comparetti, *Le antiche Rime Volgari*, Bologna, 1875–88, I
82 ff.

t it is to Group *D* that Guittone chiefly contributes; yet more
:y qualities are found in passages like this :

> E' vuole esser l'om soferente bene
> Ver tutta noia che di ciò gli avengna,
> Et quanto più la donna orgolglio tene
> Più umil far la sua parola e dengna.[1]

)ther poets commend Secrecy, Falsehood for the sake of Love,
l so on; and the figure of the steps of Love which we found first
ʒuiraut de Calanso seems to have been copied from him by the
bate di Tiboli in a sonnet which occurs in a *tenzone* written with
opo da Lentini.[2]
Ve have, however, an anonymous sonnet[3] which comes much
rer the regular Court of Love Statutes than these fragmentary
:rences.   It gives eight commandments, all on the traditional lines :

> Otto comandamenti face Amore
> A ciascun gentil core innamorato :
> Lo primo che cortese in ciascun lato
> Sia; è 'l secondo, largo a tutte l'ore ;
> Non amar donna altrui è 'l terzo onore ;
> Rilegion guardar dal quarto lato ;
> Ben provedere porre sì 'n su' grato
> È 'l quinto che de' l'omo avere in core.
> Or lo sesto è cortese al mi' parere,
> Che d'esser credentier fermo comanda ;
> Col sette a presso, onoranza tenere
> Al' amorose donne con piacere ;
> Donandoci poi l'otto per vivanda,
> Che ardimento ci dobiamo avere.

FRANCESCO DA BARBERINO.

ʌ collection of statutes with a Court of Love setting occurs in *Li
·umenti d'Amore*[4] of Francesco da Barberino, in the fourteenth

---

D'Ancona and Comparetti, no. cdxxviii.
D'Ancona and Comparetti, no. cccxxvi, and cf. *Zt. f. rom. Phil.*, X, 586.
Ibid., cmxlix, V, 253.
The account given here is drawn from an analysis by A. Thomas, *Franc. da
berino et la Littérature Provençale en Italie au Moyen Âge*, in *Bibl. des Écoles
·ç. d'Athènes et de Rome*, fasc. 35, Paris, 1883, p. 57.

century. By Amore, however, the author means, not the Cupid of the usual Court of Love allegory, but "the principle of all good." Hence the statutes are general instructions in morals, etiquette, and worldly wisdom. The plot, so far as it concerns our subject, is as follows :

At the request of Love, the poet collects the servants of the god at his castle. Then through Eloquence, Love promulgates his statutes, — the "Documenti" which are to be observed by all who aim at the glory of serving him. These have been collected by twelve ladies, with such names as Patience, Hope, Prudence, Glory, Justice, Innocence, Gratitude, and Eternity; and the poet is charged to communicate the laws to all who are not able to be present at the parliament.

Each chapter opens with a miniature representing one of these ladies, and there follows an explanation of the miniature, after which the allegory is dropped for pure didacticism.

E. GERMAN.

In Germany we do not find in connection with the statutes any such characteristic national forms as we found in the central idea of the Court of Love allegory. The numbered commandments occur several times, but the virtues insisted on are those with which we are already familiar.

In *Die Zehen Gebote der Minne,*[1] a poem of the last half of the thirteenth or beginning of the fourteenth century, the following are the points of which expositions are given: (1) Triwe, (2) Zuht, (3) Stätichait, (4) Gedulde, (5) Hübeschait, (6) Milt, (7) Verswigenhait, (8) Balthait, (9) Mass, (10) Beschaidenhait. The virtue of "Mass" or Measure, which we have not usually found in such lists, is, of course, merely a borrowing from the books on conduct in general, which it held a very important place. The poem ends by enjoining women to favor those who obey these commandments, and to be chaste and faithful.

---

[1] *Miscellaneen zur Geschichte der teutschen Literatur*, ed. by B. J. Docen, Munich, 1807, II, 171–88.

In *Ain Mynn Red von Hertzen und von Leib*,[1] which has already
en noticed,[2] Venus teaches the hero seven virtues from the Book
Love.   These are as follows :

> Die erst ist hübsch mit stättem můt,
> Die ander triu vor valsch behůt,
> Die dritt gůt sitt mit freyem leben,
> Die viert milt mit masz geben,
> Die fünfft mit rümen und verschwigen,
> So bist du lobs unuerzigen,
> Die sechszt manhaft mit gůter tatt,
> Die sibent zier mit gůter watt (vv. 213-20).

Der Mynn Regel,[3] in the same collection, similarly names Zucht,
Masz, Scham, Triu, Stätt, Verschwigen, and Rechte Vorcht.
Der Mynn Regel of Everhardus Cersne, or Cerlne (before 1404),[4]
 already been noted [5] as a close imitation of Andreas Capellanus.
The Hätzlerin *Liederbuch* has also a poem on table-manners (*Von
ch Zucht*[6]) which touches the statute about personal neatness ;
l in Germany, as in the other countries, we have an abundance
books on behavior in general.   From Wilken's and Bartsch's
ounts of the manuscripts in the University Library at Heidelberg,[7]
l from the lists given in Goedeke's *Grundriss*, it appears that a
nber of German statute poems are not yet published.

F. ENGLISH.

n bringing together the instances of Statutes of Love in Middle
glish it is important to keep in mind the fact of the translation
 wide circulation of the *Roman de la Rose*.

Liederbuch der Clara Hätzlerin, ed. by C. Haltaus, Quedlinburg and Leipzig,
o, no. 47, pp. 211 ff.
See p. 129, above.
Ibid., no. 58, pp. 238 ff.
Der Minne Regel von Eberhardus Cersne aus Minden, ed. by F. X. Wöber,
nna, 1861.
See p. 180, above.
Ed. Haltaus, no. 71, pp. 276 ff.
See the works cited p. 131, note 2, above.

CHAUCER.

In *The Compleynt of Venus* [1] Chaucer has so changed the balla
of Oton de Granson [2] which he was translating, that instead of
usual lover's praise of his mistress which the French poet wrote,
have a lady's praise of her lover. Hence the qualities which
lady selects for mention are worth comparing with the statut
She delights in the manhood and the worthiness, the truth and
stedfastness, the "gentilesse," bounty, wisdom, "governaunce," a
"noblesse" of the lover and says that

> notwithstanding al his suffisaunce,
> His gentil herte is of so greet humblesse
> To me in word, in werk, in contenaunce,
> And me to serve is al his besinesse,
> That I am set in verrey sikernesse (vv. 17–21).

The second ballade of the same poem, following the original m
closely, gives us some symptoms :

> As wake a-bedde, and fasten at the table,
> Weping to laughe, and singe in compleyning,
> And doun to caste visage and loking,
> Often to chaungen hewe and contenaunce,
> Pleyne in sleping, and dremen at the daunce,
> Al the revers of any glad feling (vv. 27–32). [3]

Apart from the translation of the *Roman de la Rose*, howev
there is no formal issuing of commandments by Love in Chauc
though many of the individual qualities occur incidentally.
Troilus, especially, is full of lover's symptoms and contains defi
directions to the lover as to patience, secrecy, etc. [4]

---

[1] Skeat's *Chaucer*, I, 400 ff., where the French also is given from Pia
Romania, XIX, 411 ff.

[2] See p. 75, above.

[3] Cf. Granson's poem in *Rom.*, XIX, 414.

[4] See for symptoms *Troilus and Criseyde*, i, 445 ff., 1072 ff.; and, for directi
the conversations of Troilus and Pandarus in i, 806 ff., ii, 981 ff., etc. Profe

THE TEN COMMANDMENTS OF LOVE.

The English *Court of Love* makes mention of certain statutes for
women which the hero was not permitted to read.   We have once
or twice found, for example, in the *Cosselh a las donas* in the *Breviari
d'Amor*,[1] and in the *Conseils d'Amour* of Richard de Fournival,[2]
instructions for ladies, but hardly anything so formal as *The X Com-
maundementes of Loue* which is printed in Stow's 1561 edition of
Chaucer.   These are :

1. Faithe. —

> Faithe is the first and principally to tell
> Verie loue requireth soche credence
> That eche beleue other as true as the Gospel
> Without adlaucion [*l.* adulacion] or flatteryng audience.

2. Entencion. —

> Your lover to please doe your busie cure.

3. Discrecion. —

> In your dealyng euer be discrete,

and consider whether a man is worthy of your confidence, and if so

> Poinct by discretion your hour, time, and place
> Conueniently methyng with armes to embrace.

4. Pacience. — Assuage your lover's wrath with soft words and
humble obedience.

Kittredge also reminds me of the qualities which the hen in the *Nonne Prestes
Tale* demands in a husband :

> We alle desyren, if it mighte be,
> To han housbondes hardy, wyse, and free,
> And secree, and no nigard, ne no fool,
> Ne him that is agast of every tool,
> Ne noon avauntour, by that god above! (vv. 93–7.)

[1] See p. 184, above.   [2] See p. 188, above.

5. Secretnesse. —

> Secretlie behaue you in your werkes
> In shewing countenance or meuyng of your iye.
>
> .   .   .   .
>
> Make priuy to your deling as few as ye maie
> For .iii. may kepe a counsel if twain be awaie.

6. Prudence. —

> Set not your loue in so feruent wise
> But that in goodly hast ye maie refreine
> If your louer list you to dispise.

7. Perseueraunce. —

> Loue him onely, and refuse all newe —

8. Pitie. —

> Be piteous to hym as womandhod requireth
> That for your loue endureth paines smarte.

9. Measure. —

> Take mesure in your talkyng, be not outrage.

10. Mercie. —

> To hym that bounde is in loues lace
> Shewe fauour, ladie, and be not merciles
> Lest ye be called a common murderes.

The anonymous composer of these commandments twice refers t
" Romance myn aucthor," which may point to an original, or ma
be merely an instance of what seems to have been a meaningles
phrase with many mediæval writers. The " Romance de la Rose
is referred to in support of Measure.

LYDGATE.

The instructions given by Venus to the knight in Lydgate's *Tem
ple of Glas*[1] belong for the most part to Group *B*. The rule to be

> Euer bisie, weies forto sech
> All trwe louers to relese of her peyne,
> Siþ þou art oon (vv. 1168–70),

[1] See p. 147, above.

might be taken as belonging to Group *A*.   The commandments here are not numbered, but are given in a loose way, the same idea often recurring several times.   The main points, however, are these :

1. To be "feiþful in hert and constant as a walle," "trwe . . . withoute chaunge."

Euer in stidfastnes
Rote thin hert, and voide doubleness (vv. 1152–8 ; cf. 1187 ff., and 1201 ff.).

Cf. *Court of Love*, Statute iii. .

2. To be "humble and meke," "lowli of þi spech to riche and poure" (vv. 1154, 1166–7).   Cf. Statutes vii and ix.

3. To be "secre" (v. 1154).   Cf. Statute ii.

4. To "haue in reuerence Thes women al for þi ladi sake . . euermore vndirtake Hem to defend (vv. 1159–63).

5. To "be curteis ay" (v. 1166).   Cf. Statute xviii.

6. To be "ai fressh and welbesein" (v. 1167).   Cf. Statute xviii.

7. "Of no wiȝt haue disdein . . . and neueȓ for cherisshing þe to mych auaunte" (vv. 1170–2).   Cf. Statute v (a).

8. To "be lusti eke, deuoid of al tristesse . . . euer be iocond" (vv. 1173–9).

9. "Al vertues biseli þou sue, Vices eschew" (vv. 1180–1).

10. "For no tales þin hert[e] not remue" (vv. 1182–3).   Cf. Statute xiv (b).

11. "None oþirs beauty lat in þin herte myne" (vv. 1188–90).   Cf. Statute iii.

12. To help all true lovers (vv. 1168–71).   Cf. Statute iv.

The substance of all these commands, with the possible exception of the last, will be at once recognized as belonging to the tradition.

THE ISLE OF LADIES.

The closing ballade of *The Isle of Ladies*[1] contains some of the usual commandments :

> Be diligent, awake, obey, and drede,
> And not too wild be of thy countenaunce,

[1] See p. 156, above.

But meeke and glad, and thy nature feede,
To do each thing that may her [do] pleasance.
When thou shalt sleep, have aie in remembrance
Thimage of her which may with lookes softe
Give thee the blisse that thou desirest ofte (vv. 2220–6).[1]

SIR THOMAS CLANVOWE.

At the end of a manuscript of *The Cuckoo and the Nightingale*, or *The Book of Cupid, God of Love*,[2] Professor Skeat has discovered the words " Explicit Clanvowe," and he identifies this person with a Sir Thomas Clanvowe who was well known at the courts of Richard II. and Henry IV.

The poem consists chiefly of a dispute about love between the two birds (the nightingale holding that from love " cometh al goodnesse "), and the statutes are implied in the following lines :

> Al honour, and al gentilnesse,
> Worship, ese, and al hertes lust,
> Parfit joye, and ful assured trust,
> Jolitee, plesaunce, and freshnesse,
>
> Lowliheed, and trewe companye,
> Seemliheed, largesse, and curtesye,
> Drede of shame for to doon amis ;
> For he that trewly Loves servaunt is
> Were lother to be shamed than to dye (vv. 152–60).

JAMES I. OF SCOTS.

The instructions issued by Venus in the *Kingis Quair* are even less formal than those in the *Temple of Glas*. Only one or two are actually stated as commands ; three or four others are quite clearly indicated in a passage where Venus charges the poet with messages to men, reproaching them for their neglect of her laws ; and one or two more are implied in the names of attendants and other persons.

---

[1] Morris's *Aldine Chaucer*, V, 153.

[2] *Chaucerian Pieces*, pp. 347–58, and Introd., pp. lvii–lxi. Cf. also E. Vollmer, *Das mittelengl. Gedicht The Boke of Cupide, Clanvowe zugeschrieben, kritische Ausgabe*, Berlin, 1898.

These are supplemented by precepts of a like nature laid down by Minerva, to whom Venus sends the poet.

I. Commandments of Venus.

> 1. Contynew in my seruise,
> Worschip my law, and my name magnifye
> That am ȝour hevin and ȝour paradise (vv. 855-7).

This command, which is parallel to Statute i of the *Court of Love*, is followed by some verses which show clearly that it was the religious rather than the feudal metaphor which the poet had in mind (vv. 858-61).

2. The general command to urge men to obey her laws (vv. 799-847) might also be considered as belonging to Group *A*, though these laws in detail (3, 4, 5, 6, here following) belong rather to Group *B*.

> 3. The songis new, the fresch carolis and dance (v. 842).
> 4. The lusty lyf, the mony change of game,
> . . . the lusty contenance (vv. 843-4).
> 5. The fresche array (v. 844).
> 6. The besy awayte, the hertly obseruance (v. 845).

This point appears also among Minerva's instructions :

> Be . . . diligent hir merci to procure,
> Noght onely in thy word, for word is noght
> Bot gif thy werk and all thy besy cure
> Accord thereto (vv. 918-22).

> 7. " Secretee " is the " chamberere " of Venus (v. 675).
> 8. And ȝit, considering the nakitnesse
> Bothe of thy wit, thy persone, and thy myght,
> It is no mach, of thyne vnworthynesse
> To hir hie birth, estate, and beautee bryght (vv. 757-60),

passage which is meant to inculcate the necessity for humility. . " be meke " in v. 918.

II. Commandments of Minerva.

1. To be virtuous and to trust in God (vv. 897-917).
2. Be trewe . . . and stedfast in thy thoght " (v. 918).
3. " Abyde thy time " (v. 927).

4. The recommendation to diligence and thoughtfulness appears in I, 6, above.

Both Venus and Minerva preach to the poet at considerable length, and embroider their precepts with similes and exclamatory passages, as, for example, that against the false lover; but the list just given embraces all the actual points made by either.

For attendants whose names imply qualities insisted on by the statutes, see pp. 153–4, above.

STEPHEN HAWES.

In *The Pastime of Pleasure*[1] Hawes puts the following instructions into the mouth of Venus in chap. xxx :

> And specially I gyve to you a charge
> To fyxe your love, for to be true and stable
> Upon your lady, and not to fle at large
> As in sundry wise for to be variable,
> In corrupt thoughtes vyle and culpable ;
> Prepence nothing unto her dishonesty,
> For love dishonest hath no certaynte.

WILLIAM DUNBAR.

Among Dunbar's poems there is a short piece of three stanzas which has no Court of Love setting, but which nevertheless consists entirely of *Advice to Lovers*.[2] The chief points are : (1) to beware of evil-report; (2) not to be miserly, "skerche in ʒour spending "; (3) "Be layth alway to do amiss or schame "; (4) to be secret (5) to be true; (6) not to be a liar; (7) not to be a tattler; (8) "Be nocht of langage quhair ʒe suld be still "; (9) "Be nocht of prowd, thinkand ye haif no peir"; (10) "Be ye so wyiss that vder at ʒow leir"; (11) "Be nevir he to sklander nor defame "; (12) "Be of ʒour lufe no prechour as a freir."

---

[1] Percy Society ed., 1845, p. 149.
[2] S. T. S., ed. by Small, II, 162; Schipper's edition, p. 323, Vienna Ac. *Denkschr.*, XLII, iv, 21–3.

CHAPTER V.

THE CHARACTER OF PHILOBONE.

THE function of Philobone in the *Court of Love* is twofold : first,
e is a guide, who shows the lover round the court and the temple,
d, second, a go-between, who introduces the lover to the lady and
'es him advice to help in winning her.

The necessity for a person to act as guide and interpreter arises
m the allegorical nature of the poem. The elaborate symbolism
mands explanation, and it is more artistic to have a *dramatis per-
a* perform this than to have the author break into the narrative in
own person.

The *Somnium Scipionis* from book vi of Cicero's *De Republica* is
ially regarded as the main source of the dream-form in mediæval
rature.[1] Guillaume de Lorris mentions it as well as the Commen-
y on it by Macrobius, in the opening of the *Roman de la Rose*
. 7 ff.), and Chaucer quotes it at least four times.[2] It is in this
rk that we have the prototype of Philobone in her first capacity.
pio the younger has been hospitably entertained by Masinissa,
l, after much talk about his illustrious adoptive grandfather,
res to rest. Scipio the elder appears to him in a vision, and
eals to him the secrets of the after life and many of the workings
the universe.

The influence of this vision upon the author of the *Divine Comedy*
generally admitted ; and the similarity of function between the
er Africanus on the one hand, and Virgil and the other figures
o act as guides in the *Divine Comedy* on the other, is not the least
ious of the parallelisms between Dante and Cicero.

Chaucer's obligation is even more clearly confessed. In the *Par-
ent of Foules*, after a Proem giving an outline of " Tullius of the
me of Scipioun," the elder Scipio appears in a vision to Chaucer
self, and leads him into the park in which the scene of the *Parle-*

Immediate source is, of course, meant. Visions occurring in Greek literature,
that of Er in Plato, doubtless count among ulterior sources.

Skeat's *Chaucer*, I, 505–6, n. to v. 31 of *Parlement of Foules*.

ment is laid. The eagle in the second book of the *Hous of Fa*
does the poet a similar service, and so, in the third book, does t
unknown man who takes him to the House of Rumour.[1] In t
German poem *Die Minneburg*[2] we have two men: first, the cha
berlain, who explains the elaborate symbolism of the pillars a
glass figure; and, second, Meister Neptanaus from Alexandria, w
interprets the allegory of the castle as a whole. In Petrarch t
melancholy shade of a fellow Tuscan [3] explains to the poet the me
ing of the different features of the *Trionfo d'Amore*.

But the business of *cicerone* in the mediæval allegories, especia
in France, is usually given to a maiden. In the procession that f
lows the God of Love in Andreas Capellanus,[4] it is one of the lad
doomed to purgatory that tells the knight the reason of the fates
those he sees. In the *Fablel dou Dieu d'Amours*[5] a nymph esco
the lover round the palace and shows him the grave of her own de
knight. In the *Roman de la Rose* various ladies, such as Idlen
and Courtesy, explain things to the hero. Influenced by this mod
doubtless, King René makes Oyseuse, "la belle amie du di
d'Amours," and Bel Acueil show to the Heart and his companio
the wonders of the palace of the god.[6]

In the *Kloster der Minne*[7] the fellow-countrywoman whom t
hero meets and with whom he views the tournament, not o
explains to him the rule of the Kloster, but gets along so well w
him that before the end of the poem they are lovers. This is
unusual development.

The lady in the English *Flower and the Leaf*[8] who tells the poet
the meaning of the costumes of the two parties of knights and lad
is herself a member of the train of the Queen of the Leaf. So a
the nymph who guides Gavin Douglas in the *Palice of Honour*, l
ing him up steep mountains by the hair, fishing him out of the m
when he falls over the bridge, and reviving him when he faints, i
lady of the court of Calliope.[9]

---

[1] *Hous of Fame*, bk. iii, vv. 1868 ff.
[2] See pp. 123 ff., above.
[3] See p. 113, above.
[4] See p. 47, above.
[5] See p. 41, above.
[6] See pp. 89 ff., above.
[7] See p. 127, above.
[8] See p. 150, above.
[9] See p. 162, above.

The other function of Philobone seems to point to an altogether different ancestry. In the *Court of Love* itself, as has been said, she arranges the meeting between Philogenet and Rosial, and gives Philogenet hints for becoming behavior; thus:

> " Well, all is well! Now shall ye seen," she seid,
> " The feirest lady under son that is :
> Come on with me, demene you liche a maid,
> With shamefast dred, for ye shall spede, y-wis,
> With her that is the mirth and joy and blis:
> But sumwhat straunge and sad of her demene
> She is, be ware your countenaunce be sene
>
> Nor over light, ne recheless, ne to bold,
> Ne malapert, ne rinning with your tong " (vv. 729–37).

Now Philobone is a perfectly proper and a very friendly young woman, and it seems almost ungentlemanly to hint that she may have low connections. Yet this match-making side of her character leads us to compare her with the obnoxious figure of the procuress who plays so important a rôle in love-stories from the classics onwards.

The most important appearance of this type of character in Ovid is that of Dipsas,[1] who, however, is represented as instructing the mistress how to gain the lover. The most frequent go-between on behalf of the man is the maid-servant, such as Nape[2] or Cypassis,[3] who is bribed to speak well of the lover to her mistress and lead her to think favorably of him.

The most important mediæval source for this type is the figure of the old woman in *Pamphilus*.[4] Her function is to prepare the mind of the girl, to arrange meetings, and to give the hero hints as to methods of attack. Many of the later examples of this type of character, such, for example, as Celestina in the tragi-comedy of that name,[5] are imitated from the hag in *Pamphilus;* while others, male (like Pandarus) as well as female, have an independent origin. Even

---

[1] *Amores*, i, 8.   [4] See pp. 173–4, above.

[2] *Ibid.*, i, 11.   [5] See p. 174, above.

[3] *Ibid.*, ii, 7–8. Cf. also *Ars Amat.*, i, 351 ff.

in *Pamphilus*, however, all the directions for seduction are not given by the old woman; the goddess Venus herself, as has been noted in chap. iv, gives precepts of no lofty ethical tone.[1] The author of the *Panthère d'Amours* also, who shows a tendency to use his divinities with somewhat scanty reverence (as in his making Cupid serve as interpreter of the symbolism of the Panther[2]), makes Venus advise with the lover, suggest the sending of rings and verses, and attempt to stir up his courage to seek a personal interview.

There is no doubt that the author of the *Court of Love* had a pretty wide knowledge of the class of literature of which his own poem is an example, so that both of these types must have been familiar to him. The situation being what it is in the *Court of Love*, it required no extraordinary imagination to combine the rôles, and thus to produce the character of Philobone.

CHAPTER VI.

THE BIRDS' MATINS.

THE *Court of Love* closes with a service sung by birds in honor of the God of Love.

> On May-day, whan the lark began to ryse,
> To matens went the lusty nightingale
> Within a temple shapen hawthorn-wise;
> He might not slepe in all the nightertale,
> But " *Domine labia*," gan he crye and gale.
> " My lippes open, Lord of Love, I crye,
> And let my mouth thy preising now bewrye " (vv. 1352–8).

The eagle sang "Venite," the falcon " Domine, Dominus noster," the popinjay " Celi enarrant," the goldfinch " Domini est terra," and the wren " Jube, Domine," as the first lesson; the robin and the turtle-dove the second and third lessons, and so on through a

---

[1] See pp. 173–4, above.   [2] See p. 70, above.

:ries of parodies of Matins and Lauds, all of which can be recog-
ized in the mediæval prayer-book.[1]   After the Amen,

> . . . furth the cokkow gan procede anon,
> With "*Benedictus*" thanking god in hast,
> That in this May wold visite thaim echon,
> And gladden them all whyl the fest shall last :
> And therewithall a-loughter out he brast,
> " I thank it god that I shuld end the song,
> And all the service which hath been so long " (vv. 1422-8).

In this passage (vv. 1352–1428) there is a combination of two
istinct features found more frequently apart in mediæval literature :
( ) the association of birds with the love-divinities, and (2) the paro-
ying of religious services.   These will first be taken up separately ;
nd then the occasional instances of their combination will be given.

A. Birds and the Love-Divinities.

The association of birds with Venus goes back, of course, to the
:assics, where the goddess is constantly represented as drawn in a
:r by doves, or as having doves flying around her.   In the sixth
:ook of the *Æneid*, Virgil, speaking of Æneas, says :

> Tum maximus heros
> Maternas agnoscit aues.

: the Triumph of Love already quoted from Ovid [2] the god cries
Maternas junge columbas."   Tibullus, in the picture of the Elysian
ields to which Venus leads him, writes :

> passimque uagantes
> Dulce sonant tenui gutture carmen aues [3] ;

d examples could be multiplied indefinitely.

Fulgentius, who explained everything in classical mythology, has
ready been quoted in his account of Venus's special guardianship
ver doves, — "quod huius generis aues sint in coitu feruidae." [4]

---

[1] For details see Skeat, *Chaucerian Pieces*, pp. 552-3.
[2] See p. 11, above.   [3] See p. 12, above.
[4] See p. 22, above, for context.

The mating of birds in the early spring as one of the first signs of
the new season, and the prominence that this phenomenon attained
in literature in connection with St. Valentine's Day, must also have
gone to emphasize the association.

The very first group of mediæval Court of Love poems shows us
the tradition firmly established. The barons forming the court of the
King of Love in *Florance et Blancheflor* are birds, and the nightingale
and parrot settle the dispute by wager of battle.[1] The nightingale in
the *Fablel dou Dieu d'Amours*[2] presides at a discussion on the worthy
lover, and in *Venus la Deesse* the same bird gives the description of
the "hom qui bien aime," already quoted among the statutes.[3] In
the *Fablel*, when the hero comes to the grave of the king's son who
was slain fighting for a maiden, he says :

> Oysiaus i ot ; por l'ame del signor
> Qui la gisoit, cantent de vrai amor (p. 31).

Venus appears with eight doves in the *Roman de la Rose*,[4] and in
the description of the God of Love we read :

> But nightingales, a ful gret route,
> That flyen over his heed aboute,
> The leves felden as they flyen ;
> And he was al with briddes wryen,
> With popinjay, with nightingale,
> With chalaundre, and with wodewale,
> With finch, with lark, and with archaungel

> (English translation, vv. 909–15

The description of the armor of Love in the *Tornoiement d'Ant
christ*[5] includes a shield with silver nightingales and other birds on
it. The approach of the God of Love to the castle in the *Roman
de la Poire*[6] is heralded by the song

> Des rossignox et des kalendres
> Et des autres oiseillons mendres,
> Oriox, merles et mauviz (vv. 1122–4).

---

[1] See pp. 36–7, above.　　　[4] Ed. Marteau, III, 396, v. 16441.
[2] See p. 41, above.　　　[5] See p. 48, above.
[3] See pp. 42 and 185, above.　　[6] See p. 56, above.

Birds sing round the God of Love as he rides at the head of his train in the *Panthère d'Amours*,[1] and round his throne in the *Parlement d'Amour*.[2]

In Chaucer, the *Compleynt of Mars*, which begins,

> Gladeth, ye foules, of the morow gray,
> Lo! Venus risen among yon rowes rede!

is sung by a bird on St. Valentine's Day. On the same day the *Parlement of Foules* is held, and there the sparrow is called " Venus sone" (v. 351). In the *Prologue* to the *Legend of Good Women*, a lark announces the coming of the God of Love, and in his meadow

> somme songen clere
> Layes of love, that ioye hit was to here,
> In worshipinge and preisinge of hir make.
> And, for the newe blisful somers sake,
> Upon the braunches ful of blosmes softe,
> In hir delyt, they turned hem ful ofte,
> And songen, ' blessed be seynt Valentyn !
> For on his day I chees yow to be myn,
> Withouten repenting, myn herte swete !'
> And therwith-al hir bekes gonnen mete,
> Yelding honour and humble obeisaunces
> To love (Version B, vv. 139–50).

It is on St. Valentine's Day also that the lark, in the beginning of Lydgate's *Flour of Curtesye*,[3] sings :

> Awake, ye lovers, out of your slombringe (v. 10),

> Take upon you the blisful holy charge
> To serve love, whyl your lyf may dure,
> With herte, body, and al your besy cure,
> For evermore, as Venus and Cipryde
> For you disposeth, and the god Cupyde (vv. 17–21).

All about the ships of the God of Love, in the *Isle of Ladies*,[4] birds

> Sate and song with voice full out,
> Ballades and layes right joyously,
> As they cowth in here harmony (vv. 716–18).

---

[1] See p. 70, above.   [3] *Chaucerian Pieces*, p. 266.
[2] See p. 86, above.   [4] See pp. 156–7, above.

The *Kingis Quair* is full of the love-songs of birds. " The lytil suete nyghtingale" sang "the ympnis consecrat off lufis vse," and "lo the text":

> Worschippe, 3e that loueris bene, this May,
>   For of 3our blisse the kalendis are begonne,
> And sing with vs, "away, Winter, away!
>   Cum, Somer, cum, the suete sesoun and sonne!"
>   Awake for schame! that haue your hevynnis wonne,
> And amorously lift vp your hedis all,
> Thank Lufe that list 3ou to his merci call (vv. 232–8).

Again, in the conceit in which Venus calls the raindrops her tears, she claims the birds as peculiarly in sympathy with her (vv. 820–3).

In the introduction to *Lancelot of the Laik*,[1] it is a bird that comes to the love-lorn hero as a messenger from Cupid. Dunbar, who calls them "Venus chapell clarkis,"[2] makes "the mery foulis, blis-fullest of chere," sing "to dame Venus, lufis mychti quene . . . ballattis in lufe, as was the gyse."[3]

In the *Hypnerotomachia Poliphili*[4] birds echo the name of Adonis around his tomb (i, 24).

Besides all these instances of definite association with Venus or Cupid, there must be kept in mind the constant presence and sing-ing of birds in the conventional May-morning landscape which intro-duces so many Court of Love poems.

B. Parodies of Religious Services.

We have noticed from time to time in previous chapters a tend-ency of the prevailing metaphor in the Court of Love to change from the feudal to the religious. A temple sometimes accompanies and sometimes replaces the castle; prayers with incense and offer-ings take the place of legal pleadings; and an altar with a statue appears instead of a throne occupied by a living sovereign. It has already been remarked also, that the religious forms that thus crept

---

[1] See pp. 158–9, above.   [3] *Ibid.*, vv. 102 ff.
[2] *The Golden Targe*, v. 21.   [4] See pp. 117 ff., above.

into the allegory were not those consistent with the worship of a pagan deity, but were rather those of mediæval Christianity. Venus, in fact, was put in the place of the Virgin; or rather, the modes of adoration of the Virgin were transferred to the shrine of Venus.

Auxiliary to this was the fashion of using the terminology of religious devotion towards a lady, in non-allegorical poetry. This was not confined to the attitude implied in the resolution in the *Livre des cent Ballades*,

J'aray Dame et Seigneur,

En ciel un Dieu, en terre une Déesse (p. 225),

but led to the use of biblical and religious phrases in quite alien fields of erotic verse. An example is found in Guillaume de Machaut's *Dit du Vergier*, where Love speaks at length on his power of making the foolish wise and the wise foolish,[1] exalting the lowly and humbling the proud, with an obvious allusion to Scripture. So Bernard de Ventador compared a kiss to the joys of Paradise, and thought a day spent in a love adventure worth a hundred. Arnaut Daniel was willing to hear masses and burn candles to gain his lady's favor.[2]

More formal and elaborate, and more strictly entitled to be called parodies, are the Paradiso, Purgatorio, and Inferno of lovers in Andreas Capellanus and the parallel passages; and the reading of Ovid and singing of love-songs instead of the Gospel and Psalms for the day in the *Romaricimontis Concilium*.[3] In *Venus la Deesse d'Amor*[4] a bier with the body of a true lover is brought in, and a funeral service is held in the temple of the God of Love.

Paternosters and *Credos* were frequently made the vehicles of love sentiments and others quite as far removed from their original meanings. Thus, in the *Patenostre d'Amours*,[5] a lover regrets the inac-

---

[1] Cf. *I Cor.*, iii, 18–20, etc.

[2] For these and other instances see P. L. Ginguené, *Histoire littéraire d'Italie*, Paris, 1824, I, 307–8.

[3] See pp. 31 ff., above.

[4] See pp. 42 ff., above.

[5] Barbazan et Méon, *Fabliaux et Contes*, IV, 441–5.

cessibility of his lady, working in the phrases of the prayer with
little enough appropriateness : e.g.,

> *Et dimitte nobis.* Por qoi,
> Dame, n'avez merci de moi ?
> *Debita nostra.* Douce amie,
> Por Dieu le filz Sainte Marie
> Vous pri qu' aiez merci de moi,
> Quar je vous aim en bone foi (vv. 57–62).

Similar instances are the *Patenostre du Vin*,[1] the *Credo au Ribaut*,[2]
in which a debauchee mixes the words of the Creed with regrets
for his wickedness, the *Patenostre a l'Userier*,[3] and the *Credo a
l'Userier*,[4] in most of which, however, the words of the prayer or
the Creed are not welded into the general sense of the passage.[5] It
ought to be said, too, that these are not in the proper sense bur-
lesques, *i.e.* there is no attempt made to ridicule the sacred things
parodied, but only a borrowing of sacred formulas to give piquancy
to the secular matter.

Somewhat more literary skill is shown in the *De Profundis des
Amoureux*.[6] Here the Latin phrases actually join in sense to the
French verse, and the "depths" of love are substituted for the
theological conception.

> Dedans le goulfre tenebreux,
> Où sont amoureux interdis,
> Plungé suis, moy, pouvre amoureulx,
> Las, ouquel lieu, *de profundis*
>   *Clamavi* à celle que j'ayme,
> Par qui suis ainsi tourmenté ;
> Las, c'elle m'y laisse en ceste flamme,
> Secours n'ay nul, sinon *ad te*,
>   *Domine* Cupido, mon maistre,
> Domine es preux et hardy.

---

[1] Jubinal, *Jongleurs et Trouvères*, pp. 69–72.

[2] Barbazan et Méon, IV, 445–52.

[3] *Ibid.*, IV, 99–106.

[4] *Ibid.*, IV, 106–14.

[5] In the *Credo au Ribaut*, however, this is done very cleverly.

[6] Montaiglon, *Recueil de Poésies franç.*, etc., Paris, 1855 ff., IV, 206 ff.

concludes thus:

> *Sicut erat* ainsi seray,
> *In principio* vueille ou nom,
> *Et nunc et semper* l'aymeray
> *In secula seculorum,*
>   *Amen.*

he same collection contains the *Patenostre des Verollez, avec une*
mplaincte contre les Medecins,[1] and the *Pater Noster des Angloys*,[2] a
litical satire.

The most elaborate example in English is the *Venus Mass*[3] of
hn Lydgate. This begins with the *Introibo* ("Introibo ad altare
ei," etc.),

> Wyth all myn Hool Herte entere
> To fore the famous Riche Autere
> Of the myghty god of Love
> Whiche that stondeth high above
> In the Chapel of Cytheron
> I will wyth gret devocion
> Go knele and make sacrifyse
> Lyke as the custom doth devyse (p. 390).

hen follow the *Confiteor, Misereatur, Officium, Kyrie eleyson, Gloria*
  excelsis: —

> Worsshyppe to that lord above
> That callyd ys the god of love,
> Pes to hys seruantes euerychon
> Trewe of herte, stable as ston
>   That feythful be (p. 392),

e Oryson, and, finally, the Epystel in prose, in which, after greet-
gs to all faithful brethren, the clerk speaks of his own life as that
" an errynge pylgrym in the seruyse of the myghty and dredful
d of loue." He calls to mind the examples of Troilus, Penelope,
olyxena, Dido, the "holy legende of Martyrs of Cupydo," and

---

[1] Montaiglon, I, 68–72.

[2] *Ibid.*, I, 125–30.

[3] Ed. by T. F. Simmons for E. E. T. S. in the *Lay Folks Mass Book*, Lond.,
79, pp. 389 ff.

many more; and ends by asking for the prayers of the brethre
that he may "sum mercy fynde, or that the god of love enspyre m
ladyes herte of hys grace what I endure for hyr sake."

In the *Parliament of Love*[1] the company "songe a balad stede
the masse."

*The Dregy of Dunbar, maid to King James the Fyift being in Striu
ling*,[2] is a parody on the *Dirige*, made "in order to relieve the Kin
out of the state of purgatory" at Stirling, where he was staying i
the Franciscan convent, and bring him back to his courtiers a
Holyrood. It begins:

> We that ar heir in hevins glory,
> To ȝow that ar in purgatory,
> Commendis ws on our hairtly wyiss.

The style of the burlesque may be gathered from the *Lectio prima:*

> The Fader, the Sone and Haly Gaist,
> The mirthfull Mary, virgene chaist,
> Of angellis all the ordouris nyne,
> And all the hevinly court devyne,
> Sone bring ȝow fra the pyne and wo
> Of Striuilling, every court-mannis fo,
> Agane to Edinburchis ioy and bliss,
> Quhair wirschep, welth and weilfar is,
> Pley, plesance and eik honesty:
> Say ȝe amen, for cheritie.

Then follow the *Responsio* ("Tu autem Domine"), second and thir
lectiones with responses, and the whole ends with an *Oremus* i
Latin.

A slight reference to the same kind of thing, probably after th
date of the *Court of Love*, occurs in Sir David Lindesay's *Testamen
of Squyer Meldrum*,[3] where the squire in ordering his funeral says,

> Se that ȝe thoill na Priest in my Processioun,
> Without he be of Venus Professioun:

---

[1] See p. 158, above.

[2] See Schipper's edition in *Denkschriften*, etc., XL, ii, 41-3.

[3] See *Works of Sir D. Lyndesay*, E. E. T. S., Pt. III, 1868, p. 371.

> Quhairfoir, gar warne all Venus chapel clarks,
> Quhilk hes bene most exercit in hir warkis,
>
> With ane Bischop of that Religioun,
> Solemnitlie gar thame sing my saull mes,
> With organe, Timpane, Trumpet, and Clarion.

Of the same period, in France, is the anonymous *Tenebres des Pauvres Prisonniers*, a parody of the matins for the Wednesday, Thursday, and Friday of Holy Week.[1]

C. Parodies sung by Birds.

The combination of the two features, the history of which has just been examined, did not begin with the author of the English *Court of Love*. The most extensive and elaborate example of the religious service sung by birds in honor of Venus is a poem already outlined, *La Messe des Oisiaus*[2] of Jean de Condé, written two centuries before our English poem.

In the work of Jean de Condé, Venus, who has been received by the birds with great joy, commands the nightingale to sing mass before they dine. So the nightingale begins with the Confession, and, immediately after it, the larks up above begin the *Introit*, the other birds joining; then, in a beautiful clear voice, all together sing the Litany. When that is finished the nightingale leads in the *Gloria in excelsis*, after which service is interrupted in order to have the cuckoo driven out. Resuming, the nightingale turns to the congregation and says "Dominus vobiscum," and they all respond heartily. The priest repeats the Collect; the thrush in his highest voice reads the Epistle; after which the larks, who never tire of singing, begin the *Alleluia* in which a chorus of about five hundred birds join. When that is finished four birds, the goldfinch, the linnet, the chaffinch, and the "chinchevens," sing another in four parts, all the birds, led by the larks, joining in again at the close. The blackbird reads the Gospels; the nightingale repeats the Creed; and, after the singing of the Offertory, the parrot preaches the sermon

---

[1] *Œuvres de Clément Marot*, ed. by G. Guiffrey, Paris, 1876, II, 519 ff.
[2] See pp. 67 ff., above.

which has already been described,[1] and absolution is bestowed. Jus
as all the lovers fall on their knees, the cuckoo comes flying over, cry
ing " Tout cuku " and causing great indignation. When they hav·
returned from pursuing the scoffer, the nightingale begins the Preface
and the *Sanctus* is sung. The priest devoutly elevates a beautifu
red rose, surpassing all flowers in beauty, perfume, and size, an·
then lowers it again. The *Paternoster* is chanted and the *Agnu
Dei* follows. The priest wishes the dove to bring the "peace,"
and he brings in his bill a green rush, from which comes a grea
sweetness. From the rose the priest takes three leaves, which h·
uses to perform cures, yet the rose remains entire. Then with win·
and water in a chalice the remaining ceremonies are duly performed
all sing the Postcommunion; the nightingale says the closing Col
lect, and the blackbird "Ite missa est." The other birds repl
with *Deo gratias*, the priest pronounces the Benediction, "et a di
l'ewangile en bas," and the service ends.

Very similar to this, though much shorter, is the poem by Lydgate
the *Devotions of the Fowles*.[2] The poet walks out in the sunshin
and hears the popinjay sing the Nativity (" A solis ortus cardine ")
the pelican the Redemption ("Vexilla regis prodeunt"), the nigh·
ingale the Resurrection ("Consurgat Christus tumulo"), the lar·
the Ascension ("Eterne rex altissime "), the dove "Veni Creato
Spiritus," and all the birds together "O lux beata Trinitas."

A Proper New Boke of The Armonye of Byrdes,[3] sometimes ascribed
without proof, to Skelton, may be later than the English *Court o,
Love*. Here the author goes out on an April morning and sees o
a tree

> Byrdes as thycke   As sterres in the skye,
> Praisyng our Lorde   Without discorde,
>   With goodly armony.
> The popyngay   Than fyrst dyd say,
>   *Hoc didicit per me,*
> Emperour and kyng   Without lettyng
>   *Discite semper a me.*

---

[1] See p. 192, above.

[2] *Lydgate's Minor Poems*, ed. by J. O. Halliwell for Percy Society, Lond·
1840, pp. 78 ff.

[3] Ed. [by J. P. Collier] for Percy Society, VII, Lond., 1843.

A long list of birds take up, one by one, a chant or psalm or hymn, — from the wren to the phœnix. Then they all fly away and

> I sayd, *In te, Domine,   Speravi cotidie,*
>   That I fall not *in infernum;*
> And than with thy grace,   After this place,
>   *Non confundar in eternum.*

Note that the service in these last two examples is not addressed to the God of Love, but may be genuinely devout.

Besides these extensive descriptions of birds' services, we have hints of the same idea in short passages.   Thus in the *Cuckoo and the Nightingale*[1] which Professor Skeat has plausibly attributed to Sir Thomas Clanvowe (beginning of fifteenth century), the author says of the birds:

> They were so joyful of the dayes light
> That they begonne of May to don hir houres !
> They coude that servyce al by rote (vv. 69–71).

Again in *The Golden Targe*,[2] Dunbar says, " Full angellike thir birdis sang thair houris " (v. 10), and he (v. 21) calls the birds "Venus chapell clarkis," as Lyndesay did after him.[3]

Thus it appears that, though the different elements which are present in the Birds' Matins at the end of the English *Court of Love* (the association of Birds with Venus, and the custom of parodying church services) were common enough in both French and English poetry, the combination of the two is found elaborately worked out only, so far as I can discover, in the *Messe des Oisiaus*.   The poet of the *Court of Love* may, of course, have worked it up from such hints as have been quoted from Clanvowe and Dunbar, or he may have combined the two elements for himself; but in view of the fact that he, like other mediæval poets, seldom invented when he could imitate, it is more than probable that the source of the last section of our poem is to be found in Jean de Condé.

---

[1] *Chaucerian Pieces*, p. 350.
[2] See pp. 163 ff., above.
[3] See p. 225, above.

CHAPTER VII.

THE IMMEDIATE SOURCES OF THE *COURT OF LOVE.*

THE foregoing chapters have furnished in considerable detail the means of realizing the extent to which the main features of the *Court of Love* were prevalent in the love-allegory of Western Europe for at least three centuries before the English poem was written. Certain of these features have proved to be so common that it is useless to regard them as in themselves means of proving any immediate relation to any particular source or sources. Thus, such conceptions as that of Venus or Cupid holding a court in which courtiers, either allegorical personages or the ghosts of famous lovers, form the retinue of the divinity; a temple of Venus in which lovers offer sacrifices and prayers; the gorgeous palace of the goddess; the decoration of walls with love-stories; the description of the mediæval type of female beauty (with golden hair, laughing eyes, red lips, fair skin, even teeth, slender figure, and so on); the May-morning landscape, with streams and flowers and birds; the presenting of "complaints" and "bills"; the nymph who acts as guide and interpreter; with a score of minor details — such conceptions occurring in any two poems tell nothing whatever about the immediate relations of these poems.

It is necessary, therefore, if we are to prove anything with regard to those sources which actually suggested certain features of the *Court of Love,* to find either striking parallelisms in detail which cannot be set aside as commonplaces, or the presence of some distinct feature which in itself is not a regular part of poems of the type.

What has been said of commonplaces in general may be said almost as strongly of the main features of the *Roman de la Rose.* A direct knowledge of that poem by any later mediæval author is to be presumed almost as certainly as a knowledge of the Bible; and even though a writer had not himself read the book, its influence would still appear in his work if he followed the allegorical tradition at all. And this tradition, it has sufficiently appeared, every allegorist did ollow.   The relations of the *Court of Love*, therefore, to the *Roman de la Rose* will not be discussed in detail.

The evidence in the case of Chaucer's influence is more tangible ; and this influence was both mediate and immediate.   Lydgate was a professed disciple, and he, for one, can be proved as an intermediary for the indirect influence.   But there abound in the *Court of Love* phrases which recall Chaucerian phrases, and it is not possible to determine whether these came directly from the master himself, or whether the *Court of Love* poet got them from one of his numerous imitators.[1]

The most important single element in the *Court of Love* traceable to Chaucer, is the prominence given to Alcestis, a prominence which seems clearly the result of an acquaintance with the *Legend of Good Women.*   The Castle of Love in our poem is :

> Within and out depeynted wonderly,
> With many a thousand daisy, rede as rose,
> And white also, this saw I verily :
> But what tho daises might do signify,
> Can I not tell, sauf that the quenes flour
> Alceste it was that kept there her sojour ;

> Which under Venus lady was and quene,
> And Admete king and soverain of that place,
> To whom obeyed the ladies gode ninetene (vv. 100–8).

The last phrase is decisive.   Alcestis is by no means a rare figure in mediæval poetry,[2] though of much more frequent occurrence after Chaucer than before, and she is mentioned by Lydgate in the *Temple of Glas* without any reference to the nineteen ladies.   This number indicates a clear reference to the *Prologue* of the *Legend of Good Women*, as also does the important rôle assigned Alcestis as Queen of Love.

---

[1] See Professor Skeat's notes to the *Court of Love* in *Chaucerian Pieces*, pp. 540–53, where such phrases are usually unhesitatingly treated as direct borrowings from Chaucer.

[2] See Schick's edition of the *Temple of Glas*, p. 74, note on vv. 70–4, for a very full list of references.

The part played by Pity in the *Court of Love* is pretty certainly also
due to Chaucer's influence. It will be remembered that Philogenet
notices (vv. 693 ff.) in the Temple of Love a jewelled shrine where
Philobone tells him, " a tender creature is shryned . . . and Pite is
her name." She had seen an eagle "wreke him on a fly" and had
died of tender heart. Since then lovers had been ill-off, and only
" hot corage spedeth the maters all of court" now. Here a reflec
tion seems to be cast on the ways of women as degenerate, and it is
natural that, when it is necessary to have Rosial relent, the author
should want to make her do so from the more womanly motive. So
he brings Pity to life again.

> Out of her shryne she roos from deth to lyve (v. 1324),

and persuaded Rosial to be gracious.

Now Pity is a frequent enough figure among the personifications
that throng the Court of Venus, but Pity dead and buried is Chaucer's
idea.[1] We have indeed, in the English version of the *Poème de la
Prison* of Charles d'Orléans some references to Pity's being asleep.

> But when a lady longe hath seyne
> Hir man in such perplexite
> Though pity full aslepe haue leyne
> She must awake him of bounte.[2]

Again, speaking of Danger and Distress,

> Allas they shulde so have ther dwelling, fy,
> In louys court, but pity slepeth fast,[3]

and again

> For loue wolde that bewte shulde it kepe,
> And she was loth, for pite was aslepe.[4]

But none of these lines occurs in the French version, and it is pos
sible that the English translator was influenced by Chaucer.

---

[1] Or an idea borrowed by him from the (lost) source of his *Compleynte*. It is
more likely that our author knew Chaucer than that he was acquainted with
this hypothetical original.

[2] *Poems written in English by Charles, Duke of Orleans,* ed. by G. W. Taylor
for the Roxburghe Club, Lond., 1827, p. 110.

[3] *Ibid.,* p. 27.   [4] *Ibid.,* p. 8, v. 6.

The situation in Chaucer's *Compleynte unto Pite*, moreover, though by no means identical with that in the *Court of Love*, is yet much closer to it than the situation in any other poem that I have found. In the *Compleynte* the poet, distressed by his love's tyranny, says:

> To Pite ran I, al bespreynt with teres,
> To preyen hir on Crueltee me awreke.
> But, er I might with any worde out-breke,
> Or tellen any of my peynes smerte,
> I fond hir deed, and buried in an herte (vv. 10–14).

Around her hearse stood Bounty, Fresh Beauty, Lust, Jollity, and others "withouten any wo" and "confedred alle by bonde of Crueltee" (v. 52). The bill he had written to present to Pity follows, and, though purporting to have been written before she died, it contains a reference to her death (v. 117). There is no resuscitation here; but it seems fair to suppose that the *Court of Love* author borrowed the idea of the shrine, and had the further development suggested by the circumstances in his own poem.

We may note also the reference to Chaucer's *Anelida and Arcite* in vv. 233–5:

> And the weymenting
> Of hir, Anelida, true as turtill-dove,
> To Arcite fals,

and sufficiently clear verbal agreements in

> For love wil not be countrepleted, indede (v. 429),

with

> For Love ne wol not countrepleted be
> (*Legend of Good Women*, version B, v. 476);

and

> Eke ye must bait on many an hevy mele (v. 194),

with

> On many a sory meel now may she bayte
> (*Canterbury Tales*, B, 466).

After the elevation of Alcestis to the position of Queen of Love, the next most distinguishing feature of the *Court of Love* is the classification of the lovers who come to present complaints to Venus. Complaints, of course, we have in abundance, and most courts of

Venus have had some one who came before the goddess with a grievance. But this elaborate description of the various classes of suitors and their causes of complaint seems to be the invention of Lydgate, from whom both James I. of Scots and the author of the *Court of Love* borrowed it. In the following table I have selected from the *Temple of Glas*, in which the list is by far the longest, those classes that are paralleled in either of the other poems. In all three cases the description of the complainants is introduced by mention of famous lovers. In Lydgate and the *Court of Love* these are painted on walls or windows, and in both Dido's is the first name; in the *Kingis Quair* no names are given, because of them

> maid is mencioun
> In diuerse bukis, quho thame list to se;
> And therefore here thaire namys lat I be (vv. 544–6)

— the *Temple of Glas*, as Schick suggests, being probably one of the " diuerse bukis."

The cause of complaint in each case is some hindrance to love, such as

	T. OF G.	K. Q.	C. OF L.
Jealousy	v. 148	v. 609	
Unrequited love (Daunger, etc.)	v. 156	vv. 607–8	
Poverty, Wealth of rivals, etc.	vv. 159, 175	v. 606	v. 1138
Loveless marriages	v. 207	v. 631	
Absence	v. 151		v. 252
Falseness	v. 168		v. 583
Death of one of the lovers		v. 645	v. 252
Monastic vows, etc., imposed in youth by guardians, etc.	v. 196	vv. 610, 624	vv. 253, 1097, 1149

Each of the poems has, in addition to the causes here enumerated others peculiar to itself, — natural developments according to the poet's individual fancy, easy enough after the general idea was once seized. It is to be noticed, however, that the only point common to the two later poems and absent from Lydgate is that of the loss of the lover by death; and this is too familiar an idea to serve as any argument for the imitation of the *Kingis Quair* by the author of the *Court of Love*.

The most striking of these parallels is that afforded by the passages in which the religious victims complain, and these are given here to strengthen the argument.

The *Temple of Glas*, vv. 196–206 :

> And riȝt anon I herd oþir crie
> With sobbing teris, & with ful pitous soune,
> Tofore þe goddes, bi lamentacioun,
> That were constrayned in hir tender youþe,
> And in childhode, as it is oft[e] couþe,
> Y-entred were into religioun,
> Or þei hade yeris of discresioun,
> That al her life cannot but complein,
> In wide copis perfeccion to feine,
> Ful couertli to curen al hir smert,
> And shew þe contrarie outward of her hert.

Cf. *Kingis Quair*, vv. 610–15, 626–30 :

> And efter this, vpon ȝone stage [a]doun,
>   Tho that thou seis stond in capis wyde ;
> ȝone were quhilum folk of religioun,
>   That from the warld thaire gouernance did hide,
>   And frely seruit lufe on euery syde
> In secrete, with thaire bodyis and thaire gudis.
>
>   .   .   .   .
>
> Sum bene of thame that haldin were full lawe,
>   And take by frendis, nothing thay to wyte,
>   In ȝouth from lufe into the cloistere quite ;
> And for that cause are cummyn recounsilit,
> On thame to pleyne that so thame had begilit.

This idea seems to have struck the author of the *Court of Love* with especial force. Cf. the following passages :

> " Ye, than," quod I, " what doon thise prestes here,
> Nonnes and hermits, freres, and all thoo
> That sit in white, in russet, and in grene? "
> " Forsoth," quod she, " they wailen of their wo " (vv. 253–6).

> " See how they cry and wring their handes whyte,
> For they so sone went to religion !

And eke the nonnes, with vaile and wimple plight,
There thought that they ben in confusion :
‘ Alas,’ they sayn, ‘ we fayn perfeccion,
In clothes wide, and lak our liberte ;
But all the sin mote on our frendes be.

· · · · · · · ·

Our frendes wikke, in tender youth and grene,
Ayenst our will made us religious ;
That is the cause we morne and wailen thus.’

Than seid the monks and freres in the tyde,
‘ Wel may we curse our abbeys and our place,
Our statuts sharp, to sing in copes wyde,
Chastly to kepe us out of loves grace,
And never to fele comfort ne solace ’ ” [1] (vv. 1100–18).

And yet againward shryked every nonne,
The prang of love so straineth thaim to cry ;
“ Now wo the tyme,” quod thay, “ that we be boun !
This hateful ordre nyse will don us dy !
We sigh and sobbe, and bleden inwardly,
Freting our-self with thought and hard complaint,
That ney for loue we waxen wode and faint ” (vv. 1149–55).

Here again it will be noted, that though the influence of Lydgate
on the two others is clearly manifest, there is no trace of the depend-
ence of the *Court of Love* on the *Kingis Quair.*

Once the point is granted that the author of the *Court of Love*
knew the *Temple of Glas,* many parallels in detail become significant
and it would not be hard to draw up lists of these to show that there
is a strong presumption that it was from Lydgate that the author got
his main outline, as well as the minor points specified. But material
for such a comparison has already been supplied in the analyses
given of the two poems, and it seems hardly worth while to insist
further on a matter already sufficiently proved.

One point more, however, may be mentioned, on account of a possible explanation it suggests for a difficulty in the construction o

---

[1] Quotation marks are inserted here in accordance with the arrangement advocated in chap. i, pp. 6–7, above.

he *Court of Love.* We have noticed that in that poem Philogenet
nakes two distinct rounds of sightseeing in the Court, and there
oes not seem to be any good reason in the nature of the plot for
his duplication. Now in the *Temple of Glas* Lydgate also intro-
uces a second description, beginning at v. 531. This, however, is
asily accounted for. The first description is introductory to the
ccount of the heroine; the second to that of the hero; and the
uplication does not strike the reader as at all out of place. But
n the *Court of Love* the author himself is the hero and is not
escribed from the outside at all. Does it not seem possible that
he *Court of Love* poet was here somewhat unintelligent in his imita-
ion, as mediæval imitators often enough were, and copied this bit of
nachinery without supplying the proper motive for its existence?

Did the author of the *Court of Love* know the *Kingis Quair*?
Mr. J. T. T. Brown says no, because, as he holds, the author of the
Kingis Quair copied the *Court of Love.* But his denial of James
.'s authorship of the Scottish poem has been sufficiently disproved
y M. Jusserand.[1] The *Court of Love* was written more than half
century at least after James's death. Yet Mr. Brown's parallels,[2]
n spite of his protests, work equally well either way; and we have
o consider whether they prove anything with regard to an immedi-
te relation between the two poems at all. The majority of these
arallels, it is clear to any one acquainted with the mass of mediæval
oetry of this sort — it would be clear merely from the material
ollected in our third chapter — are simply mediæval commonplaces;
criticism which Mr. Brown anticipated but did not forestall.[3]
)thers are due to a common knowledge of Chaucer. The most
nportant arise from the fact just proved, that both used the *Temple
f Glas* as a model. Of the existence of this poem of Lydgate's
Mr. Brown does not seem to have been aware, — unfortunately, it

---

[1] See J. J. Jusserand, *Jacques Ier d'Écosse, fut-il poète?* in *Revue Historique*,
XIV, Paris, 1897 (also reprinted separately).

[2] See Note D to *The Authorship of The Kingis Quair*, by J. T. T. Brown,
Glasgow, 1896; and cf. Henry Wood, *Chaucer's Influence upon James I.*, Halle,
879, and W. Wischmann, *Untersuchungen über das Kingis Quair*, Wismar,
887.

[3] See Brown, p. 44, n. 1.

must be added, for had he known it he would not have been im
pelled to write his book.

Yet it is not easy to deny absolutely a connection between th
poems. The very fact that both authors were diligent students c
Chaucer and Lydgate, while on the one hand it would tend to lea
us to draw false inferences as to the influence of the one on th
other, would on the other hand tend to cover up traces of such a
influence, had it really existed. The examination of the passage
on the classes of complainants failed to produce any clear evidenc
A comparison of the statutes is almost as barren. The first statut
of the *Court of Love* indeed, demanding truth to the King and Quee
of Love, which we did not find in the regular tradition of the sta
utes, and which is not formerly stated by Lydgate, is represented i
the *Kingis Quair* by Venus's tearful protest against the desertion c
her worship by men, and by the commands:

> Contynew in my seruise,
> Worschip my law, and my name magnifye (vv. 855–6).

Again the seventeenth statute of the *Court of Love*, which was no
found elsewhere, has a parallel in a stanza of the *Kingis Quai*
describing the shades of aged lovers. Cf. the following: —

> The seventeenth statut, Whan age approchith on,
> And lust is leid, and all the fire is queint,
> As freshly than thou shalt begin to fon,
> And dote in love, and all her image paint
> In remembraunce . . .
> Yet speke and talk of plesaunt daliaunce, etc., (*C. of L.*, vv. 456–66)

> Quhen thay of youth ressauit had the fill,
> Yet in thaire age thame lakkit no gude will (*K. Q.*, vv. 587–8).

Another argument is suggested by Professor Skeat who "admit
the certainty" that he [the author of the *Court of Love*] consulte
the *Kingis Quair*. He thinks the metre suggests Scottish influenc
and draws attention to the use of "celsitude" and "pulcritude,
rhyming together, as possibly due to the same source. Yet thes
peculiarities might be owing to the influence of other Scottish poet
than James I.

Thus it seems possible that we should reckon the *Kingis Quair* among the immediate sources of the *Court of Love.* If the evidence in favor of it is not conclusive, there is no important obstacle to it, so far as I have examined the case.

With regard to the relation of *Court of Love* to the *Poème de la Prison* of Charles d'Orléans the case is somewhat similar though hardly so strong. The presence of Charles in England, and the existence of an English translation of at least part of the *Poème de la Prison* increase the chances of his work's being known to an English poet. Charles is one of the comparatively few Court of Love poets who actually numbered his statutes, and it is remarkable that the somewhat rare Statute I which was found in the English *Court of Love* and also in the *Kingis Quair* is the first of the commandments in the *Poème de la Prison.* This, however, is the most definite point apart from features that are too widely spread to be available as evidence. There are coincidences in the classical examples quoted (Dido, for example, and Alcestis), but these alone prove nothing.

The *Temple of Glas* is not the only poem of Lydgate's known to our author. There is clear evidence, as Professor Skeat has pointed out, of his acquaintance with the *Balade Warning Men to Beware of Deceitful Women.*[1] Cf.

I me report to Salamon the wyse,
And mighty Sampson, which begyled **thryes**
With Dalida was . . .

. . . .

For it paraventure may right so befall,
That they[2] be bound by nature to *disceive*,
And *spinne*, and *wepe*, and *sugre strewe on gall* (*C. of L.*, vv. 536–42).

. . . Men, take hede ;
Hir *galle is hid under a sugred wede.*

. . . .

---

[1] *Chaucerian Pieces*, pp. 295–6.   [2] *I.e.* women.

> Women, of kinde, have condicions three ;
> The first is, that they be fulle of *deceit ;*
> To *spinne* also hit is hir propertee ;
> And women have a wonderful conceit,
> They *wepen* ofte, and al is but a sleight (*Balade*, vv. 25–33).

> Sampson the fort, and Salamon the sage
> Deceived were, for al hir gret corage (*Ibid.*, vv. 4–5).

Of Latin books the author seems to have known Ovid and Maximian. There are several passages where Ovid's influence is seen though there is nothing in them to prove direct knowledge; but, as Professor Skeat has pointed out, Jupiter's intrigues with Europa Antiope, Alcmene and Danaë, which are alluded to in the *Court of Love* (vv. 820–4), are also mentioned all together in *Met.*, vi, 103 13. This affords strong presumption that he actually knew Ovid at first hand.

The reference to Maximian is still clearer. In vv. 795–8 of the *Court of Love* we read :

> For lippes thin, not fat, but ever lene,
> They serve of naught, they be not worth a bene ;
> For if the basse ben full, there is delyt,
> Maximian truly thus doth he wryte.

Cf. Maximian, i, 97–8 :

> Flammea dilexi, modicumque tumentia labra,
> Quae mihi gustanti basia plena darent.[1]

The epithet "flaming" applied to the mouth in v. 793 increases the probability that the author had the actual passage in mind. I have been unable to detect further traces of Maximian in the poem.

In the *Court of Love* the following lines occur :

> Her nose directed streight, and even as lyne,
> With fourm and shap therto convenient,
> In which the goddess milk-whyt path doth shine (vv. 785–7).

The appropriateness to a young lady's nose of the figure from the galaxy is hardly clear to us, and one wonders if it were so to the

---

[1] *Poetae Latini Minores*, ed. by Bährens, Leipzig, 1882, V, 321.

uthor. The only other instance I have found of this figure used of woman's beauty is in the following lines from the *Architrenius*.[1] 'he application is quite different, but it is just possible that the ne in the *Court of Love* is the result of some such passage imper- ectly remembered. The lines occur in the description of the most eautiful of the nymphs of Venus.

> A frontis medio tractu directa superne
> Verticis ad centrum, *uia lactea surgit*, aranti
> Pectine, cuius acu geminas discessit in alas,
> Et tandem trifidum coma cancellatur in orbem,
> Diuisoque prius iterum coit agmine crinis.

The evidence regarding the sources of the *Birds' Matins* has een given in chap. vi.

To sum up. The author of the *Court of Love* was most influenced y Chaucer and Lydgate. The poems by the former which are aost used by him are the *Legend of Good Women, Parlement of 'oules, Hous of Fame,* and *Compleynt to Pity. Troilus and Criseyde* s frequently recalled by single lines, and by such episodes as the wooning of Philogenet. *The Bok of the Duchesse* may have sug- ested the painted windows near the beginning of the *Court of Love,* ut the device is common. Occasional verses show a knowledge of t least some of the *Canterbury Tales.* The total result gives the npression of a very devoted disciple.

Of Lydgate's works *The Temple of Glas* has had, of course, by ar the greatest influence on our author; and the lines proving knowledge of one of his ballades have been quoted. Professor keat quotes occasional parallels that make it probable that he was ot unacquainted with other works of Lydgate. With fair assurance e may say that he had read Ovid and Maximian, and that he knew *a Messe des Oisiaus* of Jean de Condé. The evidence with regard) Charles d'Orléans and James I. of Scots is inconclusive. In addi- on to all this we may feel sure that he knew other poems of the *ourt of Love* type, and doubtless received from them hints for his

---

[1] *Architrenius,* by John de Hauteville, in Wright's *Satirical Poets of the Twelfth 'entury,* Lond., 1872, I, 253.

main allegory and the development of his list of statutes, as well as for minute details.

Professor Skeat thinks that the coining of the names Philogenet and Philobone points to the author's being a disciple of the New Learning. But these names seem to be rather mediæval than modern in the kind of scholarship they suggest. "Philogenet," I presume, means "a lover born," and "Philobone," probably, "good to lovers"; and such a hybrid as the latter would lead one to believe that the "clerk of Cambridge" (v. 913) was more interested in making his "art of love" and songs "in honour of the King and Quene of Love" (vv. 897–9) than in reviving the study of Greek.

Nothing that I have found in any part of the present investigation seems to throw light upon the identity of the author.

CHAPTER VIII.

THE RELATION OF THE ALLEGORY TO THE INSTITUTION AND THE PAGEANT OF THE COURT OF LOVE.

THE debate (*débat*) as a literary form appears very early in mediæval literature. According to Ebert,[1] the chief influence which moulded its development was that of the classical eclogue. Yet the dialogue is a very natural form for any one to adopt who wishes to make a show of presenting both sides of an argument, and it might quite conceivably be used by writers who knew nothing of the classical tradition.

From the time of Alcuin there has come down to us a Latin *Conflictus Veris et Hiemis*[2]; and in the middle of the ninth century Sedulius Scotus wrote a *Certamen Rosae Liliique*.[3] The influence

---

[1] On the relation of the *débat* to the eclogue, see Ebert, *Allg. Gesch.*, vol. II chap. iv ; and Jeanroy, *Les Origines de la Poésie lyrique en France*, Paris, 1889 cf. G. Paris, *Journal des Savants*, Nov. and Dec., 1891.

[2] Ebert, II, 64–5.

[3] *Ibid.*, II, 220–1.

of the *Psychomachia* appears in a Latin life of St. Christopher,[1] in which the author represents Pudicitia and Libido as taking the forms of two women, and disputing with each other in Christopher's prison. Such discussions became favorite clerkly exercises, and commonly took a didactic turn. They are represented in English by such poems as the *Debate of the Body and the Soul*, and, in a different field, *The Owl and the Nightingale.*[2]

The introduction of love into these debates was only a matter of time; and we are not surprised to find "débats d'amour" among the very earliest specimens of mediæval amorous poetry. The *Romaricimontis Concilium*[3] is, of course, a debate, and the subject there discussed, the comparative merits of knights and clerks as lovers, we have traced through the whole series of poems of the *Altercatio* type down to the sixteenth-century farce played between the young monk and the old soldier.[4] In the first of these the Court of Love element is quite subordinate, appearing, indeed, only in the lady cardinal's announcement that she is sent by the God of Love; in *Florance et Blancheflor*, the god and his barons are introduced as a court of appeal, but the debate is still the main point of interest.

The growth of this kind of discussion is shown in the *Fablel dou Dieu d'Amours*,[5] in which the nightingale calls the other birds round him and complains that love has degenerated. The hawk lays the blame on the "villaine gent," but the thrush objects to the hawk's confining love to clerks and knights; while the jay thinks that to love and be well loved is to be as worthy and wise as a clerk, and to be indeed a "chevalier d'amour."

By the fourteenth century we find the love-debate a familiar type. Guillaume de Machaut wrote a *Jugement du Roi de Behaigne*,[6] in which he represents himself as overhearing a dispute between a dejected lady and an equally dejected knight, as to which is the more unfortunate. The lady has lost her lover by death; the knight's

[1] *Waltheri Spirensis Vita et Passio S. Christophori Martyris*, ed. by von Harsten, Munich, 1878.

[2] Cf. on the whole class, Raab, *Vier Allegorische Motive*, Leoben, 1885.

[3] See pp. 31 ff., above.   [5] See pp. 41 ff., above.

[4] See pp. 34 ff. and 108, above.   [6] *Romania*, XVI, 409.

mistress has given her heart to another. Machaut intervenes and proposes the king of Bohemia as arbiter. The suggestion is adopted, pleadings are made, and the judge decides in favor of the knight.

Machaut's patroness was displeased at this conclusion; so he wrote a *Jugement du Roi de Navarre* (Nov. 1349).[1] Here the discussion is between a beautiful lady and the poet on the justice of the king of Bohemia's decision, and the arbiter chosen this time is Charles the Bad of Navarre. The poet loses, and is condemned to write some *chansons*.

Christine de Pisan shows great fondness for this literary form. In *Le Livre des Trois Jugemens*[2] she submits three love cases to the Seneschal de Hainault. These are as follows:

1. A beautiful and virtuous lady, deserted by her first love, bestows her affections on a second, more sincere. Is she therefore perjured? 2. A knight has lost all hope of seeing his mistress again, since a jealous husband has shut her up in prison. May he, after an interval, seek a new love? 3. A damsel is deserted by a knight, who transfers his addresses to a powerful dame, who repulses him. The knight then returns and again seeks the favor of the damsel. Ought she to pardon him or be pitiless? To the same arbiter the following dilemma in the *Livre du Dit de Poissy*[3] is submitted: Which is the more worthy of pity — a lady grieving for a lover taken prisoner in battle, or a squire who cannot forget nor cease to love a lady who only despises him?

In Christine's *Debat de deux Amants*,[4] a discussion arises in the house of Louis, Duke of Orléans, between a knight embittered by disappointment, and a fortunate young squire. The knight acts as the accuser, and the squire as the apologist of love, and the duke acts as judge.

Distinctions are more finely drawn in Alain Chartier's *Livre des Quatre Dames*,[5] in which four ladies discuss whose plight is most pitiable, that of (1) her whose lover was slain at Agincourt; (2) her

---

[1] *Œuvres de Guillaume de Machault*, ed. Tarbé, Reims et Paris, 1849, pp. 68 ff.
[2] *Œuvres Poétiques de Christine de Pisan* (Soc. des anc. Textes franç.), II, 111 ff.
[3] *Ibid.*, II, 159 ff.   [4] *Ibid.*, II, 49 ff.
[5] *Œuvres*, ed. Duchesne, pp. 594 ff.

whose lover was taken prisoner by the English; (3) her whose lover has not been heard of since the battle; (4) her whose lover ran away in the battle.

The well-known *Arrêts d'Amours* of Martial d'Auvergne,[1] with the commentaries by Benoît de Court, which have played so important a part in discussions on the alleged institution of the Court of Love, are really only a variety of the debates of which we are giving instances, though they are worked up with a greater parade of legal machinery and in a more conscious spirit of humorous burlesque. It is strange that in the face of the fanciful Court of Love setting already quoted,[2] any one should have seriously supposed that this book contained evidence for taking the Court of Love as an established institution. The *Arrêts* themselves, indeed, are usually trivial enough to make it clear to any one that they are merely *jeux d'esprit.* The commentary by Benoît de Court is interesting on account of the mock seriousness with which he keeps the form of legal discussion and the number of classical parallels he quotes.

The influence of Martial d'Auvergne in giving a more strictly legal turn to the debates is seen in Guillaume Coquillart's (A.D. 1421?–1491?) *Playdoyer d'entre la Simple et la Rusée.*[3] Two beauties dispute the heart of a young gallant. "La Simple" claims to have been his first love and charges "la Rusée" with fraudulent interference. But "la Rusée" has him and means to keep him; so the cause is tried before a tribunal, lawyers arguing on either side. The evidence as to facts is contradictory; an inquest is ordered and the *Enqueste d'entre la Simple et la Rusée,* continuing the same plot as a framework, becomes a vehicle for satire on contemporary life. The *Jugement Definitif sur un Plaidoyer d'Amour*[4] is of a similar kind, the plaintiff being a lover who charges an unrelenting mistress with cruelty and gets a verdict in his favor.

Le Debat de Deux Demoyselles[5] (*ca.* 1490) is a dialogue between

---

[1] Ed. by Lenglet-Dufresney, Amsterdam, 1731.

[2] See p. 106, above.

[3] *Œuvres,* ed. by P. Tarbé, Paris and Reims, 1847, I, 5 ff.

[4] The authorship is uncertain. The poem is quoted in Lenglet-Dufresnoy's edition of Martial d'Auvergne's *Arrêts d'Amours,* pp. 599–600, from *Poësies de la Comtesse de la Suze,* II, 107.

[5] Anonymous; pub. by Didot, Paris, 1825.

"la Tannée" and "la Noyre," the question being which is the more miserable. The first loves a knight whose whereabouts is unknown to her; the second is so closely watched by her husband that she gets no opportunity to show favor to her lover. They finally agree to refer their case, under false names, to two renowned princesses, the Duchess of Orléans and the Countess of Angoulême.[1]

Later instances, coming down into the sixteenth century, are the *Débat de la Demoiselle et de la Bourgoise*,[2] settled in favor of the former by the president of the " Echiquier d'Amours," and the *Débat du Jeune et du Vieulx Amoureux*.[3]

In the debates of which typical specimens have just been cited, the whole piece was in each case the work of one author, the form being dramatic rather than purely argumentative. But there arose, also very early in the Middle Ages, another kind of poetical debate, one in which there was a real contest between different poets, each of whom supported only one side. The earliest form of this is the Provençal *tensos* in its double form of the simple *tensos* (in which one poet produced a stanza and was answered by another poet using the same verse-form) and the *jocx partitz* (in which the first poet propounded a question, undertaking to defend the side which the other did not choose). More than two poets might take part, and the *tensos* ended with an appeal to ladies.[4] The very earliest troubadours seem to have used this form, for Diez quotes from William IX., Count of Poitiers (*ca.* 1100), a clear reference to it:

> E si-m partetz un juec d'amor,
>   No suy tan fatz,
> Non sapcha triar lo melhor
>   Entr' els malvatz.[5]

The *tensos* is too familiar a form to call for examples.

---

[1] *Ibid.*, p. 41, note by M. de la Monnoye. In the text as published by Didot the names of the judges are not mentioned.

[2] *Recueil de Poésies franç. des XVe et XVIe Siècles*, ed. by A. de Montaiglon, V, 5 ff.   [3] *Ibid.*, VII, 211 ff.

[4] For an elaborate definition of the *tensos*, see *Las Flors del Gay Saber* in *Monumens de la Littérature Romane*, Toulouse, 1841, I, 360.

[5] Diez, *Ueber die Minnehöfe*, p. 16.

After the genuine troubadour period was over, when an attempt
as being made in Provence to revive its former poetic glories, in
323 seven citizens of Toulouse formed themselves into " La gaya
ompanhia dels .vii. Trobadors de Tholoza," and invited all Provençal
)ets to assemble at that city on May 1, to compete for a golden
olet which was to be given as a prize for the best poem presented.
his association or Academy became firmly established, granted
egrees, and drew up an *ars poetica* — the well-known *Las Flors del
ay Saber* or *Las Leys d'Amors*.[1] In the reign of Louis XIV., in
*94, new rules were drawn up and a fresh start was made. Royal
terest was again shown in 1725 by Louis XV., who increased the
umber of academicians to forty.[2]

Caseneuve says that these practices were imitated in Germany under
e Emperor Conrad I. Speaking of the time of Frederick Barbarossa
e quotes Melchior Goldast[3] thus: " Viri Principes et Equestres
onnunquam etiam Imperatores, Reges, certamina instituere poetica ;
quibus nobili familia Virgines offerebant victoriam cantus," and
ere is mention of crowns of victory. If, however, Germany got its
:ample in Provence it must have been from the society of the
oubadours themselves rather than from this later revival. The
'artburg song-contest,[4] added by Wagner to the Tannhäuser story,
es back to a thirteenth-century poem, and so quite antedates the
Jeux Floraux."

The Provençal *jocx partitz* appears in Northern France as the *jeu
urti*, and the composing of these formed the leading amusement of

---

[1] By Guilhem Molinier. On the composition and history of this work see
pecially the article by Chabaneau cited in n. 2, below.

[2] For further discussion and references on these games, see Cl. Devic and
Vaissete, *Hist. Gén. de Languedoc*, Toulouse, 1885, IX, 429 ff., X, 78, n. 19 ;
, Noulet, *De dame Clémence Isaure substituée à la Vierge Marie comme patronne
s Jeux litt.*, etc., in *Mem. de l'Acad. des Sciences . . . de Toulouse*, 1852 ; Cambou-
, *Renaissance de la Poésie Provençale*, in *Jahrbuch f. rom. u. eng. Litt.*, 1861,
I, 125 ; P. Meyer, *Bibl. de l'École des Chartes*, 5th series, V, 52 ; C. Chabaneau,
igine et Établissement de l'Académie des Jeux Floraux, Toulouse, 1885.

[3] P. de Caseneuve, *L'Origine des Jeux Fleureaux de Toulouse*, Toulouse,
59, p. 50.

[4] Cf. G. Paris, *La Légende du Tannhäuser*, in *Revue de Paris*, March 15,
98.

the trouvères in the assemblies known as "Puys d'amour."[1] The
meetings took their name from a village in Velai, Pui Notre Dam
where there was an annual festival in honor of the Virgin; but "d
l'origine," says Passy, "l'esprit littéraire dispute à l'esprit religie
la direction des Puys; souvent même avec succès." After mass ar
the singing of sacred music, the crowd entered a hall. On an elev
tion sat the president, the judges, and other important person
Hymns to the Virgin, love songs, and finally *jeux partis* were pr
sented to the audience; the subjects of these last being the passi
of love and the duties of marriage. One poet gave the challeng
another took it up, and sometimes three, rarely four, engaged in t
contest, the challenger naming a judge. Sometimes each side nam
a judge, and rarely there were three. These gave the decisions, t
crowd merely looking on; and crowns of flowers or of silver we
awarded to the winners, who gained thus the privileges of (1) bei
called "Sire"; (2) wearing the crown at these sessions; (3) bei
a judge in future — though this last point is doubtful.

The fondness for discussion on the subtler questions of love whi
is implied in the forms of poetry and social amusement just describe
manifested itself in Italy, perhaps less formally but no less frequentl
Here for three centuries the proposing of *dubbii, questioni*, or *gioc*
formed one of the chief amusements of courtly society. A picture
the way in which such discussions took place occurs in the *Filocol*
of Boccaccio.

Filocolo, driven by stress of tempest into Naples, finds in a gard
a courtly company bent on amusement, with Fiammetta at their hea
It is proposed that love-questions be discussed; Fiammetta is chos
queen and arbitress, and crowned with a garland; the company ta
seats, and Filocolo propounds the first of thirteen questions, the d

---

[1] See Louis Passy in *Bibl. de l'École des Chartes*, 1859, 4th series, V, 491-5
and cf. G. Paris, *Journal des Savants*, Nov., 1888, pp. 667 and 727 ff.

[2] Malecarni's *Trionfo dell' Amore* (see p. 114, n. 3, above) was written for
"certame coronario" got up by Leon Battista Alberti, Oct., 1441. See Veselofs
Novella della Figlia del Re di Dacia, Pisa, 1866, Appendix I.

[3] Boccaccio, *Opere*, VIII, Florence, 1829, *Filocolo*, Bk. iv.

ssion of which occupies most of the fourth book. These same
estions were worked over in verse, with additions from other works
Boccaccio and from Dante, by Jacomo di Giovanni di Ser Minoccio
the fifteenth century.[1]

Another instance is found in Castiglione's *Il Cortegiano*.[2] Here
e gentlemen of the ducal court of Urbino propose, on the occasion
festivities in honor of Pope Julius II., a series of *giochi*, the ques-
ns suggested being such as these : Which virtue would a man
efer his lady to have? If she must have some spot, which vice
uld he prefer? Why do women hate rats and love serpents? The
bject ultimately chosen, the discussion of which forms the sub-
nce of the book, is the character and conduct of the ideal gentle-
an. Thus *Il Cortegiano*, in spite of its seriousness and extent, is
t only an elaborate *dubbio* discussion.

Gli Asolani of Cardinal Bembo (b. 1470)[3] contains an account of
discussion between three young men and several ladies in the
rden of the Castello del Trivigiano. The subject is love. Perottino
ings many reasons to prove it a bad thing; Gismondo dwells on
e sweetness of its fruits, and declares it is always good; and
vinello takes up a middle position.

In the *Quattro Libri di Dubbii* of Ortensio Lando[4] (1552) we have
large collection of instances. The four books are : (1) Amorous,
) Natural, (3) Moral, (4) Religious; and the questions raised and
lved in the first are such as these : Can there be love without
alousy? Are men or women more constant in love? Which
serves love the more, the simple beauty or the clever woman who
plain ?

---

[1] P. Papa, *Un Capitolo delle Definizioni di Jacomo Serminocci*, Florence, 1887
er nozze Renier-Campostrini). Cf. Gaspary in *Literaturblatt f. ger. u. rom.
il.*, March, 1889, col. 110.
[2] Baldesar Castiglione, *Il Cortegiano*, ed. by V. Cian, Florence, 1894, p. 18, and
te V, 4, 5.
[3] *Opere*, Milan, 1808–10, vol. I.
[4] I. Sanesi, *Il Cinquecentista Ortensio Lando*, Pistoia, 1893, pp. 235 ff., in which
1556 Venice edition of the *Quattro Libri* is quoted, the first (that of 1552) not
taining the *Quesiti amorosi*. I am indebted for this reference to Mr. J. B.
tcher.

Quite similar, and pointing again to the same society customs the following:

Del regno di Ginevra Pallavicino riferisce un corrispondente dei Go zaga : " Heri la fece [Ginevra] recitare una egloga molto bella et ben dit qual se fece una disputa qual dolor fuse magiore a dui inamorati o la gielos overo l'absentia. Non se risolse el dubio." [1]

The foregoing instances sufficiently indicate the different types love debates prevalent in mediæval literature and mediæval societ Taken thus together they seem clearly enough to be the expressio (various yet constantly running into one another when we attempt draw lines of division) of the prevalent tendency to take delight subtle discussions on the subject of love. On such grounds, ho ever, as these instances afford, the belief has been built that the existed in the Middle Ages an institution called the Court of Love, which actual cases of disagreement between lovers were submitted formal tribunals, tried by formal laws, and settled by decisions whic derived their force from the sanction of public opinion. Besides tl material already given in this chapter, three other documents ha been adduced in support of this belief : the *Lives of the Provençal Poe* by Johannes Nostradamus, the book of Andreas Capellanus, and a fra mentary record of a " Cour Amoureuse," held about 1400. Seven years ago Diez [2] showed that the evidence of Nostradamus was wort less ; first, because that writer's idea of the Courts of Love was form upon a misunderstanding of passages in the writings of the troub dours which referred to the poetical amusements we have describe and, secondly, because his supposed historical examples proved examination to be inconsistent with the known dates of the alleg participants.

Diez's attempt to refute the evidence from Andreas has n stood the test of time so well as his attack on Nostradamus, becau he tried to show that the Chaplain's book was not earlier than tl

---

[1] Renier in *Giornale Storico della Letteratura Italiana,* 1889, XIII, 382, citi A. Luzio, *Fabrizio Maramaldo,* Ancona, 1883, p. 49. For further references abo *dubbii,* see notes to V. Cian's edition of *Il Cortegiano* and Sanesi's *Ortensio Lan*

[2] *Ueber die Minnehöfe,* Berlin, 1825. Cf. also Abbe de Sade, *Mémoires pour Vie de François Pétrarque,* Amsterdam, 1764-7, vol. II, note 19.

ourteenth century. Since it has been established that this work is certainly not later than the early years of the thirteenth, its contents have become the main ground on which the supporters of the older theory of the Courts of Love have founded their case. It is not part of the present undertaking to examine in detail the often-repeated and often-answered arguments on this question. Trojel and Rajna will find in Andreas certain decisions, stated by him to have been made by the Countess of Champagne, which they think point to the existence of a serious institution. Gaston Paris, however, continues to meet them with the objection which has been urged over and over again but never satisfactorily met, that the conception is inconsistent with the very conditions in which it is presented. The one essential requirement in the conduct of all affairs of chivalrous love in the Middle Ages was, as has appeared from our statutes, the necessity for secrecy. On the other hand, the only means for the enforcing of the decisions of the supposed tribunals that has been suggested by the upholders of the belief in the institution is public opinion. Now the method of bringing public opinion to bear upon a person whose very name is unknown to that public has not yet been evolved. Until it has been, it is unnecessary to seek further reasons for scepticism with regard to the institution.[1]

If then, we reject this belief in a serious tribunal, what have we left? First, we may feel sure that then, as now and always, lovers' quarrels were sometimes settled by the intervention of a third person ; and, doubtless this situation occasionally found its way into literature.[2] But this is no evidence of a formal institution. Second, and much more important for our present purpose, there existed, as a very widespread fashionable amusement, the custom of disputing on subtle points of love. This might be in connection with poetical contests, or might be merely conversation ; there might be formal judges with decisions and prizes, or there might be no attempt to designate the winners at all. But there is no proof that the name

---

[1] For references on this discussion, see p. 256, n. 4, below.

[2] For example, in Raoul de Houdan's *Meraugis de Portlesguez* (ed. H. Michelant, Paris, 1869, pp. 33, 37), in which the queen arbitrates between two rival claimants for the love of Lidoine.

"Court of Love" was used of this amusement in the time of the troubadours. The phrase belongs originally to the type of allegory whose history we have attempted to trace, and was applied to the supposed institution only after 1400.

I do not mean to say, however, that these love discussions, – whether conducted in *tensos* by troubadours, in *jeux partis* by trouvères, as *dubbii, questioni*, or *giochi* by Italian courtiers, or as mock pleadings in the courts of those ladies of whose decisions Andrea has handed down so misleading a tradition, — were without their influence upon the conduct and ideals of courtly life in the Middle Ages. As must already have appeared, the question of the existence of Courts of Love comes down to a question of jest or earnest, and the line between these is no easy one to draw. In our modern life we see men take to sport with all the seriousness of which they are capable, while others, quite literally, "play the game" of politics. An international yacht race moves men as deeply as a national election, and affects as permanently ideals of conduct and the sense of honor. There is no reason to believe that business and play were any more clearly divided in the Middle Ages [1]; and we may grant the love discussions of Eleanor of Aquitaine and her daughter an immense influence upon knightly conduct without in any way invalidating the contention that these ladies and their courtiers were only playing a game.

It was stated above that there were three documents used to support the idea of a serious Court of Love, in addition to the evidence drawn from the debates. The third of these affords an excellent example of the way in which this phenomenon of the serious influence of a pastime did occur, in connection, too, with the cultivation of both love and poetry.

There has been accessible since 1733 a partial list of the officers

---

[1] Professor Josiah Royce has drawn my attention to an interesting extension of the field over which these observations apply, in the phenomena of the play of birds and other animals, which at certain times (other than mating seasons) meet to perform dances and the like, with all the regularity and apparent seriousness which they exhibit in such necessary activities as getting food. See *The Play of Animals*, trans. from Karl Groos's *Die Spiele der Thiere* by E. L. Baldwin New York, 1899.

and members of a " Cour Amoureuse," supposed to be of the time of
Charles VI. of France.[1] But the manuscript from which this was
taken was incomplete, and the earlier pages with the statement of the
nature of the Court and its most important officers were lacking.
Recently, however, M. A. Piaget [2] has found in a collection of armo-
rial bearings in a manuscript in the Bibliothèque Nationale a complete list; and has besides drawn attention to the description of the
Charter of this Court, published in E. -J. de Turck's *Inventaire des
Archives de l' Ordre de la Toison d' Or* in 1760.

From these authorities it appears that the Cour Amoureuse was
founded in 1400 " sur l'humilité et la fidelité ou probité, et instituée
à l'honneur des dames." It consisted of (1) Le Prince de la Cour
d'amour; (2) three "grands conservateurs" (these were, at the time
of its first organization, Charles VI., Philip, Duke of Burgundy, and
Louis, Duke of Bourbon); (3) several other "conservateurs"; (4)
twenty-four "chevaliers, écuiers et autres, possédant la rhétorique et
la poésie, appellés ministres de la Cour, lesquels avoient la principale
autorité après les grands conservateurs, et étoient chargés de présenter
aux assemblées que cette cour étoit obligée de tenir dans certains
temps de l'année, des balades et autre pièces de poésies, suivant
qu'il étoit réglé par les statuts "; (5) other officers, such as treasurers,
secretaries, ushers, etc. Manuscript 5233 in the Bibliothèque Nationale
gives the names of over 600 members, including many of the most
notable people in France. From the statement of the duties of the
" ministres " it appears that the Cour Amoureuse was meant not only
to glorify and defend ladies, but also to cultivate poetry; for, as
M. Piaget says, " en 1400, c'était tout un."

We have a poem written between 1408 and 1413 by Amé Malingre,[3]
maître d'hôtel to Louis, Prince of Savoy, which makes clearer the
fantastic nature of this association.

The poet, walking in a wood, chances to enter a chapel, where he

---

[1] *Hist. de l'Acad. Royale des Inscr. et Belles Lettres,* Paris, 1733, VII, 287 ff.

[2] *Romania,* XX, 417 ff. The Vienna MS. had also been described by the
Baron de Reiffenberg in *Bulletins de l'Acad. Royale de Bruxelles,* 1840, VII, i, 339.

[3] In MS. 179 bis, *Bibl. de Genève,* fol. 88–96, described by Eug. Ritter in *Bulletin
la Soc. des anc. Textes franç.,* 1877, pp. 85–113, and summarized by Piaget,
Romania, XX, 450 ff.

finds a lady in great distress caused by jealousy and the calumnies
of certain envious persons.   In her misery she has composed a complaint against Malebouche, after reading which the poet tries to console
her by recalling the calumnies endured by the chaste Susanna and by
Our Lord, and advises her to ignore the slanderers, promising that
if she does so they will die of chagrin.   The lady takes comfort and
requests the poet to send to Pierre de Hauteville, prince d'Amour, a
letter asking him to expose the case to all the members of the Cour
Amoureuse.   The epistle follows, and is a formal statement of the
lady's grievance, with a request to the Court,

> Qu'il vuillient metre leur entente,
> Pour amour de la dame gente,
> A fayre ce qu'elle dessire.

More than twenty members of the Court are mentioned by name in
the epistle, so that we can be sure that the same institution is meant
as that described in the charter of the Cour Amoureuse, since all but
two of the names occur there also.   Malingre was himself a member
of the Court; and it seems fair to suppose that we have here an
example of the kind of poem presented at its meetings.   The influence of the allegorical *Courts of Love* upon Malingre's poem is clear,
and on the other hand we have the show of an appeal to a tribunal
for the redress of a grievance.   Yet there is a significant vagueness
about the redress asked for; and no one can suppose that anything
was done with reference to actual slanders or similar crimes, though
doubtless the institution made for the preservation of certain chivalrous ideals.

A corroboration of the statements as to the literary side of the
Cour Amoureuse is found in the following passage from Guillebert
de Metz,[1] describing notable personages in Paris about 1407 :

Item le Prince d'Amours, qui tenoit avec lui musiciens et galans, qui
toutes manieres de chançons, balades, rondeaux, virelais, et autres dictie
amoureux savoient faire et chanter, et jouer en instrumens melodieusement

---

[1] Le Roux de Lincy, *Description de Paris au XVᵉ Siècle*, Paris, 1855, p. 85 ;
Le Roux de Lincy and Tisserand, *Paris et ses Historiens aux XIVᵉ et XVᵉ Siècl*
Paris, 1867, p. 234.

If this Cour Amoureuse shows us how close the institution of the ourt of Love could come to some forms of the allegory, it suggests so how easily it becomes mere pageantry. Even the allegories are ten constructed and described in such a way as to be easily enough insformed into spectacles; and in an age that delighted in that nd of exhibition it was unlikely that the opportunity would be issed.

Thus the names, at least, of personages from the Court of Love pear in the municipal celebrations which occurred on Mardi Gras d other festivals in the great industrial towns in the north of ance. At Valenciennes there was a " Feste du Prince de Plai- nce," and we have a record of the attendance at this festival on ay 13, 1348, of two Princes d'Amour, one from Tournay and one om Lille.[1]

The influence of the allegory is even more clearly seen in the *Jeux* la Fête-Dieu, instituted at Aix in Provence in 1474 by King René Anjou, to replace certain licentious celebrations which he had ppressed.[2]

On the Monday of the feast of Pentecost the people met after iss to elect a Prince d'Amour, an Abbé de la Jeunesse, and a Roi la Bazoche. The prince who led the fêtes chose a court, and a ecial vote of money was made for their uniforms and other expenses. ie games themselves were more or less farcical representations of riptural incidents, e.g., *Le grand Jeu des Diables*, in which black and l devils baited Herod, the visit of the Queen of Sheba to Solomon, d so on, much after the fashion of the early religious drama, but thout dialogue and with more pantomime. On the third day there s a great procession, led by La Renommée on horseback, blowing rumpet. She was followed by burlesque effigies of the Duke and ichess of Urbino, Momus, Mercury, and other mythological char- ters, and by the actors in the previous plays. Among others came

---

[1] *Hist. de l'Acad. Roy. des Inscr. et Belles-Lettres*, Paris, 1733, VII, 290 ff.
[2] The account here given is based on that of le Comte de Quatrebarbes in *uvres complètes du Roi René*, Angers, 1844–6, IV, 178 ff., who drew his facts from iche et Papon, *Histoire de Provence;* Pitton, *Histoire de la Ville d'Aix;* and plication des Cérémonies de la Fête-Dieu, by "les frères Grégoire," Aix, 1777.

"dame Vénus avec un gros bouquet, et son fils Cupidon, décocha
ses sagettes aux jeunes beautés qu'il aperçoit ; les ris, les jeux, et l
plaisirs." The music for the games was written by René himsel
Quatrebarbes mentions similar celebrations at the Jeux de la T
rasque, where also the knights elected an Abbé de la Jeunesse.

Earlier discussions on the institution of the Court of Love ma
much of certain triumphal arches erected at Aix in the end of tl
seventeenth century, one of which represented a Court of Lov
"Monsieur le Comte vostre père," says Pierre de Chasteuil-Gallau
the ingenious antiquary who contrived the decorations, "m'aya
engagé de faire quelques desseins d'arcs de triomphe, pour
reception de messieurs les ducs de Bourgogne et de Berry, je
dresser une représentation, au troisieme de mes arcs, de la co
d'amour, si renommée par nos anciens troubadours, l'explicatic
desquels je fis imprimer quelque temps apres, ce qui fut ass
favorablement reçû."[1]

The "explication" here referred to is contained in a *Discours s
les arcs triomphaux, dressés en la ville d'Aix à l'heureuse arrivée
Monseigneur le duc de Bourgogne et de Monseigneur le duc de Berr*
published at Aix in 1701. This volume has not been accessible
me, but from two letters of the author's, published in the *Revue a
Langue Romanes*, and from the criticisms of the Abbé de Sade,[2]
appears that Chasteuil-Gallaup's ideas about Courts of Love we
gathered from the writings of Cæsar and Johannes Nostradamus, a
sources equally worthless for our purpose. We may, therefore, s
aside the claims made for "les arcs triomphaux dressés en la vil
d'Aix," as being without significance in the present discussion, exce
as an episode in the history of an exploded theory.

Traces of the pageant of the Court of Love in Italy appear in tl
chronicle of Giovanni Villani.[3] He tells us that in June, 1283,
the feast of St. John, there was seen in Florence

---

[1] *Deux Lettres inédites de P. de Chasteuil-Gallaup,* in *Revue des Langues Roman*
XXVIII, 259 ff. (1885). See especially p. 275.

[2] *Mémoires pour la Vie de François Pétrarque*, Amsterdam, vol. II, 1764, n
19, especially pp. 53 ff.

[3] *Istorie Fiorentine*, Milan, 1802–3, III, 159–60, chap. lxxxviii.

una nobile e ricca compagnia vestiti tutti di robe bianche con uno signore detto dello Amore. Per la qual brigata non s'intendea se non in giuochi, e in sollazzi, e balli di donne e di cavalieri popolani, e altra gente assai onorevoli andando per la città con trombe e molti stromenti, stando in gioja e allegrezza a gran conviti di cene e desinari. La quale corte durò presso a due mesi, e fu la più nobile e nominata, che mai si facesse in Firenze e in Toscana.

A hundred and forty years later, during a carnival held in Milan to celebrate the entry of Sforza, a spectacle was got up, over which a chosen lady, with the title of queen, presided. Dramatic eclogues about love were recited in competition, and the court lasted for a week.[1]

In the *Mémoires* of the French Society of Antiquaries[2] an account is given of some village games in Switzerland that seem to point definitely enough to an original connection with the Court of Love. A wooden Château d'Amour was built on the first Sunday of May, and the young people of the village divided themselves into two bands, one of which defended, while the other assaulted, the Château by means imitated from actual warfare. After it was taken, the day was finished with dancing and carousing. On account of accidents, the government of Berne in 1543 passed an edict forbidding the continuance of the custom; but in spite of this, says the anonymous historian, writing in the second decade of the present century, it continued in the environs of Echallens "tout récemment."

Very similar is the account by the same author of *le siège du Château d'Amour* in the town of Fribourg.[3] Here the defendants of the castle were pretty girls, and the attacking party young men. The assault was made to music, and the only weapons were bouquets and festoons of roses. After the surrender, each member of the captured garrison chose one of the conquerors, and ransomed herself with a kiss and a rose. Then all rode in procession through the streets, and the day ended in illuminations and festivities, in which, however, the attentive fathers and mothers were present, "à maintenir décence au milieu du bruit, et la courtoisie au milieu de la joie."

---

[1] R. Renier, *Giornale Storico della Letteratura Italiana*, XIII, 382.

[2] *Mémoires et Dissertations sur les Antiquités Nationales et Étrangères*, pub. by the Soc. Roy. des Antiquaires de France, Paris, 1817, I, 184–7.

[3] *Ibid.*, pp. 186–7.

Rolandinus Patavinus tells in his chronicle[1] of similar festivities in Italy in the thirteenth century. Here also the castle was defended by ladies, and the account of the decorations suggests the gorgeousness of the allegories. Fruits, flowers, and perfumes were the ammunition used in the siege.

The carved ivory casket described in a previous chapter[2] seems from the description given by Meyrick to conform quite closely in its design to this sort of festival. Pictures of similar carvings may be seen in an article, *Ikonographisches zu Chrestien de Troyes*, by Johann von Antoniewicz[3] and in Schulz's *Das Höfische Leben*.[4]

CHAPTER IX.

THE COURT OF LOVE AFTER 1520.

THE present chapter makes even less profession of being exhaustive than those preceding. I have here merely collected such indications of the survival or later development of important features of the allegory of the Court of Love as I have happened to meet with in my researches on the origins and sources.

---

[1] *Chron.*, i, 13, cited by A. Schulz, *Das Höfische Leben zur Zeit der Minnesinger*, 2d ed., Leipzig, 1889, I, 578. Professor Kittredge refers me to the passage itself in Graevius, *Thesaur. Antiq.*, VI, i, 10.   [2] See p. 137, above.

[3] *Romanische Forschungen*, V, 248 ff. I owe this reference to Professor Kittredge

[4] 1889, I, 577. For further discussion of the matters touched on in this chapter, see the following: H. Knobloch, *Die Streitgedichte im Provenzalischen und Altfranzösischen*, Breslau, 1886; L. Selbach, *Das Streitgedicht in der Altprovenzalischen Lyrik*, Marburg, 1886; R. Zenker, *Die provenzalische Tenzone*, Leipzig 1888; E. Trojel, *Middelalderens Elskovshoffer*, Copenhagen, 1888, and cf. G. Paris, *Journal des Savants*, 1888, pp. 664 ff. and 727 ff., and R. Renier, *Giornale Stor. della Letteratura Italiana*, XIII, 371–84; Antony Méray, *La Vie au Temps de Cours d'Amour*, Paris, 1876; P. Rajna, *Tre Studi per la Storia del Libro Andrea Cappellano*, in *Studj di Filologia Romanza*, 1891, V, 193–272, *Le Codice d' Amore*, Milan, 1890, and cf. G. Paris, in *Romania*, XIX, 372; A. R. Marsh, article *Love, Courts of*, in *Johnson's Cyclopædia*, V, 375–6.

Almost contemporary with our English poem is the *Temple de Cupido* of Clément Marot,[1] in which the ecclesiastical form of the allegory is worked out in great detail. Cupid, with the usual equipment of arrows and so forth, shoots the hero, who goes seeking Ferme Amour, and comes to a temple standing in a garden of flowers. Bel Acueil and Faulx Danger are the porters; Beau Parler, Bien Celer, Bon Rapport, Grace, Mercy, Bien Servir, and Bien Aymer are saints; the fountain and cemetery[2] reappear; Ovid, Alain Chartier, Petrarch, and the *Roman de la Rose* form the missal, breviary, and psalter. The lessons are *rondeaux*, *ballades*, and *virelais;* Genius (as in the *Roman de la Rose* and the *Confessio Amantis*) is the arch-priest; the requiem masses are *aulbades;* the candles, branches of trees; the seats, grass.

> Les sainctz motz que l'on dit pour les ames,
> Comme Pater ou Aue Maria,
> C'est le babil et le caquet des dames (vv. 390–2).

Instead of processions they have morris-dances; the Art of Love for a Gospel; and, instead of kissing a relic, each worshipper kisses his lady.

The debate survives in La Fontaine's *Parlement d'Amours*,[3] in which the influence of Martial d'Auvergne is evident. The Parliament is held for the reform of abuses in the "Isle de Cythère"; and there comes before it a lover complaining of the ingratitude of his lady. The defence is that the lady cannot love in return without losing some of her fresh beauty, and so lessening her power of producing sighs and tears, which are "les tributs de l'empire amoureux." Verdict is given for the defendant in the interest of the treasury.

Le Différend de Beaux Yeux et de Belle Bouche[4] is a similar dispute, the point being as to which is of the greater value in the service of Love. The judge decides for the Mouth, since the Eyes are useless at night. He gets a kiss for a reward.

---

[1] *Œuvres*, ed. by G. Guiffrey, Paris, 1876, II, 67–101.
[2] See pp. 88 and 91, above.
[3] *Œuvres*, ed. by H. Regnier, Paris, 1892, VIII, 421–5.
[4] *Ibid.*, VIII, 426–30.

L'Histoire Universelle des Théâtres[1] gives several examples of the Court of Love motives on the stage. In a piece by Voltaire,[2] *Ce qui plaît aux Dames*, the point of the old story of the *Wyf of Bath's Tale* appears. A council discuss the question, a queen presiding, and, of course, conclude " Il faut toujours que la femme commande."

In the *Union de l'Amour et des Arts*[3] by Le Monnier, Aglaé, President of the Court of Love, has not acknowledged her love for Floridan, who, disguised as a shepherd, comes before her to complain of his mistress's want of responsiveness. He gets a verdict in his favor, discloses his identity, and claims her love.

In an old comic opera[4] some of the *Arrêts d'Amours* can be recognized worked up into episodic scenes.

At the end of the *Veuve à la Mode*[5] by de Sainte-Foix, a vaudeville was presented by G. Panard at the Comédie Italienne in 1726 in which " Un Robin " announces a Court thus :

> Venez, accourez tous, on vous rendra justice.
> L'Amour tient ici ses grands jours ;
> Amans qui d'une Belle essuyez les caprices,
> Vous que pour prix d'un tendre sacrifice,
> On immole à d'autres amours,
> Venez, accourez tous, on vous rendra justice.

The pleading is done by advocates. A lover complaining of a broken tryst, a woman of whom her husband is tired, an actress in the Opera, a " petit-maître," an old man who wants to marry, a coquette, and others, present appropriate petitions and have them granted.

La Bibliothèque du Théâtre François[6] has record of a *Tribunal de l'Amour*, a comedy presented at Paris in 1750, written by Jean Landon.

Dinaux[7] gives accounts of several bacchanalian and licentious

---

[1] Paris, 1779–80, vol. IX, pt. i, pp. 122 ff.

[2] *Ibid.*, p. 173.   [4] *Ibid.*, p. 175.

[3] *Ibid.*, p. 174.   [5] *Ibid.*, pp. 175 ff.

[6] *Bibl. du Théâtre François*, Dresden, 1768, III, 203.

[7] Dinaux, *Sociétés Badines, Bachiques*, etc., Paris, 1867, I, 421 ; also Fournier *Variétés Hist. et Litt.*, Paris, 1863, VII, 237.

cieties founded in the seventeenth and eighteenth centuries, some
which bear traces of Court of Love influence in the nomenclature
opted.   Thus the "Ordre des Chevaliers de la Joye," founded
der the protection of Bacchus and Cupid at Mézières in 1696, had
secretary the Chevalier de Belle-Humeur, and as members the
hevaliers du Printemps, Fidèle, Sans-Soucy, de l'Espérance, Con-
ant, Complaisant, and others.[1]

The more modern developments of allegorical terminology are well
emplified in an *Assignation d'un Amant à sa Maîtresse au Tribunal
l'Amour*, mai, 1727.[2] The *Bail du Cœur de Cloris*[3] is a more
tended instance of the same class.

More comprehensive than these is a curious collection of features
rrowed from several different types of Court of Love poems.   *Les
écisions de Cythère*, or *Le Code de l'Amour*,[4] 1776, was written by
une femme de Belles Lettres."   It begins with an "Edit d'Establis-
ment de la Chambre de Justice d'Amour," which tells how Amour,
ticing certain abuses growing up in his empire — such as mer-
nariness and inconstancy — takes counsel with his good mother
enus, his dear brothers the little Loves, his dear sisters the Graces,
d his cousins "les Ris et les Jeux," and on their advice establishes
court to regulate gallantry.   Next come several cases submitted to
is court, such as a dispute among a Blonde, a Brunette, and a Spiri-
elle in a matter of precedence.   Then a group of Jurisconsults of
th sexes discuss a number of questions, e.g. :

Si celui qui aime une laide, la croyant laide, montre plus d'amour que
lui qui la croit belle, quoiqu'elle soit laide ?
Si l'on peut haïr ce que l'on a une fois bien aimé ?
Si l'amour diminue plutôt par les rigueurs d'une Belle, que par ses
veurs ?

A kind of Catechism of Love follows with questions and answers
ch as these :

---

[1] Cf. also *L'Ordre des Aphrodites*, time of Louis XV., Dinaux, I, 39, and cf.
424 ff.
[2] *Bibliothèque Universelle des Romans*, Paris, Nov., 1785, pp. 189–91.
[3] *Ibid.*, Nov., 1785, pp. 180–9.
[4] *Hist. Univ. des Théâtres*, Paris, 1779–80, IX, 179 ff.

D. Je vous demande si amours avoient perdu leurs noms, comment le
appelleriez-vous?

R. Plaisans, sagesse.

D. Qui fait aux amans jouir de ce qu'ils ont grant désir?

R. Humblement requérir et prier (p. 196).

The different kinds of love are now classified into twenty-seven
types, such as *l'amour entreprenant, sans esprit, paresseux, impérieux
jaloux, constant,* and so on.

The god also issues certain laws to be observed in his empire, and
these are the same as those versified by the Abbé Regnier-Desmarais
in his *Edit de l'Amour*[1] about a century earlier. There are eighteen
of these, and they are chiefly pieces of advice about winning and
retaining a lady's affections, commands against languor, timidity, and
jealousy, and hints about interpreting signs. Thus the seventh is
If a lover wishes to make a complete conquest and guard against
coldness, he ought to have a plan in his head as well as a passion in
his heart. The ninth is: For the reasonable time when one may best
take advantage of the favorable mood, watch the lady's eyes.

Genius as "archiprestre d'amour, vicaire et lieutenant general
pour sa Majesté," appears again in a piece by Estienne Pasquier
published at Paris in 1618, and described as *Ordonnances Generalle
d'Amour,* "envoyées au seigneur baron de Mirlingues, chevalier de
isles Hyères."[2] There are fifty ordinances of a figurative sort, forming
a kind of amorous jurisprudence rather than a code of instruction
for individuals.

Il Congresso di Citera[3] of the Count Algarotti (1712-64) shows
that in Italy the Court of Love material developed in much the same
way as in France. Love has shut himself up in the Isle of Cyther
for the purpose of settling the proper way of loving. He takes the
counsel Hope and Pleasure, and they decide to have representative

[1] See Martial d'Auvergne, *Arrêts d'Amours*, Paris, 1731, p. 601, in which are
cited *Poësies de Mme. la Comtesse de la Suze et de M. Pellisson,* p. 115, and *L.
Poësies Françoises de l'Abbé F. S. Regnier-Desmarais,* ed. 1707, p. 121.

[2] Fournier, *Variétés Hist. et Litt.,* Paris, 1855, II, 169.

[3] See *Opere del Conte Algarotti,* Venice, 1791-4, VI, 223-316, trans. into French
in *Bibl. Univ. des Romans,* July, 1786, pp. 6-83, and Aug., 1786, pp. 107-36.

f the chief modes; so an English, a French, and an Italian lady of ashion are summoned to the Congress. The allegorical framework, most of which is borrowed from the familiar mediæval tradition, and ome of which more definitely recalls parts of the *Hypnerotomachia*, is hus used as a setting for a discussion of national customs and habits f mind — "la sensibile delicatezza del cuore delle italiane, la non ncomoda leggierezza delle francesi, e la filosofica serietà delle nglesi."

From Italy, too, is said to have come the first hint for the motive f a story of Cupid that developed in France, and is found to some xtent in England also. *Les trois Contes de Cupido et d'Atropos*, ound in the work of Jean Lemaire des Belges, is alleged by Becker o go back to two sonnets of Serafino Aquilano.[1] Lemaire's first tale[2] egins with an account of a drinking bout between Love and Death, vhich results in the two gods getting their shooting gear exchanged. Lach begins to shoot, with the disastrous consequences of killing he young men, and inflaming the old with love.

The second tale brings Cupid home to his mother's palace, where he and her nymphs are having a siesta. Many of the mediæval eatures are recognizable in the description of the Castle.[3] Love's aughter Volupté is accidentally pricked by one of the deadly rrows, great excitement follows the discovery, and finally the bow nd arrows of Death are thrown into the moat and Cupid is put ut of the hall. Death comes up to the gate, driving his crowd of ovesick dotards who drag the dead bodies of Cupid's victims, and Venus urges her son, who has now awakened, to get back his bow. Cupid tries in vain to slay Death with his own arrows; but Death merely mocks him and says that in future they will take each other's ames as well as weapons. Meanwhile the water in the moat has een poisoned by Death's arrows, and Venus and her nymphs try to weeten it with flowers and honey. They make it more attractive

---

[1] *Le Rime di Serafino de' Ciminelli dall' Aquila*, ed. by M. Menghini, Bologna, 894, I, 49–50, sonnets xi and xii. But there is really no similarity between the onnets and the *conte*.

[2] See P. A. Becker, *Jean Lemaire*, Strassburg, 1893, p. 255. Becker gives a summary from Lemaire's *Œuvres*, III, 39 ff. Cf. also Goujet, *Bibl. Franç.*, X, 86–9.

[3] Becker, *Lemaire*, pp. 258 ff.

but no less deadly, and all those who drink of the water or eat of
what grows on its banks are smitten with a fearful disease.   Such
terror does this create that many are driven to virtue by fear.

The third tale is not by Lemaire, but is anonymous.   It contains
an account of Venus's appeal to Jupiter, the calling of a council of
the disorders described in the first two tales, and the presenting to
Cupid and Atropos of new bows fitted for their respective functions.
The water in the moat, however, Mercury says cannot be cured.

These stories were still further continued in the *Triumphe de Dame
Verolle*, published at Lyons in 1539.[1]   This is an allegorical procession, of the type already exemplified,[2] in which Dame Verolle, the
personification of the disease contracted from the poisoned moat,
takes the part of " Royne du Puy d'Amours."

The main point of the first of these tales — the exchange of the
weapons of Love and Death — is used by Richard Barnfield (1594)
to account for an old man's falling in love with a queen whose young
lover had died.[3]

The subtleties of love continued to furnish subjects for conversation in fashionable society long after the Middle Ages.   In England it
is reflected, for example, in certain scenes in Shakspere's earlier
comedies.[4]   In France we have an historical instance considerably
later.   In the *Mémoires d'Anne de Gonzague*,[5] written about 1660,
that Princess describes the assemblies at the Hôtel de Rambouillet,
where even Cardinal Richelieu took part in discussions on love and
poetry.   One day Mademoiselle de Scudéry told of a man who was
in great grief at parting with his mistress, and she said that he spoke
in a ravishing manner of the happiness of being loved.   The Duc
d'Enghien, however, protested that this man did not love " bien
vivement, qu'il n'étoit que personnel.   Un véritable amant, dit-il, doit

---

[1] A. de Montaiglon, *Recueil de Poésies françoises des XVᵉ et XVIᵉ Siècles*, IV,
214 ff.   See also Becker, *Lemaire*, p. 268, n. 2.　　　　[2] See p. 114, above.

[3] *The Affectionate Shepherd*, Percy Society, XX, 6, Lond., 1847.

[4] See, e.g., *Two Gentlemen of Verona*, i, 1, 2, ii, 4 ; *Love's Labour's Lost*, iv, 3 ;
Twelfth Night, ii, 4 ; *Romeo and Juliet*, i, 1.

[5] G. Sénac de Meilhan, *Mém. d'Anne de Gonzague, Princesse Palatine*, 2d ed.,
Lond., 1789, pp. 39 ff.

être plus occupé de son amour, que des sentimens qu'il inspire." A dispute followed, and Richelieu, hearing of it, gave a great dinner at Ruel to all those who had taken part. The Princess Palatine's sister was made president, and the rest took their places with great gravity. The discussion was reopened, the Cardinal collected the votes, and the decision was in favor of the opinion of the Duc d'Enghien. "Vous vous étonnerez," concludes the narrator, "peut-être des formes et de l'appareil imposant que donnoit le Cardinal à cette assemblée; mais c'étoit *l'esprit du tems*, et le sien particulièrement en amour."

The work in English which shows the most extensive traces of the Court of Love influence after 1520 is the *Faerie Queene*. It would require a quite disproportionate amount of space here to show in detail even the more elaborate instances of Spenser's borrowings from mediæval love-allegory; and we shall have to be content with a single instance of his method of treating the tradition.

In Canto xi of Book III occurs a description of the altar of Cupid, which Britomart finds in the Castle of Busyrane. The room has been described as hung with arras picturing the amours of the Greek gods :

> And at the upper end of that faire rowme
> There was an Altar built of pretious stone
> Of passing valew and of great renowme,
> On which there stood an Image all alone
> Of massy gold, which with his owne light shone;
> And winges it had with sondry colours dight,
> More sondry colours than the proud Pavone
> Bears in his boasted fan, or Iris bright,
> When her discolourd bow she spreds through hevens hight.

> Blyndfold he was; and in his cruell fist
> A mortall bow and arrowes keene did hold,
> With which he shot at randon, when him list,
> Some headed with sad lead, some with pure gold (sts. 47, 48).

> And all about the glistring walles were hong
> With warlike spoiles and with victorious prayes
> Of mightie Conquerours and Captaines strong,
> Which were whilome captived in their dayes
> To cruell love (st. 52).

The next canto (xii) contains the masque of Cupid, in which many of the old abstractions reappear.

After the action has been indicated in dumb-show by Ease, the masquers enter to music.

> The first was Fansy, like a lovely Boy (st. 7),
>
> And him beside marcht amorous Desyre (st. 9).
>
> Next after him went Doubt, who was yclad
> In a discolour'd cote of straunge disguyse (st. 10).
>
> With him went Daunger, cloth'd in ragged weed (st. 11).
>
> Next him was Feare, all arm'd from top to toe (st. 12).
>
> With him went Hope in rancke, a handsome Mayd (st. 13).

Then Dissemblaunce and Suspect (st. 14), Griefe and Fury (st. 16), Displeasure and Pleasaunce (st. 18), next a lady led by Despight and Cruelty, with a wound in her breast (st. 19).

> Next after her, the winged God him selfe
> Came riding on a Lion ravenous (st. 22).
>
> Behinde him was Reproch, Repentaunce, Shame (st. 24).
>
> So many moe, as there be phantasies
> In wavering wemens witt, that none can tell,
> Or paines in love, or punishments in hell (st. 26).

These passages are sufficient to prove how thoroughly Spenser was acquainted with the works of his predecessors in allegory.[1]

In Scotland we find occasional traces of Court of Love matter in Sir David Lindesay. Thus in the *Satyre of the Thrie Estaits*,[2] Sensuality prays:

> O Queene Venus! unto thy Celsitude
> I gif gloir, honour, laud, and reuerence.
>
> .   .   .   .

---

[1] Traces of Court of Love features are evident also in Skelton's *Bowge of Court* and *Garlande of Laurell.* See *Poetical Works of John Skelton*, ed. by Dyce Lond., 1843, I, 30 ff. and 361 ff.

[2] *Works of Sir D. Lyndesay*, ed. for E. E. T. S. by F. Hall and J. A. H. Murray pt. iv, p. 394.

> I mak ane vow, with humbill obseruance,
> Richt reuerentlie thy Tempill to visie,
> With sacrifice unto thy Dyosie (vv. 499 ff.).

Again in another poem, the *Deploratioun of Quene Magdalene*[1]:

> O Venus, with thy blynd sone Cupido,
> Fy on ȝow baith, that maid no resistance!
> In to ȝour Court ȝe never had sic two,
> So leill Luffaris without dissimulance,
> As Iames the Fift, and Magdalene of France (vv. 36–40).

In John Rolland's *Court of Venus*[2] (1575) Desperance is tried in elaborate legal form for saying rude things about Love.

The golden and the leaden arrows of Cupid, which appeared again in the passage quoted from Spenser, are found also in Richard Barnfield.[3]

> Yet, O enthraller of infranchizd harts,
>   At my poore hart if thou wilt needs be ayming,
> Doo me this favour, show me both thy darts,
>   That I may chuse the best for my harts mayming,
>   A free consent is privilegd from blaming.
> Then pierce his hard hart with thy golden arrow,
> That thou my wrong, that he may rue my sorrow.
>
> But let me feel the force of thy lead pyle,
>   What should I doo with love when I am old?

But it is in pageants and the drama that the Court of Love left most traces in England.

In a spectacle in honor of Queen Elizabeth in London (1558–9) personified abstractions appear. The Seate of Worthie Governance is supported by Pure Religion, Love of Subjects, Wisdom, and Justice, treading upon the corresponding vices.[4]

---

[1] *Works of Sir D. Lyndesay*, ed. for E. E. T. S. by F. Hall and J. A. H. Murray, pt. v, p. 553.

[2] Ed. by W. Gregor for Scottish Text Society, Edin. and Lond., 1884. Cf. W. A. Craigie in *Modern Quarterly of Language and Literature*, vol. I, no. 1, March, 1898.   [3] *The Affectionate Shepherd*, Percy Society, XX, 42.

[4] J. Nichols, *Progresses and Public Processions of Queen Elizabeth*, Lond., 1823, , 44. Cf. also I, 393 ff.

At Norwich, on a similar occasion in 1578, Venus and Cupid were represented as cast out of heaven and receiving ignominious treatment from a Philosopher, from Chastity, Modesty, Temperance, and others.[1] Elizabeth's rôle of the Virgin Queen naturally encouraged the irreverent treatment of the Love deities, and brought about an exalting of Diana at the expense of Venus.

In the tilt yard at Whitehall, in 1581, there was represented an assault on the Fortress of Perfect Beauty by Virtuous Desire.[2]

The love-quibbling custom is exemplified in a sort of pastoral performed before the queen at Sudeley in 1592.[3]

In the *Legacy of Loricus*,[4] read on another such occasion in 1592, a trace of a very old kind of allegorical fancy appears :

I bequethe to your Highnes the whole mannor of loue and the appurtenaunces thereunto belonging, *viz.* :

> Woodes of hie attemptes,
> Groues of humble seruice,
> Meddowes of greene thoughtes . . .
> Fishing for dayntie kisses with smyling countenances, etc.

In the Progresses of James I. of England the same kind of thing continues with more and more of a tendency towards the definite masque form. Thus in Ben Jonson's *Masque at Lord Hadington's Marriage*[5] (1607–8) Love has the usual accompaniments of roses, transfixed hearts, etc., and Venus is drawn in a chariot by doves and swans, and attended by Graces.

In 1619 Middleton wrote a pageant called *The Triumphs of Love and Antiquity*,[6] in which were a Sanctuary of Fame, a Parliament of Honour, and a triumphant chariot of Love drawn by two "luzerns or lynxes." Other Triumphs, such as the *Triumph of London, of Honour, of Peace*, and so on, are frequent ; likewise *Temples of Honour, Palaces of Pleasure*, etc.

---

[1] J. Nichols, *Progresses and Public Processions of Queen Elizabeth*, Lond., 1823, II, 189.   [3] *Ibid.*, III, 142.

[2] *Ibid.*, II, 312 ff.   [4] *Ibid.*, III, 212.

[5] Nichols, *Progresses of James I.*, Lond., 1828, II, 176–7. Cf. also Jonson, *Love Freed, Love Restored*, etc.

[6] *Lord Mayors' Pageants*, Percy Society, X, 45, Lond., 1843.

The literary interest is greater in a Court of Love occurring in the fifth act of John Marston's *Parasitaster,* or *The Fawn* (1606).[1]

The dénouement of this play is brought about by the disguised Duke of Ferrara, who as a fawning courtier has got up a court entertainment in the form of a Parliament of Love. Cupid is led in by Drunkenness, Sloth, Pride, and Plenty, and is followed by Folly, War, Beggary, and Laughter. After a health is drunk to Venus, Cupid says that he means to enforce his old laws, and calls for the reading of the Statutes. These are constructed with a view to the various situations in which the *dramatis personae* have been represented in the preceding acts; and after each is read, the particular culprit aimed at is called forth and has judgment passed on him. The first begins thus:

A Statute made in the 5463d year of the easeful reign of the mighty potent Don Cupid, emperor of sighs and protestations . . . for the maintaining and relieving of his old soldiers, maimed or dismembered in love, . . . etc.

An act against the plurality of mistresses;

An act against counterfeiting of Cupid's royal coin. . . .

An act against forgers of love-letters, false braggarts of ladies' favours, and vain boasters of counterfeit tokens, etc.

In Massinger's *Parliament of Love*[2] (1624) Charles VIII. of France, confronted by the complaints of his courtiers about the cruelty of the court ladies, decides to

Erect a place of justice near the Court,
Which we 'll have styled, *The Parliament of Love:*
Here such whose humble service is not considered
By their proud mistresses, freely may complain;
And shall have hearing and redress . . .

---

[1] *Works of John Marston,* ed. by A. H. Bullen, Lond., 1887, vol. II. For this reference I am indebted to the late Dr. R. A. Small.

[2] *Plays of Philip Massinger,* ed. by W. Gifford, Lond., 1805, II, 232–322. For this reference, and for drawing my attention to Gifford's valuable introduction, I am indebted to Professor A. R. Marsh.

> . . . And ladies that are wronged
> By such as do profess themselves their servants,
> May cite them hither, and their cause delivered
> Or by their own tongues, or fee'd advocates,
> Find sudden satisfaction. . . .

A month is allowed in which to arrange matters out of court. The interval is filled in with a plot of a type familiar enough at that period, and when the Court of Love comes to be held, it varies little from the usual scene for the administering of poetical justice, such, e.g., as that in *Measure for Measure*, except that the speeches on either side are slightly more formal, and a priest with an image of Cupid is introduced.

D'Avenant's *Temple of Love* and *The Triumphs of the Prince d'Amour*[1] are very fantastic things, only vaguely connected with the Court of Love.

Systematic search in literature of the modern period would doubtless bring to light many more developments and survivals of the motives which formed such an important element in the books which delighted, to an extent that amazes us, our mediæval ancestors. The present chapter is meant only to suggest how considerable has been the influence, down to even comparatively late times, of that tradition whose history we have tried to follow in this essay. The latest example I have found brings us down to our own times, and makes an appropriate enough ending to the discussion.

WHICH?

> So, the three Court-ladies began
>   Their trial of who judged best
> In esteeming the love of a man:
> Who preferred with most reason was thereby confessed
> Boy-Cupid's exemplary catcher and cager;
> An Abbé crossed legs to decide on the wager.

---

[1] D'Avenant, *Dramatic Works*, ed. by Maidment and Logan, Edinburgh, 1872-4 I, 281 ff. See also Appendix, pp. 347-8, for other instances of the name " Prince d'Amour."

First the Duchesse: " Mine for me —
  Who were it but God's for Him,
  And the King's for — who but he?
Both faithful and loyal, one grace more shall brim
His cup with perfection: a lady's true lover,
He holds — save his God and his King — none above her."

" I require " — outspoke the Marquise —
  " Pure thoughts, ay, but also fine deeds:
  Play the paladin must he, to please
My whim, and — to prove my knight's service exceeds
Your saint's and your loyalist's praying and kneeling —
Show wounds, each wide mouth to my mercy appealing."

Then the Comtesse : " My choice be a wretch,
  Mere losel in body and soul,
  Thrice accurst !   What care I, so he stretch
Arms to me his sole saviour, love's ultimate goal,
Out of earth and men's noise — names of ' infidel,' ' traitor,'
Cast up at him?   Crown me, crown's adjudicator ! "

And the Abbé uncrossed his legs,
  Took snuff a reflective pinch,
  Broke silence: " The question begs
Much pondering ere I pronounce.   Shall I flinch?
The love which to one and one only has reference
Seems terribly like what perhaps gains God's preference." [1]

------

[1] *Complete Works of Robert Browning*, Cambridge edition, Boston, 1896, p. 199.

ADDENDA.

Page 25. Guiraut de Calanso. À *propos* of the arrows of different meta[
mentioned here, cf. pp. 54 and 140, above.

Page 30. Cheltenham *Court of Love* MS. The date, according to ,
Thomas, is not later than the first half of the thirteenth century, b[
Bartsch (*Grundriss*, p. 28, MS. N.) gives it as fourteenth. On th[
poem cf., in addition to the references given in note 2, *Revue a[
Langues Romanes*, series 3, VII, 90–8, 238–9.

Page 79. Chaucer and Froissart. Professor Kittredge's article, referr[
to in note 1, will be found in *Englische Studien*, XXVI, 321–36.

Page 82. *Les Échecs Amoureux.* For an elaborate analysis of the co[
tents of this poem, with an account of the MSS., a discussion of i[
sources and literary importance, and a comparison of vv. 1–4873 wi[
the translation and expansion of them by Lydgate in his *Reason ar[
Sensuality*, see *Les Échecs Amoureux, eine altfranzösische Nac[
ahmung des Rosenromans und ihre englische Uebertragung*, by Ern[
Sieper, Weimar, 1898.

Page 120. *Königsberger Jagdallegorie.* This poem has been publishe[
by F. Schulz in the *Schade-Festschrift*, Königsberg, 1896, pp. 233–[

Page 133, note 1. The Tannhäuser Legend. Cf. also G. Paris, *Romani[
XXVII, 304 ff.

Page 165. *The Pastime of Pleasure.* The statement made here wi[
reference to the allegorical hounds should be modified by referenc[
to *La Chasse aux Médisants* on p. 74, and *La Chasse d'Amours* [
p. 100.

Page 190. Robert de Blois. See the two passages in Ulrich's edition
Chanson d'Amors, 208–10 (II, 126), 290–8 (II, 134–6).

Page 261. Jean Lemaire. Becker's statement of Lemaire's indebtedne[
to Serafino has reference to only the first of the *Trois Contes.*

INDEX.

———◆◇◆———

A leis cui am, etc., 24, 181.
Abbate di Tiboli, 203.
Abbé de Sade, 248 n. 2, 254.
Actæon, 161.
Adam de la Halle, 71.
Admetus, 3.
Adonis, 220.
Advice to Lovers, 212.
Æneas, 3, 88, 141, 217.
Æneid, 12, 217.
Affectionate Shepherd, 265.
Aiglantine, Hueline et, 37.
Ain Mynn Red, 129, 205.
Aix (Provence), 253–4.
Alanus de Insulis, 50–1, 143.
Albricus Philosophus, 22 n. 2.
Alcestis, 3, 34, 145, 147, 161, 229, 231, 237.
Alcmene, 238.
Alcuin, 240.
Algarotti, 260.
Allegorical armor, 161, 167.
—— banquet, 68, 69, 73.
—— building, 28, 36, 41, 64, 66, 99, 124, 137, 191.
—— drinking-cups, 73.
—— figures, see Personification.
—— hounds, 74, 100, 120–3, 165, Addenda.
—— steps, 24, 72, 80, 181, 194, 203.
Allegory and Mythology, 8 ff.
—— beginnings of, 8 ff.
—— founded on Scripture, 17–21.
—— in England, 135–6.
—— in Italy, 109.

Allgemeine Geschichte, etc., see Ebert.
Alphonso of Castile, 27.
Alte Swert, Daz, 130.
Altercatio de Phyllide et Flora, 34–8, 41, 43, 69, 104, 145, 241.
Altswert, Meister, 130–1, 133 n. 2.
Amant rendu Cordelier, 105, 202.
Amé Malingre, 251–2.
Amiens, Jacques d', 174.
Amorosa Visione, 115–16.
Amour dans Marie de France, 185 n. 1.
André le Chapelain, see Andreas Capellanus.
Andrea da Barberino, 134.
Andreas Capellanus, 26, 45 n. 4 and 5, 72, 150, 163, 174, 176–81, 188, 195, 201–2, 205, 214, 221, 248–50.
Anelida, 3, 151.
Anelida and Arcite, 231.
Anglo-Latin Satirical Poets, 45 n. 1.
Anne de Gonzague, Mémoirs d', 262.
Anticlaudianus, 50–2, 71, 142.
Antiope, 238.
Antoine de la Sale, 132, 133 and n. 1, 134.
Antoniewicz, J. von, 256.
Antony, 151.
Aphrodite (Pandemos), 40, 55.
—— (Urania), 55.
Apollinaris Sidonius, 16.
Apollo, palace of, 36.
April, 31–3, 62, 158, 226.
Apuleius, 14, 119 n. 4.
Architrenius, 45, 239.
Archpriest of Hita, 174 n. 1.

Arcite, 3.

Arezzo, G. d', 202.

Aristotle, 76, 139.

Armonye of Byrdes, 226.

Arnaut Daniel, 221.

Arnaut de Marueil, 183 n. 3.

Arrêts d'Amours, 105, 106 n. 2, 202, 243, 258.

Arrows (of Love), 11, 15, 22, 24–5, 27, 35, 39, 40, 42–3, 48, 54, 58–9, 61, 76, 78, 85, 88, 92, 94, 111, 115–17, 119–20, 138–40, 145–6, 148, 154, 157, 161, 188, 198, 254, 257, 261–2, 265, Addenda.

Ars Amatoria, 170–2, 175, 177.

Art d'aimer, 175.

Art d'amors, 174.

Arthur, 131.

Arthurian romances, 125, 138, 158, 178, 201.

Asceticism *vs.* chivalrous love, 176.

Asolani, Gli, 247.

Assembly of Ladies, 150–2.

Assembly of the Gods, 146.

Assignation d'un Amant, 259.

Atalanta, 116.

Atropos, 261–2.

Augustine, St., 19.

Auriol, Blaise d', 100 n. 2.

Aurora, 163.

Autos sacramentales, 20 and n. 2.

Bacchus, 116, 142, 147, 259.

Bail du Cœur de Cloris, 259.

Balade Warning Men, 237.

Bamberg, see Egen von B.

Barberino, see Andrea and Francesco da B.

Barnfield, Richard, 262, 265.

Baudouin, A. (on *Pamphilus*), 174.

Baudouin de Condé, 66, 191.

Becker, P. A., 261.

Belle Dame sans Mercy, La, 85, 88, 103 n. 1, 149, 199.

Bell's *Chaucer*, 6 n. 2.

Bembo, Cardinal, 247.

Benoît de Court, 243.

Berchta, 134.

Bernard of Clairvaux, 18, 21.

Bernart de Ventadorn, 182, 221.

Bersabee, 139.

Bertolome Zorzi, 29.

Bestiaries, 71.

Bewty and the Presoneir, 164.

Birds, 8, 11, 35–8, 41–2, 48, 52, 57–8, 61, 67–9, 78, 80, 86, 146, 152–6, 158–9, 185, 210, 217 ff.

Birds' Matins, 217 ff., 239.

Blaise d'Auriol, 100 n. 2.

Blancheflor et Florance, Geste de, 36, 38, 136, 218, 241.

Blois, Robert de, 189.

Boccaccio, 91, 115–17, 142, 145, 147, 168, 246–7.

Boethius, 142–3.

Bok of the Duchesse, 62, 79, 141–2, 239.

Book of Cupid, 210.

Bouciquaut, see Maréchal B.

Bourgoing, Simon, 100 n. 2, 105.

Bowge of Court, 264 n. 1.

Brakelmann (on Andreas), 45 n. 5.

Brant, Sebastian, 132.

Breviari d'Amor, 184, 207.

Briseyda, 88.

Brown, J. T. T., 235.

Browning, Robert, 268–9.

Brunetto Latini, 83, 111.

Brykholle, 38 n. 1.

Bunyan, 48, 63.

Calanso, see Guiraut de C.

Calista and Meliboea, 174 n. 1.

Calliope, 161–2, 214.

Canace, 162.

Canterbury Tales, 141, 148, 231, 239.

Capella, see Martianus C.

Carmen de Rosa, 176.

Carmina Burana, 34 n. 2, 39, 175.

Carvings of Castle of Love, 137, 256.

Caseneuve, 245.

Castel off Loue, 136 n. 3.

Castets, F., 110.

Castiglione, B., 247.

Castle, see Palace.

Catullus, 113.

Cavalcanti, Guido, 111.

Ce qui plaît aux Dames, 258.

Celestina, 174, 215.

Cemetery of Love, 88, 91, 259.

Cent Balades (C. de Pisan), 196.

Cent Ballades, Livre des, 196-8.

Ceres, 116, 142, 147.

Cerlne or Cersne, see Everhardus C.

Certamen Rosae Liliique, 240.

Ceyx and Alcyone, 62, 161.

Champion des Dames, 102.

Chapel, see Temple.

Chapman, J., 36.

Charles d'Orléans, 90, 93-8, 103, 142, 200-1, 230, 237, 239.

Chartier, Alain, 75, 85-9, 91 and n. 1, 102, 107, 149, 199, 242, 257.

Chartre d'Amours, 74.

Chase, Allegory of the, 74, 78, 100, 120-3.

Chasse aux Médisants, 74.

Chasse d'Amours, 100.

Chasteau d'Amour, 136-7.

Chastel d'Amors, 28.

Chastel de Leal Amour, 192.

Chasteuil-Gallaup, Pierre de, 254 and n. 1.

Chastiement des Dames, 189.

Chastity, 114.

Château d'Amour, 137, 255.

Chatelaine de Vergy, 86 and n. 2.

Chaucer, 52, 62, 77, 79 and n. 1, 102, 116-7, 141-6, 147-51, 155, 160, 163-4, 168, 206, 213, 219, 229-31, 235-6, 239.

Chaucer and Froissart, 79 n. 1, Addenda.

Chaucer and Machaut, 62 and n. 3.

Chaucer's Dreme, 62, 156-7.

Cheltenham *C. of L.* MS., 30, Addenda.

Chess, 118.

Chevalier aux Dames, 103 n. 2.

Chevaliers de la Joye, Ordre des, 259.

Chief de Joyeuse Destinée, 107.

Chivalrous ideal, realization of, 198.

Chivalrous love, see Rules of c. l.

Chivalrous love *vs.* Asceticism, 176.

Chrétien de Troyes, 44, 128 n. 1, 176, 185.

Christ, 48, 71, 252.

Christine de Pisan, 83-5, 149, 195-6, 242.

Christopher, St., 241.

Church, see Temple.

Cicero, 52, 105, 142, 213.

Clanvowe, Sir T., 210, 227.

Classification of lovers, 231.

Claudian, 14, 15, 37 n. 2, 54, 115, 117, 142-3.

Clef d'Amors, 174 and n. 3.

Cleopatra, 151.

Clerk *vs.* Knight debate, 31, 34, 36, 108, 241.

Cligès, 44, 56, 185.

Code d'Amour, 201.

Code de l'Amour (1776), 259.

Codes of love before Andreas, 180-1.

Colonna, Francesco, 114, 117.

Commonplaces of love-allegory, 228.

Complainants, 3, 5, 231-4, 236.

Complaint of the Black Knight, 146.

Complainte de Saint Valentin, 75.

Complaints, 68, 128, 142, 147-8, 153, 166, 228, 231.

Compleynt of Mars, 142, 219.

Compleynt of Venus, 142, 206.

Compleynt to his Lady, 142.

Compleynt unto Pite, 230-1, 239.

Concile de Remiremont, see *Romaricimontis Concilium*.

Condé, Baudouin de, 66, 191.

—— Jean de, 67-9, 73, 191-2, 225, 227, 239.

Confessio Amantis, 72, 138–41, 257.
Conflictus Veris et Hiemis, 240.
Congresso di Citera, 260.
Consaus d'Amours, 195.
Conseils d'Amour, 188, 207.
Conversations between lovers, 177, 184.
Coquillart, Guillaume, 243.
Corinth, 40.
Cortegiano, Il, 247.
Cosselh a las donas, 184 n. 3, 207.
Cosselh als amadors, 184 n. 4.
Cour Amoureuse, 248, 251–2.
Cour d'Amour, 184.
Cour de May, 80, 194.
Court, Benoît de, 243.
Court d'Amours, 64–5.
Court of Love allegory, development
    of, 167–8.
—— after 1520, 256 ff.
Court of Love (M. E.), authorship, 1;
    construction, 235; date, 1, 2;
    features investigated, 7–8;
    manuscript, 1; not a dream, 52;
    not by Chaucer, 1; state of text,
    5 ff.; summary of plot, 2–5.
Court of Love not a serious tribunal,
    249–50. See also Institution,
    and Pageant.
Court of the Muses, 161–2.
Court of Venus, 265.
Coutumes du Beauvaisis, 59.
Couvin, see Watriquet de C.
Credo à l'Userier, 222.
Credo au Ribaut, 222.
Cressida, 159, 161.
Creüsa, 139.
Cuckoo, 217, 225–6.
Cuckoo and the Nightingale, The, 210,
    227.
Cuer d'Amours Espris, Livre du, 90–3,
    102.
Cupid, 3, 8, 11, 14–16, 22, 34–6, 39, 45,
    48–9, 74, 78, 84, 88–9, 95, 100–1,
    105, 108, 116, 118–19, 123, 138–9,

142–7, 154, 157, 159–62, 166,
    204, 216, 219–20, 223, 228, 254,
    257, 259, 261–8.
Cupido (fem.), 124–5.
Cupido, Trois Contes de, 261.
Cursor Mundi, 136 and n. 4.
Cynthia, 159.
Cypassis, 215.
Cyprian, 19.
Cyprus, 12, 15, 115.

D'Avenant, 268.
Daisy, 78, 144, 145, 150, 229.
Dalida, 237.
Dallyngton, Robert, 118 n. 1.
Dammann, O., 24 n. 1, 25 n. 2, 72.
Danaë, 238.
Daniel, Arnaut, 221.
Danse des Aveugles, 104.
Dante, 109, 112, 213, 247.
Daphne, 140, 148.
David, 139.
De Amore, see Andreas Capellanus and
    Pamphilus.
De Arte Honeste Amandi, see Andreas
    Capellanus.
De Consolatione, 142, 143 n. 1.
De Nuptiis Honorii et Mariae, 15, 115.
De Nuptiis Philologiae et Mercurii, 16,
    148.
De Patientia, 18.
De Phyllide et Flora, see *Altercatio*.
De Profundis des Amoureux, 222.
De Republica, 213.
De Roisin, 199 n. 1.
De Spectaculis, 19.
De Venus, see *Venus la Deesse*.
Débat d'un Moine et d'un Gendarme, 108.
Débat de deux Amants, 242.
Débat de deux Demoyselles, 242.
*Débat de la Demoiselle et de la Bour-
    goise*, 244.
*Débat du Jeune et du Vieulx Amou-
    reux*, 244.

Debate (débat), 31–8, 68, 79, 136, 248 ff., 257–8.
Debate of the Body and the Soul, 241.
Décisions de Cythère, 259.
Delilah, 141.
Demophon, 88, 113, 141, 151.
Departie d'Amours, 101.
Deploratioun of Quene Magdalene, 265.
Der Mynn Gericht, 129.
Der Mynn Regel, 205.
Deschamps, Eustache, 75.
Description de Paris, 252 n. 1.
Desert d'Amours, 75.
Despartie d'Amours, 96.
Detto d'Amore, 110.
Devotions of the Fowles, 226.
Diana, 82–3, 116, 146, 150, 161, 266.
Dido, 3, 76, 87–8, 141, 223, 233, 237.
Diez, 24 n. 1, 29 n. 1, 244, 248.
Différend de Beaux Yeux et de Belle Bouche, 257.
Digulleville, G. de, 93.
Dinaux, 258.
Dipsas, 215.
Dis de l'Escole d'Amours, 194.
Dis de la Fontaine d'Amours, 72, 73.
Dis du Preu Chevalier, 193.
Discours sur les Arcs Triomphaux, 254.
Dit de la Fleur de Lis, 144.
Dit de la Fontaine Amoureuse, 62, 73, 142.
Dit de Poissy, Livre du, 242.
Dit des Huit Couleurs, 193.
Dit dou Lion, 62.
Dit du Vergier, 61, 190, 221.
Dittié de la Flour de la Margherite, 144.
Divine Comedy, 48, 89, 109, 112, 213.
Documenti d'Amore, 203.
Dotrine d'Amor, 188–9.
Douglas, Gavin, 77, 102, 160–3, 214.
Doves, 217–8.
Dream-setting, 41, 46, 48, 52, 63, 71, 73, 76, 78, 81, 86, 87, 95, 100, 102, 104–5, 130, 141–2, 144, 147, 151, 156, 158, 163, 174.

Dream-setting, Origin of, 213.
Dregy of Dunbar, 224.
Dryden, 149.
Dubbii, 246–8, 250.
Dunbar, William, 2, 163–5, 212, 220, 224, 227.
Durante, Ser, 110.

Eagle as guide, 214.
Earthly Paradise, 112.
Ebert, 18 n. 8, 19 n. 1, 240.
Ecclesiastes, 154.
Ecclestiasticus, 17.
Échecs Amoureux, 82, 195, Addenda.
Echo, 89, 141.
Eclogue, 240.
Eclympasteyre, 79.
Ediffice de l'Ostel Dolloureux, 99.
Edit de l'Amour, 260.
Egen von Bamberg, 123 n. 4.
Eleanor of Aquitaine, 176, 185, 250.
Elie, see Maistre E.
Enghien, Duc d', 262–3.
Enqueste d'entre la Simple et la Rusée, 243.
Enseignement du Dieu d'Amours, 98.
Enzo Re, 202.
Ephrussi, Charles, 114 n. 4.
Epistre au Dieu d'Amours, 84–5, 149, 195.
Epithalamium dictum Ruricio et Hiberiae, 16.
Ermengaud, Matfre, 184.
Eros, 55.
Escole d'Amours, Dis de l', 194.
Espinette Amoureuse, 82, n. 3.
Espinette du Jeune Prince, 105.
Étude sur le Songe de Poliphile, 114 n. 4.
Europa, 115, 238.
Eustache Deschamps, 75.
Everhardus Cersne *or* Cerlne, 205.
Excusation de Maistre Alain, 85.

Fablel dou Dieu d'Amours, 41, 52, 54–5, 167, 214, 218, 241.
Fabrizio Maramaldo, 248 n. 1.
Facetus, 175.
Faerie Queene, 263–4.
Faidit, Gaucelm, 30 n. 4, 182.
Fairy-lore, 125, 156.
Faits du Maréchal Bouciquaut, Livre des, 198.
Fall of Princes, 100.
Fawn (Marston's), 267.
Fête-Dieu, 90, 253 and n. 2.
Fiammetta, 246.
Filocolo, 246–7.
Fiori, 110.
Flamenca, Roman de, 27, 183.
Fleur de Lis, Dit de la, 144.
Flora, 150, 163.
Flora, De Phyllide et, see *Altercatio*.
Florance et Blancheflor, 36, 38, 136, 218, 241.
Flors del Gay Saber, 244 n. 4, 245.
Flour of Curtesye, The, 146, 219.
Flower and the Leaf, The, 149, 150, 152, 214.
Fontaine Amoureuse, Dit de la, 62, 73, 142.
Fontaine d'Amours, Dis de la, 72–3.
Fontaine Périlleuse, Livre de la, 74.
Forest in C. of L. poems, 126, 128–30.
Fortune, 51, 71, 105, 141, 152, 154–5, 160.
Fountain of Love, 53–4, 62–3, 73, 76, 80, 83, 86–7, 115, 137, 257.
Fournival, see Richard de F.
Franc, Martin le, 102–4.
Francesco da Barberino, 30 n. 2, 203–4.
Francesco di Buonanni Malecarni, 114 and n. 3.
Frau Venus und die Minnenden, 128.
Freya, 134.
Friars, nuns, etc., at the C. of L., 3, 232–4.
Froissart and Chaucer, 79 n.1, Addenda.

Froissart, Jean, 78–82, 142, 144, 194.
Fulgentius, 22, 39, 217.

Galahot, 139.
Garencières, Jean de, 98–9.
Garlande of Laurell, 264 n. 1.
Garment of Good Ladies, 93.
Gaucelm Faidit, 30 n. 4, 182.
Gäuchmatt, Die, 132.
Gawain, 79.
Gaya Companhia, La, 245.
Genius (personified), 139, 257, 260.
Ges en bon vers, 183 n. 1.
Geste de Blancheflor et Florance, 36, 38, 136, 218, 241.
Gifford on C. of L., 267 n. 2.
Giochi, 246–8, 250.
Go-between, 213, 215–6.
Goldast, Melchior, 245.
Golden Targe, 163–4, 220 and n. 2, 227.
Golden Violet of Toulouse, 245.
Goldschmidt, 202.
Goliardic poetry, 175.
Goujet, 73, 88 n. 1, 100–6 and n., 261 n. 2.
Gower, John, 138–41, 155, 164.
Graces, 12, 16, 36, 266.
Granson, Oton de, 75, 206.
Grimoald, 2.
Gringore, Pierre, 107.
Griselda, 161.
Groos, K., 250 n. 1.
Grosseteste, Robert, 136 and n. 3.
Gualterium, Liber ad, 180.
Guerino il Meschino, 134–5.
Guiart, 175.
Guide in allegories, 115, 127, 142, 213–4, 228.
Guido Cavalcanti, 111.
Guilhem (?), Peire, 26–7.
Guillaume de Digulleville, 93.
Guillaume de Lorris, 51, 53–5, 60, 185–6, 213.
Guillaume de Machaut, 60–3, 73, 91, 142, 144, 190, 221, 241–2.

Guillebert de Metz, 252.
Guiraut de Calanso, 24–6, 54, 72, 181, 194, 203, Addenda.
Guiraut Riquier, 181.
Guittone d'Arezzo, 202.

Hadamar von Laber, 121–2, 124.
Hamartigenia, 19.
Hätzlerin, Clara, 129.
Hauteville, see Jean de H.
Hawes, Stephen, 2, 165–7, 212.
Heart given as pledge, 57, 59, 95.
Heinrich von Ofterdingen, 133.
Helen, 74. See Paris.
Henryson, Robert, 2, 93, 159.
Hercules, 113, 118.
Hermann von Sachsenheim, 133.
Hermaphrodite, Love as, 76–7.
Hero and Leander, 87.
Hita, Archpriest of, 174 n. 1.
Hoccleve, 85 n. 1, 149.
Höfische Leben, Das, 256.
Holda, 134.
Homer, 9, 10, 12, 153.
Homeric Hymns, 12, 25.
Horselberg, 134.
Hospital d'Amours, 76, 87, 90, 93, 104, 200.
Hôtel de Rambouillet, 262.
Houdan, see Raoul de H.
Hous of Fame, 10 and n. 1, 13, 143–4, 146, 148, 160, 163, 214, 239.
House, see Palace.
House of Avarice, 64.
—— Fortune, 51.
—— Nature, 50, 52.
Hueline et Aiglantine, 37.
Huet, Gédéon, 34.
Huon de Mery, 48–50, 114, 187.
Hypnerotomachia Poliphili, 117, 140, 220, 261.

Idoine, Melior et, 38, 136.
Ikonographisches zu Chrestien de Troyes, 256.

Iliad, 10.
Institution of the Court of Love, 240 ff., 248, 256 n. 4.
Inventaire des Archives de l'Ordre de la Toison d'Or, 251.
Isle of Ladies, 62, 156–7, 209–10, 219.
Istorie Fiorentine, 254 n. 3.

Jacopo da Lentini, 203.
Jacques d'Amiens, 174.
Jagd (Hadamar's), 121–2, 124.
Jagd der Minne, 122.
James I. of Scots, 152, 210–2, 232, 235, 239.
Jardin de Plaisance, 106.
Jason, 79, 88, 113, 139, 141.
Jaufre Rudel, 26.
Jean de Condé, see Condé.
Jean de Garencières, 98–9.
Jean de Hauteville, 44–5, 239 and n. 1.
Jean de Meun, 51, 55, 83–4, 91, 102–3, 187.
Jeanroy, A., 38, 240 n. 1.
Jerome, St., 22, 39.
Jeux de la Fête-Dieu, 253–4.
Jeux des Fous, 90.
Jeux Floraux, 245 and n. 2.
Jeux partis, 245–6, 250.
Jocx partitz, 244.
Joli Buisson de Jonece, 79.
Jonson, Ben, 260.
Jove, 40, 115.
Ju de le Capete, 65.
Jugement d'Amour, 36.
Jugement Definitif, 243.
Jugement du Roi de Behaigne, 241.
Jugement du Roi de Navarre, 242.
Julius Cæsar, 113.
Juno, 82.
Jupiter, 159–60, 238, 262.
Jusserand, J. J., 135 and n. 1.

Kinds of love, 188.
King Hart, 102, 163.
Kingis Quair, 152–5, 220, 232, 233–7, 235 n. 2.

Kittel, Der, 130–1.
Kloster der Minne, 126–8, 214.
Knight *vs.* Clerk debate, 31, 34, 36, 108, 241.
Knightes Tale, 117, 145.
Königsberger Jagdallegorie, 120–1, 123, Addenda.
Körting, G., 82.

La Fontaine, 257.
Laber, see Hadamar von L.
Lai d'Amours, 188.
Lai de Guigemar, 175 and n. 3.
Lai du Trot, 72, 150, 188.
Lancelot and Guinevere, 76, 79, 88, 91, 113, 139.
Lancelot of the Laik, 158, 220.
Lando, Ortensio, 247.
Landon, Jean, 258.
Landscape (garden, meadow, forest, etc.) of C. of L., 26–7, 30, 35, 41, 47, 52, 61–2, 67, 72, 76, 80, 82, 86, 107, 112–3, 115, 123–4, 126, 128–30, 138, 142, 145, 149, 154, 157–8, 162–3, 219.
Lange, P., 102.
Langlois, E., 23 n. 1, 381 n. 1 and 2, 41, 51, 52 n. 1, 176.
Latini, see Brunetto L.
Laws of the Kingdom of Love, 169 ff., 194, 200, 211.
Laws of the Round Table, 201.
Lay du Desert d'Amours, 75.
Lay Folks Mass Book, 223 n. 3.
Le Caron, see Michault L.
Le Roux de Lincy, 252 n. 1.
Leaf, Walter, 10 and n. 2.
Legacy of Loricus, 266.
Legal element in C. of L., 43, 65, 68, 79, 86–7, 94–5, 103–4, 125–6, 128, 131–2, 243, 267.
Legend of Good Women, 77, 79 n. 1, 144, 219, 229, 231, 239.
Lemaire des Belges, Jean, 261.

LeMonnier, 258.
Lentini, Jacopo da, 203.
Letter of Cupid, 85 n. 1, 149.
Leys d'Amors, Las, 246.
Liber ad Gualterium, 180.
Liederbuch der Clara Hätzlerin, 129, 205.
Lincoln, 38.
Lindesay, Sir D., 224–5, 227, 264.
Lists of trees, beasts, etc., 142, 154.
Lives of the Provençal Poets, 248.
Livre de la Fontaine Périlleuse, 74.
Livre des Cent Ballades, 196–9, 221.
Livre des Faits du Maréchal Bouciquaut, 198.
Livre des Quatre Dames, 242.
Livre des Trois Jugemens, 242.
Livre du Cuer d'Amours Espris, 90–3, 102.
Livre du Dit de Poissy, 242.
Livre Morpheus, 62.
Lorris, see Guillaume de L.
Louis d'Orléans, 246.
Love, Kinds of, 188.
Love-chase, 74, 78, 100, 120–3.
Love-testament, 101.
Lovers, classification of, 231.
Lucretius, 34 n. 1.
Lydgate, John, 146, 151, 155, 164, 208, 219, 223, 226, 229, 232, 234, 236–7, 239, Addenda.

Machaut, see Guillaume de M.
Macrobius, 142, 213.
Magic pavilion, 27.
Mahiu le Poriier, 64–5.
Maistre Elie, 174 and n. 2.
Malecarni, 246 and n. 2.
Malingre, Amé, 251–2.
Mansion, see Palace.
Maréchal Bouciquaut, 196, 198.
Margivale, see Nicole de M.
Marie de France, 52, 175–6, 185.
Marot, Clément, 87, 225, 257.

Marriage *vs.* Courtly love, 179.

Mars, 113, 146, 159, 161, 166.

Marston, J., 267.

Martial d'Auvergne, 105–6, 202, 243, 257.

Martianus Capella, 16, 142, 148, 167.

Martin le Franc, 102–4.

Marueil, see Arnaut de M.

Masque at Lord Hadington's Marriage, 266.

Masque of Cupid (in *Faerie Queene*), 264.

Massinger, P., 267.

Matfre Ermengaud, 184.

Maximian, 238–9.

May and May-day, 5, 32–3, 41, 52, 67, 72, 74, 76, 78, 80, 85, 98, 106, 111, 126, 132, 138, 141, 144, 146, 149, 153, 156, 160, 163–4, 194, 216–7, 220, 227–8, 255.

Measure for Measure, 268.

Medea, 76, 141, 147.

Meister Altswert, 130–1, 133 n. 2.

Melchior Goldast, 245.

Melior et Idoine, 38, 136.

Mémoirs d'Anne de Gonzague, 262.

Meraugis de Portlesguez, 249 n. 2.

Mercury, 2, 3, 159, 253, 262.

Mery, see Huon de M.

Messe des Oisiaus, 67–9, 73, 191–2, 225–7, 239.

Metz, G. de, 252.

Meun, see Jean de M.

Meyrick, Sir S. R., 137, 256.

Michault, Pierre, 104.

Michault Le Caron, 99 n. 1.

Michault Taillevent, 99, 104 n. 1.

Middelalderens Elskovshoffer, 30 n. 4.

Middleton, T., 266.

Minerva, 154–5, 160, 166, 211–2.

Minne-Falkner, Der, 123 and n. 1.

Minne Jagd, Der, 122 n. 2.

Minne und die Ehre, Die, 131–2.

Minne vor Gerichte, Die, 132.

Minneburg, Die, 123–6, 214.

Minnesangs Frühling, Des, 123 n. 1.

Minoccio, see Ser M.

Mireoirs as Dames, 72.

Molinier, Guilhem, 245.

Momus, 253.

Monte della Sibilla, 134.

Monumenta Germ. Hist., 22 n. 3.

Morality Plays, 20.

Mörin, Die, 133 n. 2.

Morley, H., 150.

Morpheus, House of, 141.

Morpheus, Livre, 62.

Mott, L. F., 183 n. 3.

Muncker, 22 n. 2.

Murner, T., 132.

Mussafia, 58 n. 1.

Mynn Gericht, Der, 129.

Mynn Red, Ain, 129, 205.

Mynn Regel, Der, 205.

Mythographi Latini, 22 n. 2.

Mythologicum, 22 n. 1.

Nape, 215.

Narcissus, 54, 62–3, 76, 83, 87–8, 145.

Narrenschiff, 132.

Neo-Platonists, 9 and n. 1.

Nicole de Margivale, 69 ff., 103.

Nonne Prestes Tale, 206 n. 4.

Nostradamus, Cæsar, 254.

—— Johannes, 248, 254.

Nuns, friars, etc., at the C. of L., 3, 232–4.

Octavien de Saint-Gelais, 100–2.

Ofterdingen, Heinrich von, 133.

Ordonnances Generalles d'Amour, 260.

Ordre des Chevaliers de la Joye, 259.

Origines de la Poésie Lyrique en France, 34 n. 1, 240 n. 1.

Origines et Sources du Roman de la Rose, 23 n. 1.

Orléans, see Charles and Louis d'O.

Orléans contre Garencières, 98.

Orpheus, 113.

Oton de Granson, 75, 206.

Ovid, 11–13, 31, 36, 54, 76, 82–3, 91, 113, 140, 143, 148, 153, 159, 162, 167, 170–81, 187 n. 1, 198, 202, 215, 217, 221, 238–9, 257.

Ovidian tradition in Middle Ages, 170 ff.

Owl and the Nightingale, The, 241.

Pageant of Court of Love, 253–8; in Aix, 253; Echallens, 255; England, 265–8; Florence, 254–5; Fribourg, 255; Lille, 253; Milan, 255; Tournay, 253; Valenciennes, 253.

Palace of Apollo, 12, 36.

—— Beauty, 81.

—— Fortune, 71.

Palace (house, mansion, castle, tent, etc.) of Love, 11, 12, 14–16, 23–4, 25 n. 2, 30, 37, 45–6, 63, 70, 80, 92, 94, 103, 106–7, 115, 124–6, 128–33, 137, 143, 151, 153, 160, 162–3, 177–8, 228, 266.

Palace on a hill, Origin of, 143.

Palamon and Arcite, 161.

Palice of Honour, 73, 102, 160–3, 165, 214.

Pallas, 82–3.

Pamphilus de Amore, 173–4, 215–6.

Panard, G., 258.

Paṇḍarus, 215.

Panthère d'Amours, 69–73, 79, 216, 219.

Paphos, 12.

P⸗ ables of St. Bernard, 21.

radis de la Reine Sibylle, 133 n. 1.

aradys d'Amour, 78–9.

Parasitaster, 267.

Paris and Helen, 57, 63, 76, 79, 82, 86, 116.

Paris, Gaston (on Andreas), 45 n. 5.

—— (on débats), 240 n. 1.

Paris, Gaston (on Institution of C. of L.), 249.

—— (on Ovid in Middle Ages), 173, n. 1, 175.

Parlement d'Amours (Chartier), 86, 107, 219.

—— (La Fontaine), 257.

Parlement of Foules, 116–7, 142, 146–7, 164, 213–4, 219, 239.

Parliament of Love (xv. Cent.), 158, 224.

—— (Massinger), 267.

Parnassus, 30.

Parodies of religious services, etc., 5, 32–4, 67–9, 158, 192, 216, 220 ff., 257.

Pasquier, Estienne, 260.

Passy, Louis, 246.

Pastime of Pleasure, 165.

Pastourelle, 65.

Patenostre a l'Userier, 222.

Patenostre d'Amours, 221–2.

Patenostre des Verollez, 223.

Patenostre du Vin, 222.

Pater Noster des Anglois, 223.

Patristic allegory, 21, 23.

Paul, St., 21, 93, 167.

Peire Guilhem (?), 26–7.

Peire Rogier, 183.

Pèlerinage de la Vie Humaine, 93.

Penelope, 89, 147, 223.

Personification of abstract qualities, 5–9, 10 and n. 3, 11, 13–21, 23–4, 27, 30, 48–51, 53–4, 57–62, 64–5, 68, 70–83, 86–116, 121–2, 125, 129–32, 139, 142, 144–6, 148, 151, 153–4, 162–7, 190–1, 228, 241, 252, 257–67.

Pervigilium Veneris, 33.

Petrarch, 91, 109, 112–5, 163, 168, 214, 257.

Philippe de Remi, 59–60, 190.

Philobone, 3–8, 213 ff., 240.

Philogenet, 4–7, 240.

Phœbus, 140, 148, 159.

Phyllide et Flora, see *Altercatio de P. et F.*
Phyllis, 87, 141, 151.
Piaget, A., 100 n. 2, 251.
Pierre Michault, 104.
Pilgrim's Progress, 8, 48, 63.
Pindar, 113.
Pisan, see Christine de P.
Pity resuscitated, 230.
Plato, 213 n. 1.
Play of Animals, 250 n. 1.
Playdoyer d'entre la Simple et la Rusée, 243.
Poème de la Prison, 94–8, 100, 103, 142, 200–1, 230, 237.
Poësies de la Comtesse de la Suze, 243.
Poissy, Livre du Dit de, 242.
Polyxena, 223.
Precepts of Seduction, 169 ff., 172–3, 175, 186, 193, 197, 202.
Preu Chevalier, Dis du, 193.
Priapus, 142.
Prince d'Amour, 268 and n. 1.
Prison d'Amours, 66, 191.
Procession of ladies, 46, 72 and n. 1, 149, 150, 160, 162–3, 177, 214.
Procuress, 173–4, 215.
Progresses of James I., 266 and n. 5.
Progresses of Queen Elizabeth, 265–6.
Propertius, 113.
Provençal Poets, Lives of the, 248.
Proverbs, 17.
Prudentius, 14 n. 4, 19–21, 48, 55, 63, 167, 241.
Psalms, 18.
Psyche, 14, 119 and n. 4.
Psychomachia, see Prudentius.
Puech, A., 14, 19.
Pui Notre Dame, 246.
Puissance d'Amour, 188, 195.
Purgatorio, 112.
Purgatory of Cruel Beauties, 46–7, 72 n. 1, 178, 214, 221.
Puys d'Amour, 246.

Pygmalion, 89.
Pyramus and Thisbe, 56, 87–8, 116, 151.

Quatre Dames, Livre des, 242.
Quatrebarbes, Comte de, 253 n. 2, 254.
Quattro Libre di Dubbii, 247.
Questioni, 246–8, 250.

Raab, 18 n. 6, 21 and n. 1, 241 n. 2.
Raimon Vidal, 74, 184 n. 2.
Rajna, P. (on Andreas), 45 n. 5, 112.
—— (on Institution of C. of L.), 249.
Rambouillet, Hôtel de, 262.
Raoul de Houdan, 63, 190–1, 249 n. 2.
Re Enzo, 202.
Realization of chivalrous ideal, 198.
Regnier-Desmarais, Abbé, 260 and n. 1.
Religious element in C. of L. allegory, 31–4, 38–9, 47–50, 67–9, 81, 84, 88, 91, 103–4, 126–8, 136–7, 139, 142, 145, 158, 168, 192, 211, 220, 257, 259–60, 263.
Remedia Amoris, 177.
Remi, see Philippe de R.
Remiremont, see *Romaricimontis*.
René of Anjou, 89–93, 102, 144, 214, 254.
Renier, R., 248 n. 1, 255.
Resourse et Reliefvement, etc., 99.
Richard de Fournival, 188, 195, 207.
Richelieu, 262–3.
Richter, A., 9 n. 1.
Riquier, Guiraut, 181.
Robert de Blois, 189.
Rogier, Peire, 183.
Roisin, De, 199 n. 1.
Rolandinus Patavinus, 256.
Rolland, John, 265.
Roman de la Rose, 2, 41, 42, 51–6, 60, 62, 70–2, 82–3, 90, 93, 104–5, 109, 110 and n. 1, 141, 145, 167, 185–7, 205–6, 213–4, 218, 228–9, 257.

Roman de la Rose, Landscape of, 12.
Roman du Roi Artus, 201 n. 2.
Romans des Eles, Li, 190–1.
Romanz de la Poire, 56, 98, 187, 218.
Romaricimontis Concilium, 31–4, 128
    n. 1, 221, 241.
Ros, Sir R., 149, 199 n. 3.
Rudel, Jaufre, 26.
Rules of chivalrous love, 169 ff., 178–9.
    See Statutes.
Rustebeuf, 63 n. 4, 64.

Sachsenheim, Hermann von, 133.
Sackville, 2.
Sade, Abbé de, 248 n. 2, 254.
Saint-Gelais, O. de, 100–2.
Sainte-Foix, 258.
Salade, 134–5.
Sale, see Antoine de la S.
Salu d'Amours, 59, 190.
Samson, 94, 139, 141, 237–8.
Saturn, 159.
Satyre of the Thrie Estaits, 264.
Schatz, Der, 133 n. 2.
Scheler, 81.
Schick, 146, 232.
Schulz, A., 256.
Scripture allegory, 17–8.
Scudéry, Mlle. de, 262.
Sedulius Scotus, 240.
Sejour d'Honneur, 102.
Semiramis, 76.
Seneschal de Hainault, 242.
Ser Durante, 110.
Ser Minoccio, 247 and n. 1.
Serafino Aquilano, 261.
Shakspere, 262.
Sibilia, 31, 33.
Sibylle, see *Paradis de la Reine S.*
Sibyls, 135, 160.
Sicilian School, 202.
Skeat, W. W., 1 and n. 1, 5, 54, 150–1,
    210, 227, 236, 238–40.
Skelton, **226, 264** n. 1.

So fo el temps, 184 n. 2.
Sociétés Badines, etc., 258 n. 1.
Solomon, 76, 94, 139, 145, 237–8.
Somnium Scipionis, 52, 105, 142, 213
Songe et Complainte, 95.
Spenser, 263–5.
Spiegels Abenteuer, Des, 131.
Spruchgedicht, 131 n. 2.
Statius, 14.
Statutes of Cheerfulness, 174, 182, 184
    and n. 4, 186, 189, 194, 196–7,
    199, 201–2, 209–11.
—— Complaisance (obedience, etc.),
    171–2, 178, 181–2, 186, 192, 196,
    199, 207, 210–11.
—— Constancy, 178, 182, 186–7, 192–5,
    199, 200, 204, 206, 209, 211–12.
—— Courage, 182, 184 and n. 4, 187,
    189, 192–6, 200–1, 204, 206 and
    n. 4.
—— Courtesy, 178, 182, 184, 187, 189,
    193–6, 199, 200, 203, 209–10.
—— Endurance, 181–2, 192, 196, 203–4,
    211.
—— Faith, 183, 207, 210.
—— Fear, 184, 187, 209.
—— Generosity, 170, 178–9, 182, 184
    and n. 4, 186–7, 189, 193–4, 196,
    199, 201, 203, 206 n. 4, 210,
    212.
—— Honor, 181–2, 186–7, 189, 193
    195, 199, 201, 203, 209–10.
—— Hope, 184, 192, 204.
—— Love, 3, 4, 8, 168 ff., 236–7.
—— Moderation, 178, 184 n. 4, 194
    204–5, 208.
—— Modesty, 178, 184 n. 4, 186–7
    195–6, 199, 203, 206, 209–12.
—— Neatness, 171, 186–7, 189, 193–7
    200, 205, 209–11.
—— Secrecy, 172, 175, 178, 181–2
    184–5, 189, 192, 195–7, 199–205
    206 n. 4, 208–9, 211–12, 249.
—— Slander, 178, 195–6, 199, 212.

atutes of Truthfulness, 178, 194–5, 204–6, 211–12.

atutes, Classification of, 169–70.

— for ladies, 3, 184, 188–9, 194, 207.

ehlich, 56 n. 1, 58.

ejskal, 120 n. 2, 121.

eps to Palace of Love, 24, 72, 80, 181, 194, 203.

mming, 26 n. 2, 184 n. 2.

ow's *Chaucer*, 1, 207.

ife of Love in a Dream, 118 n. 1.

rrey, Earl of, 2.

sanna, 252.

mptoms of love, 169, 172, 179, 180, 183, 185–8, 190, 202, 206.

illevent, Michault, 99, 104 n. 1.

nnhäuser, 132–5, 245.

mple d'Onnour, 79, 194.

mple de Cupido, 257.

mple of Glas, 146–9, 208, 229, 233–5, 237, 239.

mple (church, chapel, etc.) of Love, 11, 39, 88, 91, 103, 116, 119, 141–2, 144–5, 147–8, 159, 166–7, 228, 230, 266.

mple of Love (D'Avenant), 268.

en Brink, 62–3.

n Commandments of Love, 207.

nebres des Pauvres Prisonniers, 225.

enson or tensos, 37, 244, 250.

ent, see Palace.

ertullian, 18–19.

eseide, 116, 142, 147.

esoretto, 111.

esoro, 83, 111.

estament of Cresseid, 159.

estament of Squyer Meldrum, 224.

heodulphus, 22, 39.

heseus, 76.

hibaut, 56, 87.

hrissil and the Rois, The, 164.

hynne's *Chaucer*, 1.

aboli, Abbate di, 203.

Tibullus, 12, 113, 217.

Tisch Zucht, Von, 205.

Tobler, 58 n. 1.

Toison d'Or, see *Inventaire*, etc.

Tornoiement d'Antéchrist, 48–50, 55, 114, 187, 218.

Trésor, 83, 111.

Tresor Amoureux, 81.

Tribunal de l'Amour, 258.

Trionfo d'Amore, 112–14, 214.

Trionfo dell'Amore, 114, 246 n. 2.

Trionfo della Castità, 114.

Tristan and Yseut, 56, 76, 79, 88, 91, 113, 115, 139.

Triumph of Love (Ovid), 11.

Triumphe de Dame Verolle, 262.

Triumphs, 114 and n. 4, 119, 266.

Triumphs of Love and Antiquity, 266.

Troilus, 79, 161, 223.

Troilus and Criseyde, 143, 206 and n. 4, 239.

Trois Contes de Cupido et d'Atropos, 261.

Trois Jugemens, Livre des, 242.

Trojel, E., 30 n. 4, 45 n. 5.

—— (on Institution of C. of L.), 249.

Troyes, see Chrétien de T.

Turck, E.-J. de, 251.

Ueber Charles d'Orléans, etc., 91 n. 1.

Ueber einige altfranz. Doctrinen, etc., (Wolf), 188 n. 4, 195 n. 2.

Ueber Vier Alleg. Motive, etc., 18 n. 6, 241 n. 2.

Union de l'Amour et des Arts, 258.

Valentine, St., 75, 94, 146, 218–19.

Van Bemmel, 27 n. 1.

Ventadorn, see Bernart de V.

Venus, 3, 8, 11, 12, 14–16, 22–3, 25, 31–4, 39, 40, 42–3, 48–9, 53, 55, 63, 67–9, 71, 73–4, 82–3, 88–9, 92, 95, 105, 113–16, 119, 123, 128–34, 138–9, 142–3, 146–8, 153–64,

166–7, 173, 175, 193, 195, 205, 208, 211–12, 216–21, 224–8, 232, 239, 254, 259, 261–2, 265–7.

Venus la Deesse d'Amor, De, 42–3, 98, 167, 185, 218, 221.

Venus Mass, 223.

Venusberg, 132–5.

Verfolgte Hindin, 123.

Verolle, Dame, 262.

Veselofsky, 246 n. 2.

Veuve à la Mode, 258.

Vidal, Raimon, 74, 184 n. 2.

Villani, Giovanni, 254.

Virgil, 109, 113, 139, 142, 213, 217.

Virgin Mary, 137, 221, 246.

Vision of Er, 213 n. 1.

Vita Nuova, 109, 112.

Voie de Paradis, 63, 93.

Voltaire, 258.

Von Tisch Zucht, 205.

Von Zwain Swestern, 129.

Vulcan, 15–16.

Wagner, 133, 245.

Waitz, G., 31.

Waltheri Spirensis Vita, 241 n. 1.

Wanastre, 38 n. 1.

Wartburg song-contest, 133, 245.

Watriquet de Couvin, 72–4, 193–4.

Which ? (Browning's), 268–9.

William of Poitiers, 244.

Wischmann, W., (on *Kingis Quair*), n. 2.

Wisdom of Solomon, 17.

Wolf, F., 188 n. 4, 190, 195 n. 2.

Wolfenbüttel MS., 199.

Wyf of Bath's Tale, 258.

Yvain, 44, 128 n. 1.

Zehen Gebote der Minne, 204.

Zorzi, Bertolome, 29.

Zwain Swestern, Von, 129.